THE CASANOVA COMPLEX

Compulsive Lovers
and Their Women

PETER TRACHTENBERG

POSEIDON PRESS, NEW YORK

POSEIDON PRESS is a registered trademark of Simon & Schuster Inc.

Manufactured in the United States of America

Library of Congress Cataloging-in-Publication Data

Trachtenberg, Peter
The Casanova complex.

Includes bibliographies.
1. Psychosexual disorders. 2. Compulsive behavior.
I.Title.
RC556.T72   1988   616.85′83   88–9886

ISBN 0-671-62048-7

1   3   5   7   9   10   8   6   4   2

Grateful acknowledgment is made to the following for permission to reprint previously published material:

Random House, Inc.: excerpts from *The Memoirs of Jacques Casanova*, edited by Madeleine Boyd. Copyright © 1929 renewed 1957 by The Modern Library. Reprinted by permission.

Applause Theatre Book Publishers: excerpts from "The Trickster of Seville" by Tirso de Molina, translated by Roy Campbell in *Life Is a Dream and Other Classic Spanish Plays*, edited by Eric Bentley. Copyright © 1986 by Eric Bentley. Reprinted by permission.

Diane Wakoski: excerpt from "The Catalogue of Charms" in *The Motorcycle Betrayal Poems*. Copyright © 1971 by Diane Wakoski. Reprinted by permission.

Jason Aaronson, Inc.: excerpts from *Internal World and External Reality: Object Relations Theory Applied* by Otto Kernberg. Copyright © 1985 by Otto Kernberg. Reprinted by permission.

Difficult Music: lyrics from "Smoke Rings" by Laurie Anderson. Copyright © 1986 by Difficult Music. All Rights Reserved. Reprinted by permission.

To the men I spoke with and the women who loved them, and to the Twelve-Step programs of recovery.

Acknowledgments

For their help in shepherding this book from its inception to its present form, I thank my agent, Gloria Loomis; her assistant, Beth Vesel; and Elaine Pfefferblit, my editor. The care they gave my work and the influence they had on my thinking make them the true godmothers of *The Casanova Complex*. For helping me formulate the questions with which my research began and then for lending shape to the answers that emerged from it, I am grateful to Dr. Michael Plautt, Dr. Eli Coleman, Dr. Jaime Nos, Dr. Barry Singer and Dr. Joseph Coltrera. I owe special thanks to Dr. Michael Weissberg, who helped me translate the alien language of psychoanalysis into one I could think and write in. Nancy Levine took on the harrowing job of typing up the transcripts of several hundred hours' worth of interviews. For his literary perspective and his copy of *Byron: A Portrait*, which I subsequently ruined, I thank Mark Rasmussen. My family, Mila Trachtenberg, Ellen Trachtenberg, Charlotte and Michael Weissberg and the late Bella Weissberg, gave generously of their love, patience and support. So did my friends and more-than-friends Peter Leviton, Shellie Leviton, James McCourt, Midge Paxton, Frederic Tuten, Jenny Keith, Richard Aberbach, Robert Reichel, Charles Wyler, Cindy Bloom, Christine Duke, Luther Miller, Raphael Rudnik, Marijke Rudnik, Gay Milius, Molly Flewharty, Will Bennett, Sheila Keenan, Helen Willis, Carol Steel, Mary Wallach, Marc Chimsky, Judy Schank, Cassi Loving, Emily Paine, Anne Trachtenberg and Mary Fuller. Thanks beyond saying go to Dineke Blom, who has loved and challenged and heartened me in ways that neither of us could have predicted, and that go on moving and astonishing me with every day that passes. Some of these people listened. Some of them guided. All of them taught me whatever I know about loving; thank God none of it was too late.

*I had intended to marry her when I loved her more than I loved myself,
but as soon as I was away from her side I found that self-love was
stronger than the affection with which she had inspired me.*
　　　　　　　　　　—Jacques Casanova de Seingalt, *Memoirs*

*Casanova loved many women but broke few hearts....That he knew
himself well enough never to take either wife or mistress must be
counted as a virtue.*

　　　　　　　　　　　　　　　　　　—Havelock Ellis

　　　　*"I think the best
　　　　Way to describe you, sir, would be
　　　　As a locust to whom girls are grass...
　　　　Whenever you're about to arrive
　　　　Towns should be warned: 'Here comes the plague
　　　　Of women in a single man
　　　　Who is their cheater and betrayer
　　　　The greatest trickster in all Spain.'"*
　　　　　　　—Tirso de Molina, *The Rake of Seville*

*He is
　charming,
　　so,
　　　be sure
　　　　that you
　　　　　keep him like fire
　　　　　beyond the tips of your fingers.*
　　　　　—Diane Wakoski, "The Catalogue of Charms"

No man who is really a man can read Casanova's Memoirs *for a few
hours without feeling envious.*

　　　　　　　　　　　　　　　—Stefan Zweig

Male promiscuity exists along a continuum.
　　　　—Otto F. Kernberg, *Internal World and External Reality*

Casanova likes being seen in the luster of a seduction; he does not hold with being recognized.... [His] untimely coquetry is tempered by the wisdom of the adage: not seen, not captured.
—Chantal Thomas, *Casanova: Un Voyage Libertin*

*Ah desire! It's cold as ice
And then it's hot as fire.
Ah desire! First it's red
And then it's blue
And every time I see an iceberg
It reminds me of you.*
—Laurie Anderson, "Smoke Rings"

CONTENTS

Introduction   13

Part One: "Mad, Bad and Dangerous to Know"   23
    Chapter One Sexual Addiction   25
    Chapter Two The Birth of the Scoundrel   31
    Chapter Three Patterns of Desire   41

Part Two: The Six Faces of Casanova   91
    Chapter Four Hitters   100
    Chapter Five Drifters   110
    Chapter Six Romantics   119
    Chapter Seven Nesters   135
    Chapter Eight Jugglers   148
    Chapter Nine Tomcats   163

Part Three: The Making of the Casanova   177
    Chapter Ten "Trying to Make Someone Love Me": The
        Family of the Womanizer   179
    Chapter Eleven The Culture of the Libertine   199

Part Four: Casanova's Women   223
    Chapter Twelve "He Broke My Heart, and Still I Love Him" 225

Part Five: Casanova Unbound   259
    Chapter Thirteen The View from the Bottom   261

Appendix   275
Notes   277

Introduction

When I was nineteen I had two girlfriends. I didn't plan it that way. What happened was that one night in my sophomore year of college I slept with a girl I knew from my writing class. The next night I slept with another woman, whom I had just met at a dorm party. Overcome by gratitude—for I was shy and sexually awkward and had spent most of my adolescence yearning for even the mildest recognition from the opposite sex—I decided that I was in love with both of them. That is how I fell in love in those days. And because I thought I loved them and, more important, desperately wanted them to love me, I never told Iris about Cathy or Cathy about Iris and continued to see them in secret. This was a peculiar practice in the early 1970s, when sex was a public entertainment and most people wore, not their hearts, but their genitals on their sleeves. I still have no idea how Iris or Cathy felt about me. From the very first I reduced them to the roles they played in my erotic life: the women I slept with; the women I loved; the women whom I

13—

wanted to love me; the women I betrayed, each with the other—the objects I acted on.

Although they were physically different and attractive in different ways (Iris was short, buxom, dark-haired and a gifted writer; Cathy a tall art major with a lioness's golden skin and hair), they aroused in me the same feelings of excitement, triumph, omnipotence and guilt. And they elicited from me the same euphoric and panicky busy-ness that cocaine induces in the addict. For six months I saw them on alternate nights, dashing between their rooms like a harried urban commuter, never quite sure whose room I was leaving and whose I was heading toward. In bed with them, I flogged myself into heroic displays of imagination and endurance. Yet for all the attention I gave to the body parts I was licking or caressing, I scarcely knew whom those parts belonged to. The more frenziedly I tried to plunge into the carnal, the more abstract the carnal became.

I presented each of these women with an edited version of myself. With Iris, I came across as a severe, sharp-tongued intellectual, the kind of kid who had won his schoolyard fights by quoting Nietzsche. With Cathy, I was all skinless vulnerability, overflowing with poetry and tears. And for all the affection and sexual nourishment these women gave me, I felt unfulfilled with both of them, as though some essential part of me were languishing unseen and untouched.

It never occurred to me that I might have something to do with this, that what felt neglected was precisely what I kept hidden. Instead, I sought fulfillment through more sex, more intrigue and emotional fireworks. I went from seeing Iris and Cathy on different nights to seeing them both in the space of a few hours. I took more elaborate measures to deceive them, until I was no longer just lying about where I had spent the previous evening, but about who my friends were, what courses I was taking, when I visited my family. I developed a separate itinerary for each girlfriend and dared not take either any place where the other might show up. I took to migrating between trysts with my head down and my shoulders hunched, like an embezzler scurrying to make the next flight to Rio. I stopped answering my phone unless I was alone. I was perversely convinced that discovery would mean the end of both affairs and a loneliness keener than any I had felt before. So I tried to make my lovers give me some assurance of commitment. To Cathy, I fantasized out loud about having her move in with me the next year; with Iris, I talked about us spending the spring break together in

Montreal. And over and over I told both women how much I loved them, hoping only that they might love me back—love me enough, perhaps, to stay with me no matter what I did to them.

But the assurances they gave me always felt hollow and conditional. The fact that neither of my girlfriends loved me as much as I thought she should became my justification for having two of them, for I saw myself as entitled to a set quota of tenderness that it was these women's job to provide. I also felt increasingly resentful of both of them. They couldn't love me enough to make me feel loved. And in exchange for what they gave me, they "forced" me to lie to them, to spend hours attending to their sexual whims—to anticipate those whims before they came into existence—and, worst of all, to ask for what was mine by right. If I was haggard and sleepless and transfixed with guilt it was their fault, and infidelity became my payback, an exhausting and schizoid retribution for itself.

I have no doubt that some part of me was relieved when I was finally found out. I don't remember who it was who knocked on my door when I was in bed with the other or how I tried to explain it. I remember that my stomach sank, but that a moment later I had the sensation of hitting bottom, of achieving a solidity I had been missing for the past six months. For the first time I felt not guilt, but embarrassment, as I realized that what I had been living was the kind of bedroom farce that nobody finds titillating or even funny anymore. Who wants to be trapped in anything as ... farcical ... as farce? When Iris asked me what I wanted to do, I said, "I don't care. Do what you want to do." When Cathy said, "I don't want to go out with someone who lies to me," I answered, "Nobody's forcing you." By the time both women had given me up as hopeless and I was once more spending my evenings drinking and studying alone in my room, I was convinced that that was what I had wanted all along.

Within weeks, though, I was involved with another woman, whom I dated steadily and exclusively but cheated on any time I found someone willing to join me in a zipless fuck. When that relationship began to feel too confining, I ended it, on the theory that it was better to leave than to be left. I found others: one-night stands with women whose names I forgot as soon as they left my house the next morning; three-week affairs that began with a date and escalated to declarations of love and plans for a future that might have been science fiction for all its bearing on reality; long stints of housekeeping with women whose emerging humanness became more galling to me with every month until it finally made them monstrous, triangles, quadrangles, a fragmented geometry of desire, tenderness and loathing. I was occupied in this fashion for the next fourteen years, and in all that time I spent no more than a few weeks without some consuming sexual and romantic attachment. My behavior changed. For three years I was faithful to one woman. After our breakup, I slept with at least two different partners a week for close to two years. I was married. I was divorced. My vision of my erotic life fluctuated between picaresque adventure and soap opera. My vision of myself oscillated, sometimes in a single night, from liberated cocksman to contemptible sneak, from victim to victimizer, heartbreaker to heartbroken.

What strikes me most in my recollection of those years is not the range of my behavior or the number of lovers I took. In so many ways I was heeding the social imperatives of the times: free love, sexual openness, coolness and skittishness. Rather it is the unvarying cycle of feeling that accompanied each affair. When I met a woman, my desire for her was immediate and crippling—a hammer blow to the heart. Whether I wanted to sleep with her or marry her and give her children didn't matter: it usually took me some time to figure out what I wanted. In the beginning there was just that longing, and the sense of myself as a starved orphan gazing through a window at a room where a happy family is sitting down to dinner. To attain that happiness I would do anything, say anything, make myself into whatever kind of man I thought most likely to be admitted into it. At the moment I first knew that she would sleep with me, I felt a triumph as galvanizing as a rush of cocaine. This sense of grandiose aliveness was better than sex. In time, it became my main reason for having sex, for my penis increasingly was just a tool, an aid to my partner's enjoyment and to my further mastery of her. If I reached orgasm at all, it was only an interruption of the siege: I did not consider my triumph complete until my partner was begging me to stop.

But in the next moment, triumph turned into something else. Sometimes it immediately gave way to the old yearning, fiercer now and coupled with the suspicion that my lover had just been playing with me, feigning attraction, faking her orgasms, and that she would now write me off as some creep she'd taken home in a weak moment and couldn't wait to get rid of. To lay that dread to rest, I had to see her again and again, to conquer her in different ways, to win her heart or her mind or her hand or whatever else I imagined there was to win. It might take anywhere from a few days to a few years—a whole relationship based on hunger and frustration. Or triumph might give way to a sense of being drained yet paradoxically filled to the point of sickness, and I would look down at the woman beside me as though she had violated me and be certain that she would want more at any minute. She would want more, and I had nothing more to give her; she had taken all of me and left me as withered as a used condom, and I would scramble out of her bed and into my clothing, trying to be polite but trembling inwardly with panic and the rage of someone who feels he has been horribly cheated.

This finally was the summation of my erotic life. It got so that even as that life slowed and became outwardly more stable, the cycle of desire, triumph and dread accelerated. If I cut down on my sexual partners and tried to stay faithful to them for as long as possible, it was partly in the hope that I could slow down the treadmill whirling inside me. In the last months of that life, I had only to meet an attractive woman to go through the entire cycle in a few moments—longing to fulfillment to uncertainty to panic and disgust, flickering like so many riffled cards while I was still framing my come-on. Those feelings were now compounded by a growing sense of insanity, for I knew that all of them were self-induced. There was no room for a real woman amid the whir of my compulsion. I yearned for something that no woman could give me. I was avenging injuries that no woman had ever dealt me. I was living a life whose sole attraction was the fact that it was familiar, as prison is familiar to the convict. None of which, in itself, was enough to make me stop, until it was a question of stopping or killing myself.

When I first told an acquaintance about this book he replied, "You're describing ninety percent of American men!" This was not what I meant—or thought I meant—at all. Did the term Casanova comprise every man who had ever had a one-night stand or cheated on a wife or girlfriend? Did it include everyone who had dated a woman once and decided that she was not his type? Was I going after every patron of singles bars, sex clubs or prostitutes? Would I end up indicting every man who just happened to prefer being single? In the beginning my sole guide was my own experience, and I was pretty sure that what I had done and felt was not normal— whatever normal is.

I therefore limited my definition of Casanovas to men who have a repeated history of one-night stands, abortive love affairs or broken marriages; who continually end their romantic relationships; who are chronically polygamous or unfaithful: men like myself. At the onset of my research, I left terms like "repeated," "continually" and "chronically" vague, preferring to clarify them through actual observation. If I knew anything when I began this book, it was that I was not looking for a norm but rather for an extreme that sometimes masquerades as normal. Most men, I imagine, have at some point in their lives dreamed of being Casanovas, and many have tried to act like them, but the men described here are far rarer than my friend believed, and far more disturbed than either he or I initially suspected.

For similar reasons, I decided to exclude women and male homosexuals from this study. Although there are women who are habitually seductive, unfaithful or abandoning—who might be said to suffer from a "Catherine the Great complex"—such women are less common than their male counterparts. In this culture the strictures against promiscuity and infidelity still bind women more closely than they do men. A woman who takes many lovers is likely to be called a nymphomaniac. A wife who cheats faces social penalties from which an unfaithful husband would be exempt. Above all, I could not identify with women as I did with male Casanovas and suspected that I could only study them at a serious disadvantage.

Nor was I equipped to discuss objectively the sexuality of gay men: the desire for someone of my own gender seemed at once too alien and too threatening. Furthermore, in studying gay men I would also have to study a gay culture, whose sexual mores often seem like exaggerations of the codes governing straight men. Until the advent of AIDS, a good portion of gay society seemed to treat promiscuity and erotic instability as public and highly political badges of affiliation. Was that pattern a collective response to centuries of repression or an expression of male sexuality at its purest and most unfettered? It seemed to me that I would have to view both gay Casanovas and female Catherines at too far a remove and through too many psychological and cultural lenses, and that whatever vision emerged would be blurred and diffuse.

Through ads in several magazines, I sought out heterosexual, or predominantly heterosexual, men whose relations with women were characterized by brevity, instability and frequent infidelity. I spoke to some fifty men, for anywhere from two to four hours each. I began by asking them about their behavior: how many women they slept with in a given year; where, when and how they met their partners; how they went about their lovemaking and how their relationships ended. More important, I wanted to know how they *felt* about their behavior. What traits attracted them to women? Which ones repelled them? How did their feelings change in the course of a relationship and what events, if any, triggered those changes? Did these men choose to act the way they did, or did they feel compelled to do so? I asked them about their childhoods, their families, their health, their work habits, their fantasies and dreams. Each interview comprised more than a hundred questions and yielded a detailed psychosexual portrait of its subject, one that often revealed far more than he had intended.

I interpreted these conversations on the basis of extensive reading in psychiatric and psychoanalytic literature and discussed my hypotheses with psychiatrists, psychoanalysts, sexologists and counselors. What I learned about Casanovas challenged many of my original assumptions. For the most part, the men I spoke with were not suave playboys, but accountants, doctors, businessmen and carpenters. Most were in their thirties and early forties. A few were in their sixties, and carrying on their philandering in spite of the complaints of their families and the warnings of their doctors. They were not always handsome; many of them complained of weight problems and thinning hair, body odor and bad backs. For all their conquests—some of these men had slept with hundreds of women —and the apparent pleasure they took in them, none of my Casanovas impressed me or my consultants as especially enviable. Their happiness seemed strained and self-willed, like that of someone who keeps prodding you in the ribs and demanding, "Isn't this *fun!?*"

At the same time what I saw struck me as highly consistent. Among the men I interviewed I found four basic themes—instinctual approaches to women and to sex—which I call "thrill seeking," "game playing," "escaping" and "devouring." These motivations differ: womanizing is the thrill seeker's attempt to give meaning and resonance to an arid life; for the escape artist, it is a flight from life itself, an attempt literally to "fuck my life away," as one man told me. But in all four themes, one encounters an underlying hunger and impoverishment of spirit and an unconscious view of women as faceless instruments of pleasure, ego gratification and relief. All women are interchangeable and divided into two rigid categories: those to pursue and those to run from.

In the chapters that follow, six types of behavior typical of Casanovas are identified, ranging from the promiscuity of hitters to the routinized infidelity of tomcats, who shuttle maniacally between wives and mistresses. In between are the men I call drifters, romantics, nesters and jugglers. These behavioral styles overlap and change: a Casanova may in the course of a lifetime become a hitter, a romantic and a tomcat. But each type of Casanova has specific motives and preferences, both conscious and unconscious, which these chapters attempt to make clear.

Among these types, however, I discerned a recurring childhood pattern, characterized by an absent or remote father and by a mother who was at once intrusive and narcissistically self-involved. The kinds of families that are likely to produce Casanovas and the psychic parallels between the Casanova complex, fetishism and addiction will be explored in a later chapter.

It is hard to single out Casanovas in a society that often treats infidelity and promiscuity as masculine norms, and this dilemma will be addressed. I will offer evidence that Western culture has from very early on afforded men sexual options that it forbade women and that our cultural institutions continue to equate a virile and effective manhood with bachelorhood or polygyny. (The more commonly used "polygamy" describes the practice of having many wives; a polygynous man, by contrast, may have many wives or just many female sexual partners.) Male monogamy, on the other hand, has long been portrayed as comical or sexually ambiguous, the mark of the patsy and the wimp. From Chaucer's barnyard philanderers to Warren Beatty and Mick Jagger, our masculine ideal has been predominantly freewheeling and sexually exploitive. And in recent years our culture as a whole has entered a phase of triumphant narcissism, in which sex is a commodity and a mode of performance, and all relationships—romantic, economic and political—are characterized by cynicism and expediency. If such times do not actually spawn Casanovas, they provide them with a hospitable environment.

I also spoke with thirty women, whom I sought out through magazine ads and personal referrals, in an attempt to see what traits make Casanovas attractive to the opposite sex and to examine the role women play in their relationships with them. Almost as a rule I learned that women respond not to these men's looks or prestige but to their innate seductiveness—their urgency, their obsessive focus on their partners in the early stages of their affairs and their driven sexual virtuosity. In addition, certain women seem particularly susceptible to their appeal: they fall for Casanovas passionately and without reservation; they put up with their infidelities and wait for them hopefully when they leave. Lady-killers' ladies often come from families remarkably similar to those that produce Casanovas and indeed seem to suffer from a parallel compulsion. A grotesque dance—a heartbreak tango—binds these men and women together through repeated desertions and betrayals, its steps ritualized and unchanging.

The final chapter discusses treatment for and recovery from the Casanova complex. It outlines the options available to Casanovas who wish to achieve "sexual sobriety" and suggests what women can do to avoid involvements with them or make current relationships with them less painful. What this chapter does *not* do is tell women how to make their partners change. Nor does it attempt to tell Casanovas how to "manage" their erotic lives—this strikes me only as a way of having one's cake while eating it. If you see yourself or someone you love within this book, you are halfway home. I wish you well on the rest of the journey.

PART ONE

---◆---

"Mad, Bad and Dangerous to Know"

CHAPTER ONE

—◆◆—

Sexual Addiction

THE EXAMPLE OF GARY HART

He was a United States senator and he might very well have been the next president, but it is as a candidate—as the candidate—that we most easily picture Gary Hart. A candidate is someone who runs for office, a petitioner for public favor. In recent times, the role has called for instincts that are as much personal as political, seductive as persuasive. During his 1984 campaign for the Democratic nomination, Hart made scant reference to his legislative background. His platform consisted not of positions but of broadly invoked "new ideas." The operative word was "new." It reminded us that Hart was young, the self-appointed spokesman for a generation that still dreamed nostalgically of the sixties, the decade when youth was at a premium. It made us perceive Walter Mondale, his principal opponent, as old, much older than he really was. Like Ronald Reagan and Jimmy Carter before him, the candidate cast himself as a political outsider. The scenario evoked was as old as Oedipus: the virile maverick kicking down the doors of the Washington gerontocracy. Gary Hart's platform was—and has largely remained—himself, his charm, his good looks and his messianic belief in his fitness for the presidency.

By 1987 Hart was once again the front-runner. He seemed hardly to have relinquished his status, as though he had only stepped backstage to freshen his makeup. Walter Mondale, and with him the old Democratic ideals, had been effectively eliminated in 1984. New rivals like Albert Gore and Michael Dukakis were blander versions of Hart himself, technocrats without charisma. In April, as his campaign geared up for an early caucus in Iowa, a poll showed Hart garnering 65 percent of the state's Democratic votes.

Just as Hart made his campaign a showcase for his personality, the questions that haunted it had less to do with his ideology than with his character. In 1984 it came to light that he had lied about his age and falsely denied changing his name. Like Jay Gatsby, he had invented his past, portraying himself as a mischievous prankster in the small town where he grew up, when in reality he had been straitlaced, in thrall to his fundamentalist mother and so afraid of getting dirty that he would not play outside. At the time these incidents suggested that the candidate was more than a little vain, with a cavalier disregard for the truth. Only later did one see in them the evidence of a divided spirit (was it just coincidence that Hart had coauthored a thriller called The Double Man?), a man in violent rebellion against his personal history.

The timid boy had become a dazzlingly handsome man who reveled in the company of women. By 1987 his sexual conduct had become the subject of anxious questioning. If Hart had modeled himself after John F. Kennedy and Warren Beatty, two notorious womanizers, just how far did the emulation go? If he enjoyed the racy environs of Hollywood and Turnberry Isle, was it only as a spectator? While working for George McGovern in the early seventies, he had been renowned for seducing college coeds into joining the campaign and discarding them once they were stuffing envelopes in a back room. "He had a real Don Juan complex," an associate recalled. "Women weren't people to him at all." Since then,

Hart and his wife, Lee, had separated twice. There were rumors that he was still unfaithful.

Lee Hart ignored the rumors diplomatically. The candidate was outraged by them, as though he were a private citizen arbitrarily singled out for a moral inquisition. To his staff, he protested, "I'm not [president], that's twenty months away. You can't take my privacy away from me!"At the same time, he seemed confident of his innocence—or invulnerability. In an interview in The New York Times Sunday Magazine Hart challenged reporters to "Follow me around. I don't care...if anybody wants to put a tail on me, go ahead."

The article appeared on May 3, 1987. On the same day the Miami Herald disclosed that it had placed the candidate's Washington town house under surveillance and that a young woman had apparently spent the night there alone with him. Although Hart and his guest—a part-time model and actress named Donna Rice—insisted that their relationship was innocent, it soon emerged that they had spent a previous night together on board a yacht docked in Bimini. There was a photograph of them snuggling on the deck, the candidate's face strained and sunburned. Hart tried to convince anyone who would listen that Rice was only his political confidante, but the woman had been the lover of a convicted drug dealer and a fixture in the female entourage of the Saudi arms magnate Adnan Khashoggi. She had boasted of her affair with Hart to friends, and one of the Herald's reporters had actually followed her to the assignation in the capital. None of this was airtight proof of adultery, as the candidate kept arguing, but within days the Washington Post announced that it had evidence of his ongoing romantic involvement with another woman in Washington.

Hart gave up his candidacy—only briefly, as it turned out. When he reentered the race that November, it was as though he had popped up from the grave, the Politician Who Wouldn't Die. It was months before he acknowledged that his own behavior had at least temporarily derailed his ambitions. In Hart's eyes there was no connection between his indiscriminate pursuit of women and his loss of the presidency. He continued to portray himself as naive but morally spotless, and he turned his retreat from public life into an assault on those who had in large part launched him into it. The press, he said, had capriciously severed his link with the American people. It had hounded and maligned him. His was the anger of a man who has been robbed of his due, of a suitor libeled by a scan-

dalmongering duenna. His belligerent self-confidence in some way was still intact, and it translated into a belief that he was still above the rules. Yet Hart's capacity for self-destruction could not be underestimated. A political consultant who had known him for a decade observed, "Gary Hart has been writing in lipstick for years, 'Stop me before I fuck again.'"

At the center of every addiction, as at the center of every cyclone, is a vacuum, a still point of emptiness that generates circles of frantic movement at its periphery. By "addiction" I do not mean the physical necessity that binds a junkie to heroin or a smoker to nicotine. I use the word to connote a psychic state that often predates the addict's first encounter with his drug and that remains unchanged throughout the career of his substance abuse. It is characterized not only by feelings of worthlessness, the conviction that one deserves nothing more than the destiny of a drunk or junkie, but by a blurred and tenuous sense of self—a fundamental uncertainty about one's own existence. That uncertainty breeds hunger, a ravenous desire to be filled, to be validated, to be made whole. When the addict takes his fix or the alcoholic his drink, what he experiences is not so much pleasure as a sense of completion that has been missing until that moment. His drug gives him a brief assurance of his own boundaries and substance: it tells him, "Here you are." The void calls out for satisfaction—a satisfaction that must be repeated endlessly, since the void is finally unfillable—and that cycle of hunger, momentary completeness and renewed emptiness comes to be the sole drama of the addict's life.

The experience of addicts who give up heroin only to become alcoholics suggests that addiction is not a matter of a particular drug. Rather, the drug fills a slot in the scenario of hunger, ingestion and emptiness. For a certain time, it becomes the focus of the addict's quest, the source of his momentary satisfaction, the thing he rebels against even as he craves it. Not only substances but activities— gambling, eating and work—can serve the same function. "Addiction," Stanton Peele writes in *Love and Addiction*, "is not a chemical reaction. It is an *experience*—one which grows out of an individual's routinized subjective response to something that has special meaning for him—something, anything that he finds so safe and reassuring that he cannot be without it."

For the men in this book, the primary object of compulsion is women. To Casanovas, women are at different times objects of maddening desire, sources of sexual pleasure and self-validation, and focuses of overwhelming dread. For all their outward insouciance—their air of men surveying the canapé tray at a cocktail party—they pursue women with an urgency and single-mindedness that make ordinary courtship seem casual and desultory and with a recklessness that often jeopardizes their marriages, careers and health. With the advent of AIDS, some of them are undoubtedly risking their lives. Some of these men are indiscriminate womanizers; others have rigid criteria of attractiveness. But all of them to some extent seem powerless in their frenzied pursuit of sexual opportunity.

Powerlessness is not the same thing as helplessness. Many addicts and alcoholics are at least superficially successful and effective individuals. One need only point to the examples of Hermann Goering, F. Scott Fitzgerald or Judy Garland to realize that such people may radiate charisma and authority while remaining in thrall to their disease. The examples in this book suggest that the same is true for Casanovas, among whose numbers I include Lord Byron and Gary Hart, Frank Sinatra and Ernest Hemingway. Indeed, what impresses anyone who studies such personalities is the radical split between their outer and inner selves, the one assertive, elastic and assured, the other frail, insecure and fearful.

Paradoxically, their compulsion and its psychic concomitants give Casanovas a great deal of power over women—a persistence, an urgency, a persuasiveness and sexual authority that many women find overwhelming. These men are as adept at finding sexual partners as alcoholics are at finding a drink when the bars are closed, as skillful at seduction as drug addicts are at getting money for their next fix. Unconsciously viewing women as objects whose sole purpose is to satiate and adore them, Casanovas often have the unhappy facility of making women briefly conform to their inner scenarios—and of choosing those women who are most likely to comply. If they are victims of their compulsion they are also victimizers, whose exploitation of women is no less pernicious because it goes by the name of love.

By calling their condition a compulsion, I have implied that Casanovas are sick people. In our time sickness has become the fashionable explanation for what used to be called wickedness; sometimes it has been used to excuse it. I offer no excuses for these men, and my explanations of why they act the way they do are basically informed hypotheses, the kind that any student of human nature is forced to make do with for lack of a surer blueprint. The condition that I call the Casanova complex—the compulsive pursuit and abandonment of women—encompasses a number of psychiatric disorders, much as addiction does. Among these men one sees the neurotic quest to possess the mother and unseat the father played out in the adult world; one finds the alternating grandiosity and insecurity of narcissism and the primitive psychic states that characterize the borderline personality: megalomania, paranoia and the tendency to see other people—women, especially—as all good or all bad. A neurotic Casanova can feel tenderness and compassion for the women he loves and is often tormented by guilt when he loses them. A Casanova with a borderline personality barely recognizes women as separate beings and is as guilt-free as a sociopath. To paraphrase an old saying of Recovery, some Casanovas are sicker than others.

It takes no great effort to diagnose someone as emotionally ill. Most of you who are reading this book are probably neurotic to some degree, as am I: Freud would say that this is the price we pay for living in an industrial society. A psychoanalyst named Jaime Nos has identified several of the men in this book as probable borderline personalities. In diagnosing, however, we run the risk of reducing human beings to *cases*. Where before we viewed them with disapproval or perhaps with loathing, the act of diagnosing encourages us to see them clinically, as walking illustrations of a particular condition. But both the moral and clinical perspectives are simplifications, defenses against complexity and ambiguity. Rather than diagnose Casanovas, among whose number I count myself, I would rather recognize them in all their otherness, their unpleasantness and their humanity. See them. See me.

CHAPTER TWO

The Birth of the
Scoundrel

The historic prototype is Jacques Casanova de Seingalt, who in the eighteenth century made a virtual career of seducing women. In his *Memoirs* he described himself as "a bachelor whose chief business in life was to cultivate the senses." The description was accurate. In the course of his seventy-three years Casanova made forays into the Church, the theater and the military, supported himself as a gambler and swindler, but practiced nothing so constantly as the pursuit and seduction of the opposite sex.

By the standards of his time—an age when the Pill, the telephone and penicillin, those staples of the libertine's survival kit, had not yet been invented—he was phenomenally successful. By his own count he slept with 122 women in thirty-nine years. He conducted love affairs in his native Venice, in Rome, Naples, London, Paris, Madrid, Berlin, Vienna, Corfu, Constantinople and St. Petersburg. His tastes were eclectic, his lovers ranging from married women to girls barely past puberty, and from aristocrats to actresses and innkeepers' daughters. He once had a ménage à trois with two nuns, echoing the exploit of an ancestor who had carried off a bride of Christ on the day after she had taken her vows. On a Greek island he collected a harem of "nymphs." When aroused he was utterly audacious. He would approach a woman who was being chaperoned by her uncle and so completely ingratiate himself that her guardian willingly left them alone. The presence of fiancés and husbands only inspired greater perseverance. To Casanova every woman was a potential paramour.

Women responded with equal interest; he was rarely rejected by those he desired. At the age of seventeen, Casanova hesitated to bed a friendly chambermaid and so lost her to a more forceful rival. After that he forswore timidity and viewed all feminine reluctance with suspicion. "If she tries to play the prude," he once vowed, "I will not be her dupe." Few lovers have been blessed with such self-confidence. We do not know whether Casanova was handsome, though he evidently devoted much attention to his clothing, favoring the elaborate military uniforms and decorations that one could buy in those days like so many Armanis. He left no record of his sexual techniques: as instructive matter, the *Memoirs* are no match for *The Sensuous Man*. Certainly he was a romantic figure, well-traveled, well-read and physically fearless, a man who never shied away from a duel. He was a free-handed spender who would buy a woman a complete wardrobe before they had even spent a night together and entertain her family sumptuously the morning after. Above all, we can attribute his success with women to the single-minded intensity with which he pursued them. "I am neither tender nor gallant nor pathetic," he once remarked. "I am passionate."

But his passion was always short-lived. Casanova prided himself on knowing his nature and following its dictates. Part of his nature was to avoid attachment, to remain forever at liberty for the next affair. On a few occasions he became engaged, but separation always restored him to a proper sense of his inclinations. At the end of one betrothal, he recalled: "I had intended to marry her when I loved her more than I loved myself, but as soon as I was away from her side I found that self-love was stronger than the affection with which she had inspired me." For all that, he wasn't the kind of man who simply runs out on his fiancées. Chivalrous even in retreat, Casanova often recruited new and more suitable husbands for the women he abandoned. "Casanova loved many women but broke few hearts," wrote the pioneering sexologist Havelock Ellis. "That he knew himself well enough never to take either wife or mistress must be counted as a virtue."

For all the good-natured breeziness of the *Memoirs*, Casanova was nevertheless a complex and perverse man. His remark on the triumph of self-love points to an unhealthy narcissism, a self-absorption with which no real woman could ever compete. He seems to have been fascinated by women disguised as men or boys, which suggests that women may never have been the true objects of his desire. In his old age, he raped a girl who turned out to be his estranged daughter and who may have borne his child. And although he was never much burdened by conscience, he was sometimes troubled by the awareness that his desires lacked depth and staying power. By his thirties, he realized, "I could still love passionately, but some of the delicacy and power of idealization, which alone justifies the excesses of passion, had passed from me."

To Casanova we must add the fictional archetype of Don Juan or Don Giovanni. He first appears in the seventeenth-century play *The Rake of Seville* by Tirso de Molina and was taken up years later by Molière. He was the subject of Mozart and Da Ponte's opera, *Don Giovanni*, of plays by Goldoni, Pushkin and Montherlant, and of a narrative poem by Byron. In his earliest incarnation Don Juan seduces four women. The librettist Da Ponte endows him with a hefty track record—a thousand and three conquests in Spain alone.

Don Juan is a darker figure than Casanova, a liar as well as a libertine, a rapist as well as a rake. His modus operandi is to propose marriage and leave as soon as the seduction is complete, but he is not above disguising himself as a woman's cloaked fiancé in order to gain access to her boudoir. His obsession is not so much with sex as it is with deception and humiliation. The Don takes ungentlemanly pleasure in ruining the innocent and robbing other men of their brides' virtue. Only Byron, himself an avid seducer of women, portrayed him as a naif who keeps falling in love only to be parted from his mistresses by a capricious fate. In most versions of the story Don Juan gets his comeuppance. Unlike Casanova, who lived into a senile old age, he dies young, dragged down to hell by the ghost of a man he murdered, the father of one of his abandoned lovers. Fiction is neater than life.

A FREED SLAVE

Around these tirelessly seductive figures there has evolved an even more seductive myth. It is the myth of the eternal ladies' man, insatiable and irresistible. His love of women is so great that it can never be confined to one: we can no more expect this man to be faithful than we can expect the wind to blow in one direction. Indeed, the Casanova is sometimes seen as an elemental force. He might be a lesser descendant of Zeus, who was at once the personification of heaven and the lover of goddesses and mortal women, a suitor so persistent that he would change himself into a bull, a swan or a shower of gold just to make a date. Casanova has the resilience, the mercurial temperament and the anarchic humor of the Trickster figure, the Coyote of Navajo legend. To Havelock Ellis, Casanova's constantly changing appetites embodied "the instability which marks only the most intensely vital organisms."

Even if we overlook such inflationary rhetoric, we cannot deny that Casanova sometimes seems like the archetypal male—or at least the kind of man that many men would like to be. The Casanova's virility is unimpeachable: any man who makes love to so many women must be overflowing with testosterone. Indeed, his maleness is what draws women to him in the first place. They recognize it instinctively. If we rate men by their appeal to the opposite sex—as *People* magazine does with its "Sexiest Man of the Year"—Casanova is a top-of-the-line model. We see his polygamy (or polygyny, since he is not the marrying kind) as a reflection of the male's innate tendency to scatter his seed as widely as possible. As the old rhyme has it:

> Hogamus, higamus
> Men are polygamous
> Higamus, hogamus
> Women monogamous.

In this view of things, the Casanova represents man in his true state, a noble savage frolicking with his harem. "Casanova's name, unlike those of de Sade or Sacher-Masoch, is not used to designate a perversion," says the French writer Chantal Thomas. "On the contrary, it refers to a sort of tacit agreement on normality."

In his adherence to his nature, Casanova sometimes resembles a product of the romantic imagination of Rousseau. Or he might be an exponent of the revolutionary and anarchic individualism espoused by the Marquis de Sade. We tend to forget that de Sade was an ideologue as well as a deviant, his manifestos calling for a republic of the senses in which everyone has the right to everyone else and sex is both an imperative and a medium of exchange. In such a state, says the critic and cultural historian Christopher Lasch, "pleasure becomes life's only business.... All freedoms ... come in the end to the same thing, the same universal obligation to enjoy and be enjoyed." Similar ideals inform the rhetoric of the sexual revolution of the 1960s and 1970s. It is not impossible to see the apolitical Casanova as an early guerrilla of the pleasure principle.

The Casanova's willingness to invent his own morality hints at a naive existentialism. Take away his wig and Italian courtesies and he might be an antihero from the novels of Henry Miller and Norman Mailer. For these writers sexual license is more than brute pleasure. Sex has *meaning*. It is an avenue of self-assertion and self-definition, all the more crucial for the two thousand years of Judeo-Christian injunctions that would seal it off. Every time the Casanova embraces a new partner, he seizes his own existence, his prerogatives as a being with pleasure centers and a penis. And when he evades domestication, he also flees the constraints that seem to go hand in hand with marriage. He reminds wistful husbands, ensnarled in the claims of wives, children and creditors, that the Latin root of "libertine" is *libertus*—a freed slave.

THE TORCH-SONG AESTHETIC

Part of the Casanova's appeal to women lies in the threat he represents. As Lady Caroline Lamb wrote of Lord Byron, he is "mad, bad and dangerous to know." In the romantic novels of the eighteenth century—*The Fair Penitent, Clarissa* and *Les Liaisons Dangereuses* come to mind—the threat he posed was to the heroines' virtue. This dashing and elegant figure was the ideal suitor in every respect but one: he had no interest in marriage and, like Don Juan, he was out to steal the thing that no young woman could marry without. His intentions were often clear, but his sexual appeal was so great that his victims rarely could resist him.

The heroines of today's bodice rippers—and of more serious novels like Sue Kaufman's *Diary of a Mad Housewife* and Anne Roiphe's *Torch Song*—are no longer virginal and have nothing against a fling with the right man. The problem is that Casanova is so obviously Mr. Wrong. The danger he poses to today's women, in fiction and in life, is that of abandonment. But the fact that he will depart—after a night, a weekend or a few glorious months—only adds to his glamour, the glamour of the dream. The woman who loves a Casanova knows that she will never have to compete with "Monday Night Football," squabble over the bills or inhale sour male breath. Those, after all, are the liabilities of husbands and boyfriends. Casanova is too much of a good thing. When he leaves, he continues to haunt his lovers, as a vampire lingers in the blood of his victims.

The different threats the Casanova embodies in different popular fictions spring very much from the cultural climates of the times that produced them. To the bourgeois readers of the eighteenth century the worst thing that could befall a woman was disgrace, which destroyed her chances for marital happiness and exiled her from her class. Sexually savvy yet emotionally vulnerable, the fans of Judith Krantz and Janet Dailey dread being dumped. For rejection is not just painful, it is the ultimate humiliation in a society that makes a fetish of success. When the Casanova leaves his girlfriend, the common assumption is no longer that the man is a rotter but that the *woman* has somehow failed, intellectually or sexually. Two hundred years ago, the Casanova only jeopardized a woman's class status; now he calls her very femininity into question.

But his sexual menace is also mesmerizing. The heroines of romantic novels—and their real-life readers—are often perversely drawn to men who are mad, bad and dangerous. When they stare into those smoldering eyes, all their alarms go off. But instead of fleeing they rush forward, even if to do so means losing their virtue and self-esteem. Part of this is due to the torch-song aesthetic that informs so much of popular women's fiction. In this aesthetic, passion is redeemed by heartbreak. It even depends on it, if it is to be recognized as passion and not as simple lust, which even in our zipless decade remains something of a taboo. A woman need not be a saint to love a Casanova or to suffer at his hands, but hopeless love and suffering will ennoble her, transfigure her, in much the same way as they ennobled and transfigured legions of female saints. Casanova offers her a shot at secular martyrdom.

Female masochism, though, plays only a small part in the mystique of the Casanova. Female pride is responsible for much of his allure. Inherent in his elusiveness is a challenge that few women seem able to pass up. Meeting his insouciant gaze and surveying his track record of broken hearts, ambitious women see Casanova the way some men see virgins—as rare and formidable game whose capture will affirm their own sexuality. Oscar Wilde observed that all men aspire to be a woman's first love, while women, being more practical, want to be the last. The Casanova is rarely coy about his past. He often advertises it, as though daring each new woman to succeed where her predecessors failed. Everything about him seems to say "catch me if you can." Is it any wonder that so many women take him up on it?

THE BABY AND THE BRUTE

In our century, however, the Casanova has become the subject of a countermyth, or really, of two countermyths, inspired by the psychoanalytic and feminist movements. Few of the early psychoanalysts devoted much attention to the compulsively seductive and unfaithful man (a major exception is Otto Rank, whose *The Don Juan Legend* was of major help in formulating my ideas on the Casanova complex). Freud was too preoccupied with the adverse consequences of repression to consider those whose sexuality seemed unfettered. "A man who abstains, for whatever reasons, from satisfying his strong sexual instinct, will also assume a conciliatory and resigned attitude in other paths of life," he observed.

Freud blamed repression for two baffling characteristics of masculine sexuality: the need to degrade the love object and the inability to be satisfied with one partner. What was repressed, he argued, was an incestuous attachment to the mother, the male child's first love object. In normal development, that attachment is eventually relinquished and, after a period of latency, the boy transfers his desire to other women, who inspire in him the tenderness and passion that he originally felt for his mother. But some men, Freud believed, remain maternally fixated. Unable to acknowledge their incestuous wishes, they deny their sexuality altogether or, in less extreme cases, sunder their sensual feelings from their feelings of affection. The result is that any woman who arouses tenderness or esteem is sexually taboo: they can only feel passion for women whom they despise. In assessing this dilemma, Freud permitted himself an analytic shrug: "Where such men love they have no desire and where they desire they cannot love."

The repression of incestuous desires exacted other penalties. According to both Freud and Carl Jung, men who have failed to give up their mothers as sexual objects can never find satisfactory replacements for them. Although the original desire is repressed, it prevents new bonds from forming. Such men are condemned to shuffle eternally among many women, unable to find one who is "just right," who evokes in them the same combination of sensuality and esteem that mother did. In the glare of Freudian scrutiny, the image of Casanova suffered a diminution. Inside every ladies' man there now seemed to be a mama's boy struggling to get out.

More recently, feminists have identified the Casanova as an agent of the undeclared patriarchy that has victimized women for millennia. He is as much an oppressor as the brute who uses his wife as an unpaid whore, brood mare and scullery maid. He may be worse, for he doesn't even give his partners the emotional and financial security of marriage. By this reckoning, the Casanova uses women as little more than sexual pit stops, each one indistinguishable from those before her. As he practices it, seduction is only a more genteel form of rape. And just as rape has more to do with power than with sex, so the Casanova's erotic gamesmanship is really an endlessly repeated assertion of masculine supremacy.

Myths, of course, need not be logical or consistent. The mythical Casanova can play as many contradictory roles as we care to pile on him: man's man and lady's man, masculine paradigm and mama's boy, liberator and oppressor, urbane courtier of the bedroom and sexual outlaw. Nothing requires him to conform to any one pattern —Casanova is a myth.

HOW ARE THESE MEN DIFFERENT FROM OTHER MEN?

Yet just as the mythical Casanova grew out of the life of a real man, so there are real men who reenact the myth. These latter-day Casanovas have an insatiable appetite for women and seem irresistibly attractive to them. They rarely lack for female companionship. Some of them are forever at liberty, with a different partner every night and a hundred names in their address books. A steady date may last them a month, a significant other three, but there are always new women on the horizon—or tucked away somewhere in their schedules. However much they desire women en masse, they have a phenomenal aversion to individual commitment and are phenomenally nimble at avoiding it.

Of course, some Casanovas do marry; indeed, some men become Casanovas only after they settle down, as though they need to be assured of a home base before they can play the high-risk game of musical beds. These erring husbands may fall deeply in love with other women, whom they see regularly for years. Others limit themselves to one-night stands or brief flings. But for all such men, adultery is neither a traumatic symptom of mid-life crisis nor a scratching of the seven-year itch: it is a habitual practice. In the Casanova's marriage vows the phrase "forsaking all others" is conveniently penciled out.

Who are these men, really? How do they interact with women and why do they appeal to them? Why are they unable to settle with one partner or stay faithful to women they claim to love? How do Casanovas see themselves?

We might begin by distinguishing Casanovas from other men—a difficult job since, as previously mentioned, they sometimes seem to embody all the stereotypes of the polygamous, unfaithful and oversexed male. Among the world's cultures polygyny—the union of one man with several women—is far more common than monogamy or polyandry, under which one woman is permitted several men. In the industrial West men generally become sexually active at an earlier age than women and take more sexual partners in the course of a lifetime. In the United States men are more likely than women to engage in extramarital sex. The pattern seems almost universal. How then are Casanovas different?

THE DECADE OF DETUMESCENCE

In recent years we have come to revise our notions of conventional sexual behavior. For one thing, more and more women are having sex earlier, more often and with more partners, both before and after marriage. And according to some studies, women are more likely than men to leave an unsatisfactory marriage or relationship. Women are catching up.

At the same time, men seem to be slowing down. In present-day America relatively few men make a life-style of polygyny or cheat regularly on their spouses. For most men, promiscuity is rather like the Times Square of twenty years ago: an exciting but slightly dangerous neighborhood that we pass through en route to the suburbs of monogamy. In the 1980s the epidemic of sexually transmitted diseases such as herpes and AIDS has curbed our sexual appetites; we are uncomfortably aware that the most transient pleasures may carry a terminal price tag. Our society as a whole has entered an age of sexual retrenchment, a decade of detumescence. The baby boomers are graying. And whether we attribute it to Jerry Falwell or falling testosterone levels, men as a whole increasingly value stability over stimulus, security over abandon. If the ideal of the seventies was a nonstop orgy in a hot tub, the dream of the eighties is marriage and a five-room condo.

In the decade of detumescence, Casanovas are anachronisms, acting on the discredited sexual assumptions of an earlier generation. Compared to other men, they have more sexual contacts with a greater number of partners, sometimes with three or more different women a week for extended periods of their lives. If married, they are frequently unfaithful. They do not see adultery as a lapse, but as a norm, a continuous counterpoint to the theme of marriage. As one of the men I interviewed said to me: "I felt like being married was having my entrée, but where was my dessert?"

We recognize Casanovas by the fragility of their relationships: theirs is a brotherhood of the sundered and divorced. We recognize them by their vast, shifting entourages of lovers, mistresses and girlfriends. Casanovas are not one-woman men, and those who take one partner at a time prove incapable of sustaining the relationship. And it is usually the Casanovas who leave. They may fall in love with other women; they may simply decide that their present ties are too boring, too limiting or demanding. And so they go, as they always have, as they always will. We know them by the explanations they leave behind:

"It just wasn't working out."
"I met someone else."
"I wasn't ready to be tied down."
"She was getting too possessive."
"I needed more space."

CHAPTER THREE

---◆---

Patterns of Desire

Baby,

I'm still feeling racked about Friday. I never thought I'd let you walk out my door so easily. Or could see you in the morning without having to have you right then. I'd thought you'd given me a reprieve from myself; that you'd managed to strike the fault line that would shear the good from the dross, pleasure from pain, strength from cruelty, love from need. I should have known that some sentences can't be commuted. You serve your time or you break out. I should have known, but I didn't and now I'm furious, because you cheated me. You made me believe that caring for you would make me whole.

I agree that I wasn't seeing you, or acknowledging your needs as I

acknowledge my own. I can't be a lover without exalting my own
selfishness and then scourging myself half to death for it. I can't be
a lover without turning into someone awful and lashing out at the
woman who witnesses the transformation. I can't be a lover—or
simply don't want to be.
                    —from the author's letter to a former girlfriend, 1978

To speak of Casanovas is to speak of many different kinds of men,
whose outward behavior seems varied and contradictory. Casanova
is an urbane bachelor who collects beautiful women as though they
were objets d'art, only to tire of them once their novelty wears off.
He is the embittered survivor of a divorce who views each new
partner as a potential adversary, allowing her only a grudging mite
of closeness before he banishes her. He is an aging married man
who goes on sexual benders during which he couples with any
woman who will have him. He is a nice Italian boy who still lives
with his parents but spends his nights in a frantic and endlessly
frustrated search for love.

What these men share are unconscious attitudes about women
and sex—and about the self—that make their behavior necessary
and perhaps inevitable. For Casanovas women are not individuals.
Rather, they are a race of necessary but nonetheless threatening
beings who inhabit a borderland between the inner world of the
psyche and the outer world of people and things. Sex is not "about"
sexual pleasure, a set of enjoyable sensations in the erogenous
zones. Nor does it have much to do with love—however we choose
to define *that*. Sex is a vehicle, a means of attaining the sense of
wholeness and completion that lies at the bedrock of most of our
identities, but which Casanovas usually lack. Sex is their only way
of easing a disquiet that is otherwise always present and virtually
crippling.

These attitudes are most easily expressed as metaphors. "Thrill
seeking" describes the Casanova's endless, escalating search for sexual and emotional experience. His obsession with mastery and control translates into a continuous "game playing" in which women
are alternately prizes and pawns. Once we realize the depth of his
psychic unease, we can easily envision his promiscuity as a kind of
"escape." And the very language in which he describes desire and its
objects suggests that he does not make love to women so much as
he "devours" them, using his partners as sources of temporary
nourishment and then disposing of them with the finality and dis-

gust with which one disposes of the body's wastes.

Not every Casanova displays all these attitudes. Escaping and devouring, in particular, are often signs of grave character disorders. At the same time, it is possible for one man to exhibit all four attitudes at different times and to varying degrees: a man who seems to pursue women for excitement may, on closer investigation, turn out to be satisfying a hunger that is almost physical; his boredom is a metaphor for emptiness. The apparent self-assurance of a game player may mask the panic of an escape artist. It is chiefly for the sake of clarity that I have illustrated each pattern of desire with a different case history. I have changed the names and altered the histories of the following Casanovas in minor ways in order to protect their privacy.

LOVE IS THE DRUG: THRILL SEEKING

Saul, thirty-six, most closely lives up to our expectations of the successful Casanova, cultured, well-spoken and dripping with attitude. He gives a simultaneous impression of torpor and great busyness—he interrupted our conversation several times in order to answer phone calls. Although he spoke with me in a well-modulated purr, his voice seemed to speed up when he addressed his other callers: he barked at them frantically, as though he had just sucked up a lungful of helium. I wondered which voice he used with his girlfriends.

Saul is an executive for a high-fashion clothing manufacturer in New York City. He spends most of his workday surrounded by good-looking women—models, designers, wealthy customers. In his office, he tells me, even the bookkeepers are stunners. He still sees women as "glorious creatures. They're God's greatest creations. My business is glorifying women. Our clothes make women feel good about themselves. But it doesn't stop there. Sometimes I think that my reason for living is to satisfy women, to make them happy."

Women have been a constant in his life since he left college. He has always had what he calls "lovers," women whom he sees at least three times a week and to whom he devotes most of his time and attention. He squires them to the city's most chic restaurants and clubs. He proudly introduces them to his family and friends. He takes them with him on vacations to places like Muscat and St.-Tropez. Sometimes he considers marrying them. Usually, he ends up living with them, in his lavish apartment on the Upper East Side.

Most of Saul's lovers have been fashion models. "They're the best-looking, of course. They know how to dress and how to act in social situations. They won't embarrass you. And to be honest, models are good at taking direction. It's important that a woman follow my lead. She's got to live up to my standards; she should be someone who, if I feel like going to the Philharmonic or to Nell's, isn't going to want to stay home to watch 'Family Ties.'" As exacting as his standards are, Saul has always found women who met them—at least for a while. He almost married three of his live-in girlfriends.

But he is still single. To his regret and bewilderment, none of his relationships has lasted more than two years. "I'll tell you," he says, "I'd do anything to meet the right woman. I mean, I'm pushing forty. If you want to know the truth, the loneliness is sometimes a bitch. Sometimes I feel like a failure. I think to myself, I'm not a loser. I've got good looks. I'm a good lover—women tell me that all the time. I'm intelligent, I've got two degrees. I make a good living. And if I say so myself, I'm basically a decent human being. Why can't I find someone I can stay with?"

Saul has parted with his lovers for different reasons. Some failed to satisfy him sexually. Some were too possessive. A few he wrote off as "hopeless neurotics." But the most common problem is his own boredom. Once he starts living with a woman, his early excitement—"that overcharged, superalive feeling that we're driving somewhere at ninety miles an hour"—turns into routine and obligation. Nights on the town yield to squabbles about housekeeping and the evening's menu. The fierce clamor of the heart gives way to the ticking of the clock.

Most of us look forward to learning more about the people we love. Saul believes that familiarity breeds disappointment: "At the beginning every woman is a mystery. I don't know what she does when she's alone. I don't know how she makes herself so beautiful. I don't know what she's thinking about when she's not talking. I want to know everything about her. But then the mysteries disappear. Every time I walk into the bathroom, I can't turn around for all the makeup she's got on the sink and the panty hose hanging in the shower stall. And when she's quiet it turns out she's just wondering what she's going to get her cousin in Des Moines for a wedding present. It completely turns me off. I mean, is that all there is? I feel like she's cheated me."

When mystery goes, so does desire. "The first few months it's sex four times a day. Then it starts to turn into companionship. Now I look at my relationship as though I had a roommate—a roommate with sex." Paradoxically, as lovemaking loses it ardor, it becomes the subject of many more arguments. One night Saul wants sex and his girlfriend doesn't; the next night the tables are turned. Saul likes to see himself as perpetually turned on: the waning of desire is a severe blow to his pride. For a time, he tries to restore it with exotic scenarios and positions, brandy and cocaine. Then he begins blaming his diffidence on his partner. He often complains that his girlfriends are too passive.

"My last lover would do anything I'd ask her to. The problem was, I always had to do the asking. I always felt like everything she did, she was doing just to please me: she'd have been just as happy to clean the house or bake me a pie if she thought that would please me more. She could tell I was disappointed. She'd say to me, 'Tell me what you want.' How could I tell her that what I wanted was for her to want me—wildly, desperately? But she wasn't that kind of girl."

Why does such a virile and sexually demanding man end up with passive women? Part of the problem must lie in the kind of women he chooses. Saul prefers models because they're good at taking direction, but a woman who is submissive on the runway may well be submissive in the bedroom. Furthermore, Saul seems most attracted to women who possess "the scrubbed Kelly Embree look," whose appeal, in other words, is more wholesome than erotic. It may be that those women appeal to him precisely because of their lack of overt sexual threat—that the last thing Saul really wants is a woman who might demand more than he can give her.

Yet as his primary relationship cools from passion to companionship, Saul begins to look for other women. In his business he finds them easily. "It's not like I'm searching for a replacement," he says. "The last thing I want at this point is another relationship. I just want some good, uncomplicated sex, sex that's dirty and exciting, that gives you a buzz. I don't think of it as cheating. Do I tell my girlfriend? You've got to be kidding! What good is telling her going to do? I don't want to hurt her feelings."

Although he believes that what he does in bed is his business alone, these involvements take an inevitable toll. Lying becomes a necessity, and each lie breeds others. Deception breeds contempt for the one deceived. It also engenders anger, for Saul only lies for his partners' sake. After a while that unappreciated, unrewarded effort comes to feel like drudgery. Contempt and anger breed their own fatally persuasive logic: why stay with a woman you have to lie to?

And so finally Saul decides that his relationship is more trouble than it's worth and breaks it off. "Usually I tell her, 'It's not you. It's just that we're not going anywhere. It's getting stale.' I don't like scenes. Most of the time, we stay friends. In a good relationship, you can get together for drinks a year after it's over and laugh about it. There's nothing to regret. It's just that you both had to move on."

But if Saul's relationships usually end on a benign note, their cumulative legacy has been bitter. Although he keeps searching for new lovers, he speaks of love with the sour bleakness of a man who keeps losing at it: "Falling in love is always a big letdown. It's like doing cocaine. You get high, but sooner or later you know that you're going to run out and you're going to come down. And it's the same with love: the rush ends after three or four months."

A GAME OF LIVING OUT FANTASIES: GAME PLAYING

Howard, fifty-two and divorced eight years, lives in a suburb of Chicago. It doesn't take long to realize he is a lawyer: he has a lawyer's gift for semantic acrobatics, for finding a loophole in every sentence and leaping nimbly through it. "Yes, I was an adulterer, in the technical sense," he admits. "But so, arguably, were most men of my generation—all the guys who got married between the end of World War Two and the sixties, when people finally had other options. We were conned. You have to understand that when Linda and I got married, we didn't know anything about sex, except for what we'd learned in the backseat of my Plymouth. I was twenty-one, horny as hell and scared shitless. Linda was the first girl I'd scored with, and there was no choice but to marry her. What else was I supposed to do? But already I was wondering if that was all there was to sex. I was curious; all kids are curious at that age. And even then I knew that one woman wouldn't be enough for me."

For the next twenty-odd years Howard satisfied his curiosity with hundreds of different women. He quickly adds that not all of them were women he sought out: a lot of his encounters were accidents. He'd be alone in a coffee shop, an airport or at a business function and meet someone who struck him as attractive and available. Like most Casanovas, he is quick to spot the cues that women use to advertise their interest and availability. He has codified female walks, glances and attire and can tell you what it means if a woman primps in a shop window as you pass by, or how many opened blouse buttons constitute a sexual invitation.

As much as the sex itself, he enjoyed the protocol of seduction. He liked "the whole Rock Hudson–Doris Day thing—soft music, fine wine and a perfectly timed kiss." He prided himself on being a smooth talker, and while not especially handsome, he dressed with care and moved well on the dance floor. He made a point of never rushing his partners into bed. He let the situation carry them there, as though they were both surrendering to forces beyond their control.

Above all, he was relaxed and confident. For in addition to all his other skills, Howard had "the Pete Rose theory" of seduction: "There were so many available women that I didn't *have* to have anybody. There was always another one out there. I figure that I actually slept with about half of the women I was interested in: that's one out of two. Now Pete Rose usually hits .333: one for three. So my score was good enough to win a championship, if I say so myself."

Howard's baseball metaphor betrays a view of sex as gamesmanship. In that game, numbers definitely counted. He could afford to be sportsmanlike as long as his average exceeded a certain figure, the average of the other players in the field: "What you call adultery was attractive because it was challenging. It was a game of living out fantasies. Most men fantasize and don't do anything about it. I did."

For a long time Howard was a cautious player. He kept the game separate from his life with his wife and children. Although he describes himself as a romantic, I was struck by the businesslike way in which he conducted his flings. At the onset of an affair—a word he is reluctant to use—he would tell his partner that he was married, to avoid later misunderstandings. And he would warn her not to expect a deeper involvement. "I had a nice secure existence with the wife and the house with the white picket fence and the kids and the cat and the dog and the Little League—the whole nine yards. So as soon as another woman threatened my marriage, I had to end it. Getting laid wasn't worth it to me."

Howard's measured infidelity resembled a game of emotional chicken, that competition in which two cars race toward each other and veer away at the last minute. He was constantly testing limits, skirting foul lines. How often could he come home at midnight without arousing his wife's suspicions? How far could he stray from his role as a respectable husband before he crossed the border of respectability? How long could he see a woman before she became stickily involved with him—or he with her? How far could he strain the fabric of his marriage until it was irreparably rent? To play this game, he had to place rigid limits on his time, his conduct and his feelings. The precautions he took might seem even more constricting than the codes that govern most marriages. To Howard, even daydreaming about a woman was off-limits: it might be the prelude to obsession.

Finally, in spite of all his rules, Howard fell in love with one of his extramarital partners. Magnetic, unpredictable, Annette was a "Babe Ruth of sex," a woman who would try anything twice. She spurred him on to greater risks: he would stay with her until two or three in the morning; he called her from his home. Eventually, Linda found out. She demanded that he end the affair. He refused; he couldn't give Annette up. In the divorce that followed, he lost his house and most of his money. His children stopped speaking to him. To meet his alimony payments and keep up his extravagant life with his mistress, he had to moonlight in a legal clinic, working seventy-hour weeks. A few months later, he had a small but terrifying stroke; he was forty-nine years old.

He was almost helpless now, and pathetically dependent on Annette. But although she loved Howard, she refused to be tied down by him. She insisted on her right to take other lovers. She exercised that right whenever it pleased her. "Suddenly," he recalls, "I was the jealous one, the one who was always whining about commitment." After years of fighting and infidelities, Annette called the affair off.

The chaos and humiliation of that episode have made Howard wary of entanglement. In his relations with women he now resembles an overcautious boxer, one who feints, jabs and bobs but avoids the clinches. He is still courtly and attentive; he still prizes the trappings of romance. But before he beds someone for the first time, he meticulously states his terms for the relationship: he will see her only when he feels like it; he will date other women; he will not make a long-term commitment. He refuses to plan a date more than two weeks in advance. Declaring his intentions, he feels, signifies a new honesty. His affairs now should be as orderly as a game of baseball.

But few women are willing to play by Howard's rules. His relationships always end after a few months, in peevish squabbles over excessive demands and broken promises. "I'll tell you what the problem is with women today," he says, "at least with women of my age. They all have this sense of *entitlement*. All these fortyish ladies who call themselves 'liberated'—they're still playing by the old rules: that if you want their companionship and their sex, you've got to give up your privacy and independence. But ladies, ladies, *the rules have changed!!*"

THE ESCAPE ARTIST: ESCAPING

Fred, sixty-three, is a retired army officer who now lives in a suburb of Washington. During the early part of our interview his language was formal and precise, the language of the military dispatch. He had been married for thirty-eight years and five months; he had had his first sexual encounter at the age of fifteen; since then he had had relations with 862 women in five countries. He rattled off the figures without hesitation, as though he had memorized them along with his serial number.

As we spoke, though, he seemed to sink through the ranks until his language was as foul as a drill instructor's. Where once he had referred to women—even to prostitutes—as "ladies," he now sometimes called them "bitches." His descriptions of lovemaking became pornographically lurid but lacked pornography's power to arouse: they sounded too much like descriptions of beatings. Phrases like "I fucked her" or "I gave it to her" abounded.

Basically Fred has just one story to tell. He meets a woman someplace; they get drunk together (most of his encounters seem to have taken place in an alcoholic fog); they go somewhere—to her house, or to his, if his wife is away, to a hotel room or a parked car—and they have sex. Sometimes, they see each other again. More often the women seem to vanish. He cannot tell me how any of his affairs ended. One woman segues into the next, or he and his lover "just drift apart." It may be a condition of military service—a year at one base, three years at another—but for Fred all sexual relations end with a drifting apart. This is in marked contrast to his relationships with other men, some of which have endured decades over many postings. It is only women who are expendable: here for a time and then gone forever.

The women, whether congressmen's wives or Okinawan B-girls,

all sound the same, stripped of everything but the meager facts of sex. When he first meets them, he wants them with a blinding, monomaniac urgency: "She drove me crazy," he says of a recent partner. "Here I was supposed to be buying groceries for the wife and instead I'm buying her one drink after another, hoping she'll get drunk enough to let me slip it to her for ten minutes. I'm two hours late. I'm not supposed to be drinking. And I don't care. If she asked me to rob a liquor store, I'd do it if it helped me get into her pants."

But that's as far as passion goes. A half hour later, she will have dropped from consciousness. Fred's women have no identity outside the bedroom. While stationed in Thailand, he had a four-year affair with a woman who worked for the U.S. consulate. The most he can tell me about her is that "she was a splendid woman. We got along splendidly." "Why?" I ask. He starts telling me about something she did in bed; I can't tell if he means it as a digression or an explanation. When she was transferred, he felt sad for a while, but he made no effort to contact her once he was back in the States. "She knew I was married. What good would there be in seeing her again?"

The only real woman in Fred's life is his wife. He talks about her with a courtly deference. He calls her "a lady," "my better half" and "Mrs. S." He says she is the only person who really knows him, the only person he feels comfortable with. He has taken great pains to give her a good life, sending her expensive gifts from every foreign posting, remodeling their kitchen by hand to her specifications. Although he claims to feel no guilt over his extracurricular activities, he says he tries to keep them hidden from her: he doesn't like to hurt her.

For an army officer, frequently away from home and always protected by a closed masculine society, secrecy should be easy. But Fred is a shamefully careless adulterer, who has done everything but issue printed announcements of his indiscretions. One can't help asking whether he *wants* his wife to know about them. But why? For all the brutality of his language, Fred doesn't strike me as a sadist, at least not where his wife is concerned. Perhaps, like Howard, he is playing a game of chicken, whose object is to see how openly he can flaunt his adulteries without losing his wife's affection.

Or perhaps Fred's infidelity is not the risk it seems, but something that actually guarantees his marriage. How else can we account for his wife's patience? Once, after walking in on his tryst with another woman, she threatened to divorce him. Fred sweet-talked her into staying. That was years ago, and although his infidelities still hurt her, she no longer talks about leaving: "If Mrs. S. finds out I've been playing around," Fred explains, "she'll cry a little, and she won't let me bother her for a few days. But it's just her pride. She knows she means the world to me and there's not going to be anyone else." He stammers a bit and suddenly, in spite of his age, he sounds very young to me, like Jimmy Stewart toeing the dust and saying "Aw, gee whiz!": "And she knows that I'm just—oversexed, that I've just got to have other women. It's how I am."

Adultery thus takes place within the context of a tacit understanding. Fred is oversexed, that understanding goes. He needs other women the way other men need to get drunk every so often or go fishing with their buddies. Infidelity is his escape valve, a licensed departure from a marriage that in all other ways seems extraordinarily, even repressively, close: "My wife and I are compatible in everything. You take sex. If I climax, she climaxes. If I don't climax, she can't. Sometimes I don't know if I'm screwing or masturbating." Is this a boast or a cry of panic? It's as though Fred and his wife had fused into a single organism. Their lovemaking is not the joining of separate individuals but the masturbation of a beast with two bodies, a Siamese twin. Fred's infidelity is more than a way of kicking up his heels: it's his only escape from a nightmare of togetherness.

If we look beyond his marriage to the rest of his life, all those years of obeying orders and repressing mutinous impulses, Fred's erotic escape route makes painful sense. Sex is his reprieve from the suffocating closeness of his marriage, from his life sentence of duty, honor, country. Sex for this man is not about pleasure, it's a grinding necessity, a liberation that constitutes another kind of imprisonment. "I wish I knew what turns me on to women," he muses. "I'll be honest with you, for me that kind of desire is a painful thing. It's like a nagging itch that you can't get to and you can't relieve. Or it's like you're drowning and you're fighting to get to the surface for that one gulp of air. When you finally do, your lungs are bursting, and breathing is pure torture. But what are you going to do? You're in pain, but you've got to breathe or you're going to die. That's what sex is to me: a mental anguish."

THE HUNGER ARTIST: DEVOURING

At twenty-six, Anthony is a little too old to be called a good boy. But that's how his parents see him. After all, he still lives at home with them in a suburb of Pittsburgh, does his share of the chores and works diligently for his father's trucking company. When I ask him if his parents mind his hyperactive sex life, he replies: "They've never had any complaints." I, too, can't help thinking of him as a good boy. He's so sunny, polite and eager to please. He responds to questions with studious thoroughness, as though he were anxious to get the answers right. He corrects himself when he thinks he might be exaggerating and, until I reassured him that I'm not easily shocked, he kept saying "thing" instead of "penis" or "vagina," "we did it" instead of "we had intercourse."

Anthony had a steady girlfriend through most of high school, but she wouldn't sleep with him. When his efforts to coax her into bed proved fruitless, he relieved his frustration by picking up girls at parties and grappling with them for a fevered half hour in a parked car or an unused bedroom. "None of them meant anything," he says. "They were just pieces of meat to me." His girlfriend, in contrast, was "a good girl. Too good. She wouldn't give me what I needed."

In college, he dated several women, with whom he had full sexual relations, but he would always end these affairs after a few months: "I guess they were nice girls, but they all wanted something. Sooner or later they'd start pressuring me: 'When are we gonna get together again?' 'When are you gonna get serious?' 'Don't you ever think about getting married?' I'd try to be nice to them, but then they'd get like sharks. So I'd have to dump them." A good-looking boy, Anthony had no trouble finding replacements.

Today, he says, he wants something more than a quick sexual fix. "Sex is okay," he says, "but there's got to be something more. Too many times I look at a girl and that's all there was between us, just us doing it. And I feel, What a waste!" Anthony will settle for nothing less than being in love, and he looks for it several nights a week, as methodically as though he were looking for a job. His routine is unvarying. He comes home from work, showers, eats dinner with his parents and does the dishes afterward, then changes into fresh clothes and drives to one of a half-dozen clubs or discos. He makes the rounds of his friends, chats with the bartender, but all the time he is scanning the tables for a woman, someone young, single and preferably attractive. He knows her the moment he sees her: "It's total. Like suddenly, I've found what I was looking for all my life. Yeah, I know there's not supposed to be such a thing as love at first sight. But that's what happens to me."

Approaching this woman is like plunging into a vortex: the closer Anthony gets, the more he wants her. Everything about her delights him. No matter what she says to him, she sounds brilliant and sensitive and sweet of heart. He doesn't just want to have sex with her; he wants to make love with her, to taste her, to hold her tightly and never let her go. His yearning is a distillation of every pop song written since 1954. In her presence he feels small and clumsy, terrified that she won't like him. On the few occasions a woman turned him down, he felt like crying or hitting her. He had to flee from the club and sit trembling in his car for a few minutes before he could drive somewhere else for another chance.

But this rarely happens, he assures me. "I know how to talk to a girl. I'm fun, I'm considerate. Usually there's no trouble. We go to her place and we party." I ask him if he ever takes girls home with him. "Oh no," he says, shocked, "that would be showing disrespect to my folks." It so happens that most of the women he hooks up with are older, with their own apartments. "I like the sophisticated type." Their lovemaking goes on a long time. Unlike many men his age, Anthony has no trouble with premature ejaculation, especially if he has had a few drinks beforehand. If anything, he has difficulty reaching orgasm. He gets more pleasure from oral sex, he says, which allows him to concentrate on his partners' pleasure. "They give me what I need," he delicately sums things up, "I give them what they want."

If the sex is good, Anthony knows that he is "really" in love; he often has to struggle to keep from blurting it out right then. His breathing has scarcely returned to normal before he asks his partner for a date and maps out an entire strategy of courtship: dinner at the right restaurants, dancing at the right clubs, roses, perfume, hours of balletic lovemaking with a gram of cocaine on the night table. Later on, he imagines introducing the girl to his parents and meeting her family, a weekend in New York—all the way up to a videotaped wedding, where his best friends serve as ushers and the bride is caparisoned in lace as white and stiffly frilled as the icing on the wedding cake.

But this scenario has never come to pass. On several occasions, the women Anthony wanted felt unduly pressured by his daily phone calls and premature declarations of love. A few were dating other men and wouldn't give them up just because he wanted them to. Sharing a woman with others is unacceptable to him. "She's got to choose," he says. "If I like a girl, right away I want to have her all to myself." More often, though, Anthony himself begins to have second thoughts. Usually, it happens somewhere between the second and fifth dates: "One time I was with a girl and she said something that was a little dumb. I don't even remember what it was. But after that, I started seeing her differently and thinking, What am I doing with this bimbo, me with my 3.5 grade average? Another time, I'm doing it with a girl and I notice that her pubic hair is kind of long, and that turned me off. Another one, she had these awful stretch marks. There's always something. I start asking myself what I'm getting into."

Disillusionment has an insidious effect. Suddenly, it's Anthony who feels pressured. His partner's enthusiasm—the enthusiasm that he nurtured so carefully—now feels like an assault. He grits his teeth at every request for a date, shudders at every phone call. A girl's "I love you" is no longer a gift: it's a dunning letter, a demand that fills him with rage. For the women in question, it's a no-win situation. If they sense his growing coolness and ask for reassurance, he feels importuned—"like I'm being panhandled." If they ignore it, he feels pushed around.

He has ended affairs in a moment of anger; he has dragged them out for weeks, making dates and then breaking them at the last minute, leaving calls unanswered in the hope that his caller will finally get the message. He sometimes feels hypocritical, worries that he's "just been taking advantage" of women who made the error of taking him at his word. For all his remorse, though, Anthony has a gift for forgetting his "mistakes": he can't remember the names of girls he loved a year ago. "I don't know why I make such a big deal about it," he says of one recent three-week fling. "We had a thing, and it was good for a while. I thought the girl was right for me, but she wasn't. That doesn't mean I didn't show her a good time. I'll tell you, her problem was that it wasn't enough. She had to have more. She wanted a bigger piece of me, and she got pushy about it. And I guess it's too bad that I was harsh with her—I'm like that sometimes. But the whole thing was a mistake."

THE LOVE OF THE MOMENT

These men and the stories they have to tell demolish our stereo-types of the Casanova. Translated into a contemporary idiom, ex-otic settings replaced by the bedrooms of suburbia and the singles bars of the inner city, Casanova's erotic exploits become the one-night stands of a would-be swinger, the grapplings of a nervous adulterer. The language of love is replaced by the language of nego-tiation. Passion gives way to the calculation of a man trying to choose between his penis and his picket fence. Ecstasy is ony a brief respite from anguish. The contemporary Casanova is not a roman-tic figure, but the prisoner of a viciously circular compulsion, a man driven to possess women only to flee from them, to accumulate sexual experience that teaches him nothing.

There is a poem by Wallace Stevens called "Thirteen Ways of Looking at a Blackbird." Saul, Howard, Fred and Anthony repre-sent the Casanova's four ways of looking at desire, his four skewed visions of the interactions between men and women. For Saul, love is thrill seeking—each of his relationships is a quest for a transcen-dent, peak experience. A thrill, by its very definition, is short-lived, a stimulation of the nerve ends that lasts only as long as it takes for the roller coaster to complete its circuit or the rail of coke to zoom into the bloodstream. It is not continuous or self-renewing. Each new thrill requires a new stimulus: once your heart has stopped hammering, you have to get back on the roller coaster, snort an-other line or move on to stronger drugs.

For men like Saul a love affair is not a continuity but a series of thrills, of heightened moments. The intensity of these moments de-pends largely on their novelty. But novelty fades quickly, and soon they require new thrills, new "firsts," if their excitement is to be sustained. Each moment must be followed by one of even greater freshness and intensity, and it is this flickering progression of thrills that makes up a liaison. There is no time to stand still, to simply savor their feelings and the presence of the beloved. Things must move *forward*—from dating to sex, from sex to falling in love and, more important, to being loved. Saul isn't content until his partners want him "wildly, desperately," even if that kind of love is totally alien to their nature. Like many Casanovas, he casts women as Galateas and himself as the Pygmalion who sculpts them from rough stone. His romantic process is a movement toward total possession of the beloved: Galatea is not complete until she has been chipped and polished into a female replica of her creator.

In the same way, Casanovas often view sex as a progression of thrills, each of which must somehow surpass the one before it. When talking with them, one often hears that they are seeking an "ultimate sexual experience." For some, that ultimate is associated with a particular erotic scenario. For others it's a fantasy so vague that it can never be realized. Many men told me that once they have had intercourse with a woman, they must then know her in other ways—orally, anally, in ménages à trois with another woman or another man. The joy of such variations lies less in the sensual pleasure they afford than in what they represent—the breaking of new ground and a continuation of the process of sexual conquest and possession. If their partners balk at certain acts, Casanovas tend to feel cheated of something essential. Implicit in their approach to love and lovemaking is the question "What next?"

But when the next moment arrives, they are likely to ask, "Is that all there is?" Once attained, the ultimate sexual experience proves disappointingly pallid. Every peak is necessarily followed by a lull, the time when the breathing slows and rapture gives way to repose. But for Casanovas the lull is a devastating crash. Not surprisingly, a great many of these men are uncomfortable immediately after sex, especially with a new partner. It isn't just the unease of sudden intimacy: they don't know what to do or how to feel in the postcoital hush. "It's as if all of a sudden I don't know what I'm doing in bed with this woman," one man said to me. "The moment my penis goes down, my thoughts come back. And what they tell me is, 'Let's get the hell out of here, buddy.'"

It's not surprising that Saul compares love to the fleeting rush of cocaine. What he calls love, with its nonstop, ecstatic lovemaking and its idealized vision of the beloved, belongs to the subtype that one psychologist calls Eros. Erotic love is marked by intense physical attraction and powerful sexual chemistry but is inherently short-lived. Like an atmosphere of pure oxygen, it induces rapture but cannot support life. Recent studies suggest that the intoxication of Eros is more than a metaphor. In test subjects, falling in love is accompanied by increased levels of the neurotransmitters dopamine and norepinephrine. The same neurotransmitters are released by cocaine. When a Casanova falls in love, it's not so much with a particular woman as with the sensation of love itself—with the exhilarating rush of his own brain chemistry.

OBSCURE OBJECTS OF DESIRE

Erotic love requires a beloved, but who the beloved is matters little to the Casanova. In Roland Barthes's words, she may be "a colorless object...placed in the center of the stage and there adored, idolized...covered with prayers...as if she were a huge motionless hen huddled amid her feathers, around which circles a slightly mad cock." For most people, loving is a process of discovery. We come to know and delight in our partners' smallest idiosyncrasies—the saddle of freckles on one woman's nose or the way another drinks water directly from the faucet. Casanovas as a whole seem to miss those features. They describe the women in their lives in terms that are at once glowing and blurred, as though squinting at them through a glare of sunlight. For these men, women exist only as the hallucinatory by-products of an erotic high.

The high has its inevitable letdown. Eros may provide the first white heat that bonds a man and a woman together, but if their bond is to endure it must evolve into something else. Eventually love entails companionship and the sharing of goals and experiences. Above all, it means recognizing the other person as an autonomous entity. To love someone, as Saint Augustine defined it, is to say "I want you to be." Most Casanovas seem incapable of such recognition. After the first weeks or months of erotic rapture, Saul's love cools into companionship. But companionship gives him no comfort. As his partners lose their mystery and emerge as individuals—as people who worry about wedding presents and hang underwear in the bathroom—their attraction vanishes. It's replaced by disappointment and revulsion at the all too human beings who seem to have materialized in his apartment overnight.

The polar extremes of idealization and violent disillusionment are fundamental aspects of the thrill-seeking mentality. Casanova has a tendency to fall in love, not with real women, but with fantasy creatures who, when they are finally "exposed" as human, automatically lose their appeal. He does not find the objects of his heart's desire so much as he *creates* them, projecting his unconscious longings onto the screen of another being. What makes his perceptions so vague, what blinds him to the other's humanness, is the radiance of projection. What entrances him is the sight of his own reflection briefly shimmering on a woman's form. The reflection is not necessarily accurate. More often, what the Casanova sees is a self idealized beyond recognition or a composite self made up of bits of longed-for others—mother, father, sisters, all the portraits that hang in the gallery of his unconscious. Psychiatrists call these processes "primitive idealization" and "projective identification" and generally associate them with the severest narcissistic character disorders.

THE SHOCK OF SEEING ANOTHER

A man who falls in love with his own idealized reflection—or with the other projected contents of his psyche—is bound to be disappointed with a real person. A living woman is an unsuitable screen; sooner or later, her humanity breaks the surface tension of illusion. But the thrill seeker's disillusionment is also a disillusionment with self. If he expects too much from his lover, how much greater are his expectations of himself. As I spoke with Saul and other men like him, I recognized many of my old beliefs about what was required of me in the act of loving: men like us were supposed to be eternally erect and capable of making love for hours at a time; we were not supposed to be irritable, selfish or unkind. Our unconscious definitions of love ruled out a night spent cuddling or the petty squabbles that other people take for granted. Love was supposed to make us kinder, more passionate and attentive. Instead, we found that there were times when we couldn't satisfy our partners sexually; there were times we didn't want to touch them. We caught ourselves speaking sharply and even cruelly to women we thought we loved. At those moments, we heard the death knell of our relationships. If we were disappointed by the humanity of our lovers, we were disgusted by our own.

Typically, the Casanova recoils from what he sees. If he is a pathological narcissist or borderline personality, he may be incapable of recognizing his own imperfections. Such recognition might shatter his delicate, yet rigidly defended, self-image. Instead, he lashes out at the woman he once adored: his obscure object of desire becomes his scapegoat, the repository for all that he loathes and fears in himself. When Saul's desire ebbs, he accuses his girlfriends of being frigid. When he is unfaithful, he blames them for forcing him to lie. Another man, who struck me as a tyrannical perfectionist, kept describing his exes as "nags" and "nitpickers." When one hears only one side of a relationship, it's hard to tell which problems are real and which imaginary. Not every Casanova projects his defects onto his partners. But to such a man, women's human shortcomings are all the more hideous because they mirror his own.

A DEATH BY BOREDOM

In thrill seeking, negative feelings—anger, fear, disappointment—are often experienced as boredom, which serves as a buffer against psychic unrest and provides the Casanova with an illusion of superiority. Once the loved one is no longer a mysterious temptress but "a roommate with sex," once every avenue of desire has been trodden smooth, he is left with only himself and a stranger who reflects and magnifies his own worst defects. It's here, at the butt end of romance, that the brevity of his attention span is most evident. Instead of confronting his partner, he retreats into silence. Rather than try to renew his sexual relationship with his wife or girlfriend, he uses other women to sate his hunger for novelty and confirm his potency. Loving is no longer worth the effort—if it ever was to begin with. When he speaks about his relationship, it's in the language of exhaustion and ennui. His lover is "a drag," "old news," "a broken record." Their union is "stale," "played out," "in reruns" or—in the arid phrase of a man named Alan—"no longer viable."

This state of affairs cannot last long. Regardless of their chronological age, the men who engage in thrill seeking are paradigms of the video generation: they cannot live without novelty and excitement and are used to getting them from women as easily as one flicks the channel selector on a television. Chronically bored and unable to engage the "program" in any deep or meaningful way, they change channels quickly. Once they have exhausted the possibilities of their current partners, and often long before, Casanovas look for replacements. A middle-aged man told me that he spent half his wedding ceremony scanning the church for potential mistresses. Some of these men are so keenly aware of the multitude of women in the field that they can barely concentrate on any one of them. A young actor I spoke with always meets his dates at dimly lit restaurants so that he won't be distracted by the women at neighboring tables. "When it comes to women, I've got the attention span of a three-year-old," he says, "a *hyperactive* three-year-old."

Implicit in this rapid turnover of desire is a sense that all its objects are interchangeable. As the psychoanalyst Otto F. Kernberg observes, "the narcissistic person learns from experience that the 'exciting new' is one more edition of the 'disappointing old.'" To these men, a woman's particular flaws and shortcomings are finally of little real consequence. What matters is that she has lost her novelty, and the sight of her no longer makes the pulse race or the brain hum with dopamine and norepinephrine. Where once she served as a mirror for her lovers' fantasies, she now only reminds them of their insufficiencies or is simply depleted, a blank screen in an empty theater. The thrill is gone, and because Casanovas define love in terms of thrills, they must seek them elsewhere, in other women who will inevitably turn out to be as boring as their predecessors.

In *The Professor of Desire* Philip Roth eloquently captures the dilemma that confronts every thrill seeker:

> ...Within a year my passion will be dead. Already it is dying. ...It's stupid! Idiotic! Unfair! To be robbed like this of you! And of this life I love and have hardly gotten to know! And robbed by whom? It always comes down to myself!

PLAYING SAFE

Howard's pursuit of women is in part a search for thrills, but what stands out most clearly in his attitude and behavior is the theme of gamesmanship. From the moment he first sees a good-looking woman, the encounter becomes an absorbing exercise of luck and skill, a contest in which she is both a goal and an adversary. All his actions, from come-on to climax, are maneuvers within a sexual arena. Throughout, he measures his behavior by precise— and essentially amoral—standards of achievement and performance. And when he finally disengages, it is at once a signal that the game is over and an acknowledgment that it has brushed dangerously close to real life.

This seems to contradict the very purpose of games, which above all are supposed to provide a respite from the demands of reality. Most games are played in a marked-off space, whose boundaries protect the players from the rigors and chaos of the world outside. No matter how furious the action on a ghetto basketball court, it is still safer than the street beyond the fence: you can jostle an opposing player on the court without getting a knife in the ribs. At the same time, the playing field is subject to well-articulated rules. Within these limits grown men and women can, at least in theory, re-create the freedom and innocence of their childhoods. While they play, they are exempt from the crushing standards of maturity.

Yet our games are not as carefree as the ones played by earlier generations. To the players and spectators of the twentieth-century West, nothing is more serious, more fraught with the imperative of success and the fear of failure. Increasingly we approach games in the spirit of work. On the playing field as in the office, winning is the only thing. Even amateurs—as anyone who has survived Little League can testify—are expected to perform like pros. When we are not competing with other players we compete with ourselves, breaking our previous speed record or doing yet one more set of leg lifts on the Nautilus machine. The only vestiges of childhood today's players are allowed are vindictiveness and temper tantrums.

If Howard treats love and lovemaking as a game, it's a game characterized by that same paradoxical state of playfulness and grim perfectionism. On one hand, desire, sex and love are stripped of emotional value: marriage is little more than an insurance policy for sex; adultery is just a technicality, motivated not by passion but by casual curiosity. A separation is simply the dissolution of a contract that's no longer convenient. On the other hand, the most trifling moves of the game now throb with tension: every seduction is reckoned toward a strict ratio of success; the bedroom becomes the primary arena of performance. Every relationship, no matter how casual, is a showdown in which whoever walks out first wins and whoever is left behind is a humiliated loser.

What rewards does the game offer its players? For children, games are a way to master skills like running, throwing, catching and, most important, getting along with others. For adult Casanovas, games are a way of shoring up a tottering ego, of instilling an inner sense of potency, attractiveness and power. In the game of seduction, Casanovas seek to control their feelings, their physical responses and the feelings and responses of their partners; they accumulate conquests like merit badges. Through practice and repetition—and sometimes through a personal set of rules—they hone seduction into a science, replacing romance with technique and passion with precision. This bargain doesn't sound that satisfying —unless we remember that passion is inextricably aligned with risk. For all their apparent love of adventure, men like Howard don't handle risk well.

The first risk in any relationship between the sexes occurs at its onset, when a man approaches a woman and expresses interest in her. There's always the chance that she'll say no. For game players such rejection can be excruciating, a lethal slash at the ego. Yet Howard seems devoid of fear. He has conquered it through rationalization, for his Pete Rose theory assures him that for every woman who turns him down, another will accept him. No loss is unbearable when measured against a probable gain. Of course, there's no reason why Howard's luck should hold firm. But he doesn't rely on luck alone. He has developed a game plan that minimizes the danger of rejection.

Like many Casanovas, Howard makes advances only toward women who seem available. Some women are ruled out in advance: a wedding band, for instance, might be an automatic damper on desire. Many game players approach women who are not knockouts. Scoring takes precedence over desire. Better to sleep with a woman who doesn't really matter than to be turned down by one who does.

SMOOTH OPERATORS

What strikes me about such rules is the calculation behind them. There are men who describe seduction as something that just happens, a spark of erotic electricity that leaps unbidden from one person to another. But sexual gamesmanship requires concentration and self-control. Although Howard portrays himself as a born lover, he consciously models himself after romantic screen heroes like Cary Grant and Tony Curtis, those masters of the perfect cocktail and insinuating repartee. He makes up for his average looks with a charm that seems natural but is actually quite deliberate. Even flattery is a demanding art. One man told me that he begins by complimenting a woman on her dress and, depending on how she responds, then moves on to her body, praising her hair or lips or throat: his rap is a way of undressing his partner verbally, a dry run for what will transpire later in the bedroom.

Performed with panache and proper timing, such rituals make sex far more enjoyable. Romantic protocol redeems a one-night stand in the same way that candlelight and an elegant place setting turn fast food into a meal. A successful game player is an erotic gourmet, whose pleasure derives in large part from the care he devotes to the feast. But for this man, the techniques of seduction are also *necessary*. They not only heighten the pleasure of conquest; they make conquest possible.

One often senses that the game player's reliance on technique arises from feelings of inadequacy. He may lack—or feel he lacks— the physical charms that women find attractive. Few of the men I spoke to described themselves as handsome. They complained of spare tires and receding hairlines, sloping shoulders and concave chests. Lord Byron was tormented by a clubfoot. My own womanizing was in part a delayed compensation for my years as a fat child and teenager, a boy who could never find someone to dance with him during the slow songs. But the sense of inadequacy is more than skin deep. The more one listens to these men, the more one is struck by the undertone of failure in their voices. They rarely acknowledge it as such: most Casanovas present themselves as successes, in every sense of the word. But the very insistence with which they do so gives their self-promotion a wishful and even poignant quality. They are so eager for admiration and approval.

And what higher form of approval than the surrender of an attractive woman? For these men every conquest is an affirmation of the self. Their come-on lines and smoky stares are adaptive strategies that enable the small, the weak and the psychically wounded to acquire as many sexual partners as men who are stronger, better-looking and more self-assured. Game players always seem to be anxiously eyeing the other contestants in the arena, those they have overtaken and those they haven't. There's an element of aggression here that recalls the Oedipal rivalries of the nursery, the forgotten time when little boys challenged big, strong fathers for the love of the only women who mattered. In the singles bar, Casanovas avenge the humiliations of the office and the locker room but fight older battles as well. The men they outscore now are often convenient surrogates for the men who defeated them in childhood.

This is not to say that Casanovas are wholly dependent on technique. These are not the "wild and crazy guys" of "Saturday Night Live"; they know that a smooth dance step and a pimp's cap are not enough to make a woman keel over in an orgasmic faint. Most of these men have cultivated an aura of defensive self-confidence that borders on the grandiose. Many describe themselves as innately seductive; one man told me: "I know how to handle women the way other guys know how to handle machines. They're my element." Through repetition and inner necessity Casanovas have mastered the rules of their game and integrated them into a body of learned reflexes. Seduction comes to them as easily as pitching does to Dwight Gooden.

THE LOVER AS SPECTATOR

If the Casanova's rituals were meant only to seduce women, we might expect them to stop at the bedroom door. They don't. Men like Howard practice the sex act as assiduously as they do the rituals of seduction. Of course, some Casanovas are perfunctory and even selfish in their lovemaking. But in game playing, sex is usually a continuation of the act of conquest. Thus, it is a mode of performance, and like any other performance, it demands self-consciousness and an almost altruistic attention to the responses of the audience.

Game players are acutely aware that in the arena of sex one's audience is also one's partner. In bed they are crowd pleasers who try to guarantee their lovers as many orgasms as possible. As Howard says, "When I get into bed with a woman it's with the idea that I'm going to make her as happy as I can. I'm going to make her come a lot, and in ways she never imagined. If I have only one orgasm, that's okay—I'm not greedy. But where women are concerned, I'm generous to a fault."

Hand in hand with this obsessive attention to their partners' pleasure comes a peculiar indifference to their own. For Casanovas the joy of sex has more to do with the assertion of power than with the stimulation of nerve ends. They are often slow to reach orgasm and may take special measures to delay it: a great many of these men regularly use alcohol, marijuana or cocaine as sexual aids. The very emphasis on performance may serve as a partial anesthetic, a sort of psychological novocaine. When all your senses are fixed on the woman beneath you—when you monitor the rate of her breathing, the loudness of her cries and the hardness of her nipples like a surgeon taking vital signs—your own responses become so much wallpaper and you are unlikely to reach climax until your partner has, many times over.

It's nice to have a generous lover. But game players tend to be a little *too* generous. They treat sex as a favor granted to women instead of as a mutual need or expression of love. The quality of their performance takes precedence over anything they actually feel, and the less they feel the more highly they rate their performance. While performance carries its own anxieties ("Was it as good for you as it was for me?"), it allows these men to see their encounters in comfortably unambiguous terms. Any sex act that lasts x number of hours, includes x minutes of foreplay and yields x orgasms is automatically counted as successful.

By imposing such rigid criteria on sex, game players avoid the complex and shifting demands that are the true substance of Eros. They need not wonder if they really connected with their partners or made them feel recognized and desired. Most of all, they needn't wonder whether they themselves were satisfied. In extreme instances, Casanovas seem unable to experience pleasure directly, to know it only by observing the pleasure of others. One man, a systems analyst, describes good sex as "a feedback situation. Knowing that I'm stimulating my date stimulates me." For this man and others like him, lovemaking is a kind of voyeurism, in which he raptly studies his partner in order to discern his effect on her. His own body, his own sensations, are left far behind, observed from a safe distance by a coldly watchful ego.

As Casanova withdraws from the center stage of desire, he forces his partners to its periphery. In game playing the most desirable lover is an anonymous stranger, who can be reduced to the mere sum of her sexual responses—a barometer of the Casanova's performance. For some, sex is a conversation, a feverish exchange of yearning and energy between two human beings who for a few hours try to escape solitude and inhabit each other's skins and hearts. For the game player it is never sex, but the "sex act"—a one-man show carried out for the benefit of a female spectator who, no matter how demanding, is finally only a spectator, a passive witness to his virtuoso display of power, stamina and invention. No matter how eagerly he courts her applause, her feelings carry little weight. He has banished her to the shadowy regions on the other side of the footlights, where nothing is quite real.

THE DICTATORSHIP OF RULES

What goes on in the bedroom is mirrored elsewhere in the game player's relationships. His transactions with women are always governed by rules that are all the more confining because he himself has formulated them. On dates he is usually a stickler for protocol, the kind of man who can't imagine going Dutch. He schedules his trysts as carefully as he would a business meeting, although he is not above breaking a date at the last minute. He insists on controlling the romantic agenda, determining when, where and how often he will see his lovers. His marriage, too, is informed by an ironclad sense of protocol and duty. Summing up his years with his wife, Howard says, "We always acted the perfect young married couple; then, when we had kids, the perfect young family. And now we're the perfect divorced couple, civil, supportive in emergencies, everything according to Miss Manners."

But there's little pleasure in this perfection. The Casanova's relationships seem fundamentally mechanical and joyless. When Howard talks about his marriage, it's with the distant air of someone who's learned to dance by following a chart and who still counts the steps under his breath whenever he takes the floor. His marriage seems to have been shaped by his wife's expectations—or by his beliefs about what those expectations were. No matter how adroitly he fills his roles as boyfriend, lover or spouse, the game player remains bound by the rules and paradoxically dependent on the women who play the game with him.

The game player's underlying dependency often goes unnoticed, because he is so adept at controlling his relationships and so determined to see himself as the partner who gives. After all, it is he who picks up the restaurant tabs and delivers orgasms on tap. But although he often complains that his lovers are pushy and demanding, Casanova needs to be needed. His frail self-image requires the reassurance that he is necessary to his partners' happiness. A woman who doesn't need him is likely to threaten his self-esteem, as he faces the intolerable depth and intensity of his own yearnings. With Annette, who made few demands and jealously guarded her independence, *Howard* became "the jealous one, the one who stayed up waiting for her to call, the one who was always whining about commitment." The transformation seems to have taken place by default, as though every relationship had only two possibilities: to be jealous or to arouse jealousy, to ask for commitment or to evade it, to want or to be wanted. Such rigid dualism points to a pathological narcissism, for the narcissist defends himself from feelings of dependency by projecting those feelings onto a convenient other. Incapable of seeking satisfaction, he seeks only to satisfy. Unable to express his needs, he finds a needy woman. Unable to love, he seeks instead to be loved and admired.

Yet the love and admiration he gets can never be enough. They are only the spoils of a game, the rewards for the gamesman's artful and seductive behavior. As such, love is always suspect. Do women love him for what he is or only for the things he gives them? He often feels unappreciated, as Howard did in his marriage: "I went from being Linda's lover to being her husband. Then I became the father of her kids. And finally, I was just the breadwinner, the guy who made the payments for the house and the picket fence and the kids' clothes." Any relationship that lasts too long can trigger similar feelings of obligation and resentment. Increasingly seduction comes to feel like drudgery, his lover or spouse like a tightfisted boss.

THE LOVER AS ADVERSARY

The only way these men can stop playing this losing game is to shift it to new arenas. And while some game players simply walk out in a self-righteous fury, most make sure that there are other women waiting for them. Because their self-esteem hinges on female adoration, they require a constant supply of new admirers. Howard's depression after his breakup with Annette is typical of Casanovas who find themselves alone. Even in the absence of conscious grief, they often display symptoms of depression—loss of appetite or compulsive overeating, sleep disturbances and fatigue. Deprived of women, they are prone to bingeing on drugs or alcohol, on anything that will fill the vacuum of self. To be without a woman is to be out of the game, unmoored from one's identity as a man. To be without a woman is to face how badly one needs them.

Thus game playing means being constantly on the make. The game player cannot have too many conquests. Polygyny and infidelity are his instinctive strategies, and in the course of the game, his original partner is transformed from a goal into an adversary. If his primary object is to take new lovers, his secondary aim is to keep his wife or girlfriend in the dark.

Adultery has its own rules, as complex as the codes of seduction. Howard, for example, always made a point of spending the night with his wife, even if that meant sliding stealthily into bed at four in the morning. He forbade his lovers to call him at home and carefully destroyed all evidence of his affairs. Gamesmen act out all the dreary rituals of infidelity: the nightly search for incriminating phone numbers which are then transferred to a safe place, the scrupulous use of cash for dinners and hotel rooms, the compulsive postcoital shower. Even those men who pursue their extracurricular activities openly—as so many did in the 1970s—maintain a rigorous set of rules. A fiftyish academic told me that his wife had overlooked his affairs with other women as long as he restricted himself to other college teachers. Their shared rules turned infidelity into something as innocuous as a departmental seminar.

Rules are always a defense, a way of channeling chaos into a semblance of order. Casanova's rules of seduction defend him from the anxiety raised by the possibility of rejection. His codes of infidelity provide him with a safe way of expressing aggression toward his partners, while warding off the guilt that accompanies every betrayal. Howard loved his wife, and he would have you believe that he concealed his adultery in order to protect her. Yet he describes Linda as "a martyr," a word that connotes an infinite capacity for pain. Every martyr needs a tormentor. When Howard and Linda fought, usually over the amount of time he spent away from home, he would "tear her apart" with lawyerly sarcasm. On the rare occasions he lost, he would stalk out of the house for what he calls a "vengeance fuck" with another woman. Even when he describes the pains he took to cover up his affairs, it's with the suppressed glee of a small boy who has stolen change from his mother's purse.

All marriage breeds some hostility between partners whose lives are so intimately bound. Casanova, that man who loves women, tends to express that hostility in the arena of sex. Infidelity serves him as a genteel form of violence, an assault on a victim who is unaware that she is being assaulted. For men like Howard, coitus fuses passion with brutality. To "fuck" one's mistress is simultaneously to "fuck over" one's wife. But to express rage in this fashion usually arouses guilt. My own infidelities were always followed by wicked moral hangovers; it's probably the chief reason that I finally sought help. But the most profoundly disturbed Casanovas often seem immune to guilt, which is instead repressed, rationalized by the comforting thought that they are playing by the rules. Game playing is characterized by obsessively repeated mantras: "I don't get involved"; "I take care of her"; "What she doesn't know won't hurt her."

One would think that the gamesman's other women get the best part of him. And at first they do. He approaches them as fresh conquests, with the enthusiasm of a sportsman playing on a new field. Because his primary relationship—with its weight of obligations and resentments—lies elsewhere, his extracurricular affairs are initially exciting and carefree. They are, for the time being, games.

But Casanova often ends up blurring the realms of the game and real life. He needs a validation greater than that offered by casual sex; he needs nothing less than adoration, and he may court it without quite meaning to. And, as we shall see later, he has an unconscious affinity for women who will fall in love with him. For all his awareness of the rules he plays by, he doesn't always spell them out. His girlfriends don't know when they can expect to see him; they don't know about his other lovers; they don't know that he has no intention of leaving his wife. Eventually, they begin taking the game too seriously. Howard complains that all his lovers ended up becoming "naggy," plaguing him with demands for time, attention and consistency. They refused to play by the rules he had never bothered to explain to them.

Thus, even the most compliant mistress is transformed into a demanding shrew—a wife without a wedding band. There is very little she can do to avert this devaluation, for it is written into the nature of the game. Casanova loves conquest but has little desire to hold on to what he has conquered, for holding on to someone entails being held in turn. There is no such thing as free love. Once this man has mastered a new woman, she inevitably loses value and becomes a liability. The game moves only in one direction, in an unending search for zipless gratification.

Superficially, game playing seems rather glamorous, the men who engage in it the true heirs of Casanova and Don Juan, Lothario and the Marquis de Valmont. They are not common womanizers but connoisseurs, who have transcended the pickup and the quick bang for the airy realms of seduction, where style outweighs gratification and a partner's pleasure takes precedence over one's own. Because they are so skillful at what they do and so acutely sensitive to their lovers' desires, they are often seen as men who love women. Their only fault would seem to be loving them to excess.

Yet the game player's chief concern is really the game itself, with its progressive stages of seduction, conquest, infidelity and abandonment. Women are only the stakes of this game, the external measures of the player's prowess. They are not even sex objects, but props for a ego that is at once inflated and without a durable center. That impoverished sense of self compels the gamesman to look outside for confirmation and approval. His barren psychic landscape—an arena in which there exist only the player and his pawns—prevents him from ever attaining satisfaction. How can he trust the love that he has won through role playing and manipulation? And what will become of that love when he gets tired of playing a role? Whatever pleasure he derives from conquest is finally hollow, for his Byzantine transactions with women are only acts in an endless performance whose greatest reward is the applause of a shadow.

In Milan Kundera's *The Unbearable Lightness of Being*, we find a chillingly precise description of this game and of the man who plays it:

> ...Tomas desired but feared [women]. Needing to create a compromise between fear and desire, he devised what he called "erotic friendship." He would tell his mistresses: the only relationship that can make both partners happy is one in which sentimentality has no place and neither partner makes any claim on the life and freedom of the other.
>
> To ensure that erotic friendship never grew into the aggression of love, he would meet each of his long-term mistresses only at intervals. He considered this method flawless and propagated it among his friends: "The important thing is to abide by the rule of threes. Either you see a woman three times in quick succession and then never again, or you maintain relations over the years but make sure that the rendezvous are at least three weeks apart."

THE DICTATORSHIP OF DESIRE

When Casanovas use women as an escape, they seem to turn into the products of a feminist's nightmare: thoughtless, driven and hypersexed. Like Fred, they may sleep with hundreds of different partners, but their liaisons are usually brief. Nothing suits them better than a one-night stand with a total stranger. In escape, they treat women as they would paid professionals, coupling with them for an hour and then disposing of them without tenderness or guilt. Inveterate escape artists shun relationships; any they may enter into are determinedly superficial. They are often strangers even to the women they live with, sharing a roof, a bed and a bank account but nothing that resembles intimacy or passion.

Both thrill seeking and game playing gravitate toward obvious goals: a moment of perfect pleasure or a validation of the self. Fred, however, uses women only as vehicles of flight. His lovers are refuges from his marriage. Sex is a momentary relief from torment but is itself a mental anguish. He enjoys women as sexual beings but seems unable to relate to them in any other way. They pass from his life without occasioning a ripple of regret. His erotic career has been a scrambling, treadmill race for a safety that lies forever out of reach. At the age of sixty-three, he is still cheating on his wife, so eager for new partners that he solicits them in swingers' magazines.

Men like Fred often blame their behavior on an overactive sex drive. And there *is* something compulsive about their sexuality, a merciless insistence that won't be denied or delayed. When Fred wants a woman, he tells me, "I'm like a dog that's sniffing after a bitch in heat." Another Casanova compares desire to drunkenness: "You see a woman and something comes over you. You just have to have her. You'll go to the most insane lengths to get her—lie, skip work, anything. Your better judgment goes flying out the window. It goes out for just about thirty minutes, and then, the moment you're finished, it comes back and smacks you in the head. It's like an instant hangover. Suddenly you're disgusted, at her, at yourself. A few minutes ago she was a princess; now she might as well have tentacles. But you know that a week later you'll see someone else, and you'll do it all over again." In *Portnoy's Complaint*, Philip Roth also invokes the idea of sexual stupefaction, using a Yiddish aphorism, *Ven der putz shteht, ligt der sechel in drerd:* "When the prick stands up, the brain gets buried in the ground." In game playing, sex is a mode of mastery, a way of proving one's strength and skill by manipulating one's partner. In escape, sex seems to entail surrender, a loss of control to a torrential overflow of libido.

The idea that one may be constitutionally "hypersexed" provides many Casanovas with a handy excuse for promiscuity or infidelity.

But it seems to have no physiological basis. Even Dr. John Money, a leading proponent of biochemical theories of sexual behavior, finds no correlation between hormone levels and the kind of hypersexuality that used to be called satyriasis. If escape artists are oversexed, their desire would seem to be located in the psyche rather than the gonads: for these men, as for most of us, the brain is the chief erogenous zone.

But the psyche is at least as dictatorial as the flesh. In escape, any woman can be an object, regardless of her looks or appeal. If you bed anyone who is willing, chances are you will sometimes be revolted when the act is finished. Fred's first sexual partner was his next-door neighbor, a woman old enough to be his grandmother. But although he was repelled by her sagging breasts and grizzled pubic hair, he continued to sleep with her throughout his fifteenth summer. A man named Nick complains that many of his one-night stands are "coyote fucks—women who, when you wake up next to them, make you want to gnaw your arm off if that's what it takes to get away without their knowing it." Revulsion can be moral or aesthetic, as well as physical. I can hardly count the men who told me horror stories about women whom they found stupid, shallow or sluttish—all conveniently after the fact.

Escape artists will sleep with women who repel them; they will act repellently to do so, and the disgust that overwhelms them after climax sometimes comes from facing their own behavior. They are inveterate liars when it comes to sex, and unlike game players, whose deceptions are not without elegance, escape artists lie crudely, outlandishly. Like Fred, who has taken girlfriends to his officers' club and left his black book where his wife could easily find it, they often seem to court discovery. There's a great deal of hostility in such recklessness, and guilt as well. But in escape, recklessness is a general pattern, an outward sign of a chaotic psyche acting in the sexual realm.

"I'LL ... FUCK MY LIFE AWAY"

In escape, the Casanova can become genuinely self-destructive, jeopardizing far more than his marriage or relationship. Several men I spoke with had compromised their careers by sleeping with their female coworkers: the affairs had become common knowledge, with humiliating results. Another acquaintance actually lost a profitable business because he had slept with his partner's wife. Escape artists rarely take responsibility for birth control or protect themselves from sexually transmitted disease. This insouciance seems almost suicidal in the age of AIDS. But then, these men's desire for sex sometimes resembles a yearning for death. Fred, who had open-heart surgery a few years ago, was chasing women not long after his operation: "When the doctor told me I had to cut back on the ladies, I said, 'Don't tell me how long I've got to live, because I don't give a damn. If it comes down to that,' I said, 'I'll go out and fuck my life away.' "

Something about this phrase was chillingly familiar to me. I myself had said something much like it in the weeks after I left my wife, as I hurled myself into a series of short, pleasureless affairs. At the same time, I began to drug my life away with deliberate effort. I was no longer satisfied with getting "high"; I no longer bothered with the niceties of seduction: I charged headlong into the regions of blackout and sexual d.t.'s, where forgetfulness gives way to oblivion and every orgasm really feels like a little death. What I sought now was at once comfort and punishment—a denial of what I had done and a penance for it. Every time I made love, I tried to reenter my partner's womb, to possess it and be possessed by it. I wanted nothing less than to be annihilated in the sleep of the unborn.

To fuck one's life away, then, is to turn sex into a drug, with the imminent possibility of overdose. The excess that characterizes the sexuality of escape—the accumulation of hundreds of partners in a single year, the fevered rush from bed to bed, the bullying urgency of desire—springs in part from an impulse toward self-destruction. There's an element of resignation in the Casanova's surrender to the call of Eros, as though he were saying, "I know I shouldn't, but what the hell." Fred was fully aware that sex could kill him so soon after surgery; he pursued it anyway. Gary Hart, for all his magical belief in his immunity, must have realized that his fling with Donna Rice could have disastrous repercussions: the face in the photographs taken in Bimini is that of a man staring back at the firing squad. Hart may have seen his affair as a prerogative of power, but it was also an abdication of power: when he spent the night with Rice, he threw it all away. It sometimes seems that the men who use women as vehicles of flight are precisely those who have the most to lose by doing so—candidates and convalescents, men with marriages and careers that hinge on a semblance of rectitude. For these men, sex is a leap off the edge of a cliff, an act that combines Eros and Thanatos.

THE FLIGHT FROM CLOSENESS

The affair that ended my marriage was significant in its timing. The week before I had learned that my father had terminal cancer. When I heard the news I started crying, but stopped as soon as my wife entered the room. I cringed a little when she touched my shoulder; I couldn't stand her seeing me like that. Crying in her presence made me feel weak and diminished, as though she'd caught me changing from a man into a little boy. On the day I placed the phone call to the woman who would become my next lover, I had just gotten back from visiting my father. My wife hadn't been able to come with me, and a part of me was angry with her. But more important, I was afraid to come home to her, knowing I would collapse in tears the moment I walked in the door. I went to the only place I felt safe, the bed of a strange woman. I rarely cry in front of strangers.

The escape artist's promiscuity is not a chase after pleasure but a flight from pain and fear. I used sex to escape from my father's death and from the shame of grieving over it; Fred used sex to deny his mortality; Gary Hart may have been trying to escape from the pressures of his campaign and the terrifying prospect of the presidency. Above all, Casanovas use sex as a flight from intimacy. Intimacy, after all, means seeing the other as she really is and allowing oneself to be seen in turn, and Casanovas in general suffer from an occluded vision of others and a damaged sense of self. For such men, a one-night stand can seem the perfect substitute for closeness, a way of touching without seeing or being seen. To sustain a longer relationship with a single partner fills them with the dread of discovery. Like spies in enemy territory, they can afford only the briefest and most neutral contacts with the native populace.

When one lives with a woman, the pressures toward intimacy are all the greater; so, consequently, is the need for flight. Married Casanovas, shuttling frantically between the marriage chamber and the motel room, often seem far more promiscuous than their single counterparts. When speaking with these men, I was repeatedly struck by the contrast between the outward stability of their marriages and the intricacy of their extramarital lives. Men who have been wed placidly for years and never so much as fight with their spouses report sleeping with four or more different partners in a week. Men who claim to cherish their wives spend most of their nights with other women. In this context we can see the enduring but chronically adulterous unions of men like H. G. Wells and Marcello Mastroianni, John F. Kennedy and Donald Manes, the New York City politician who committed suicide when his graft and clandestine sex life were about to become public. The more solid the relationship, the more Casanovas feel compelled to flee from it.

Not surprisingly, the flight from intimacy goes on within marriage itself. Usually, it takes the form of silence. Although Fred describes his marriage as close, it seems terribly noncommunicative, devoid of sharing and open conflict. He has told his wife little about his childhood and adolescence, has never discussed his career with her and refused to "trouble her" with the news of his heart condition until a week before he was due for surgery. He keeps secrets in order to protect his wife from worry and in order to avoid fighting with her; he keeps secrets because she "will not understand" the truth. Implicit in this silence is a sense that women are fundamentally untrustworthy—weak and unforgiving, if not actually stupid. The placidity of such a union turns out to be a disguise for the contempt in which one partner holds the other.

Such silence actually conceals very little. An escape artist's marriage is full of open secrets, not the least of which is his infidelity. Game playing may require tact and artfulness; escape is reckless and clumsy, and its infidelities are poorly hidden, if not blatantly advertised. The knowledge of infidelity forms a bond between the betrayer and the betrayed. Like sex itself, pain and guilt become substitutes for intimacy. Fred's guilt is part of what keeps him with his wife: how can he leave the woman who has put up with so much from him? I suspect that Fred's wife is at least intuitively aware of how he feels and tolerates his affairs because she knows they pose no threat to her marriage. Indeed, his infidelity is a guarantee: never mind that the guarantee is written in tears and bile. Escape artists and their live-in partners are coconspirators sharing the secret of infidelity. The very thing that would blow most alliances apart holds theirs together.

DANGEROUS SECRETS

Silence is also a way of denying the bad news to oneself. To keep something secret is to pretend that it doesn't exist—and by extension, to wish it into nonexistence. This is exactly the kind of magical thinking that one encounters among Casanovas. If Fred could keep his heart ailment hidden from his wife, perhaps his heart would heal of itself. If I could keep from crying in front of my wife, I might stop being sad and my father might somehow be restored to health. If we pretend that our marriages are without conflict, perhaps these conflicts will spontaneously disappear.

The men who engage in sexual escape often seem burdened with painful secrets that prevent them from having any but the most transient and noncommittal relations with women. In the course of talking with Fred, I discovered that his account of his sexual initiation was really a cover story: his first sexual experience had taken place at the age of four, when he was molested by an aunt. In Fred's mind the two episodes blur to form a single image of incest, a word he will not use. To call his seduction by its proper name would be to recognize it as a violation. To tell his wife about either episode would be to make their trauma real.

A striking number of the escape artists I spoke with are veterans of the war in Vietnam. They saw, and took part in, all the usual horrors of combat, but then returned to a country that wouldn't acknowledge them. The price of coming home was to pretend that they had never left, to join in the silence of their countrymen. As one man told me, "When my girlfriend asked me why I scream in my sleep, how could I tell her what I was dreaming?" There is no need to explain his nightmares to a woman he sleeps with once and will never see again.

I also spoke with Casanovas whose compulsive promiscuity seemed to arise from an underlying homosexuality or served as a defense against homosexual panic. One man, for example, had long, essentially platonic relationships with women but regularly slept with partners of both sexes. As long as he lived with women, he could wishfully describe himself as heterosexual, while gratifying his true inclinations elsewhere. Another man, married for several years, was periodically tormented by homosexual fantasies. He denied these by seeking out new women. The more urgent his fantasies, the more he had to reassure himself with a manic display of heterosexuality.

What the Casanova hides and runs from is not necessarily so dramatic. His denial stems mostly from the merciless rigidity of his self-image. For this man, the most basic frailties—the fear of his own death or grief at another's—are intolerable. Not only does he deny their existence in himself, he flees from any situation that evokes them, from any woman who has the bad luck to witness them. Priding himself on his independence, he recoils from women who make him feel needy. Clinging nervously to his manhood, he runs the moment he feels less than wholly masculine. Even the threat of exposure fills him with continual unease, so that he is always on the verge of bolting, scanning every bedroom for the nearest exit. Like his historical namesake, the Casanova is an impostor whose greatest fear is being unmasked.

THE IMPERILED SELF

In extreme instances of escape, one sees a bizarre confusion of identities, a blurring of the boundaries between man and woman, self and other. Fred complains that he sometimes can't tell the difference between his wife's orgasms and his own or between intercourse and masturbation. A few of the men I spoke with disclosed a similar uneasy sense of fusion with their partners. Such a confusion recalls the dreamy symbiosis of infancy, when the child perceives his mother as an extension of himself, with desires and responses indistinguishable from his own. It's extremely rare for adults to make this confusion. Its presence points to severe psychopathology, a state that might be called prepsychotic. A blurred sense of self can be comforting, leading to delusions of grandiose omnipotence, but it's also terrifying. To be so tightly interwoven with another human being raises the prospect of losing oneself.

At the bottom of the Casanova's need for sexual escape lies precisely this fear: that his closeness to the women in his life may dissolve the boundaries that mark him as a separate being. It's important to realize that the fear is not always so naked: I would hesitate to label every escape artist a prepsychotic. But these men frequently suffer from a tenuous and constantly imperiled sense of self. Their hunger for sexual union disguises a dread of emotional interdependence, of anything that might erode the shell of the ego.

In escape artists' unconscious fantasies, women are endowed with enormous power. A woman can make a man abandon his scruples and hop into bed with her with a twitch of her hips. A woman can make a man do whatever she wants him to. A woman—as so many Casanovas have told me—will turn you into her possession, her breadwinner and personal stud. If loving one woman does not necessarily mean a loss of identity, at the very least it threatens these men with passivity and subservience. Love too much or too long and you might change into a woman yourself or become a little boy again.

We often sense that Casanova is a man who has invented himself. More accurately, he has edited himself, suppressing the traits and feelings he cannot accept and consigning them to the trash bin of the unconscious. The danger of intimacy lies in the threat it poses to his scrupulously composed persona. Beyond the safe anonymity of the one-night stand lies the region in which he may be seen and known. In the glare of intimacy, the discarded self may suddenly emerge, and the escape artist may find himself becoming all that he tried so hard to cast aside: a monster or a homosexual, a weakling or a failure, a child or even a woman.

In the story "Six Inches," Charles Bukowski taps the primitive fears of emasculation and engulfment that underlie sexual escape. Henry, his protagonist, marries a woman who shrinks him by degrees into a tiny, struggling puppet:

> I stayed home with Sarah. Which made it worse—she fed me. It got so I couldn't reach the refrigerator door anymore. And then she put me on a small silver chain.
> ...I had to use a potty chair to shit. But she still let me have my beer, as promised.
> "Ah, my little pet," she said, "you're so small and cute."
> Even our love life was ended. Everything had melted in proportion. I mounted her but after a while she'd just pick me off and laugh.

THE ORIGINS OF DESIRE

The sexuality of adults is the desire of one person for another. I want a woman whom I recognize as a separate being, complete in and of herself. I desire her precisely because she is *not* me, because she is herself and no other. At times, I may see parts of myself reflected in her and love or hate them as the case may be. But I never truly lose sight of her otherness, and even if we should spend a life together, she will always be a partial mystery, for how can I ever presume to know another being fully?

Freudian psychiatrists call such sexuality genital, partly because its aim is genital union with the other person and partly because it arises during the genital phase of child development, the time when children discover their genitals as sources of pleasure and conceive a sexual desire—inarticulate, but nonetheless real—for other beings, whom they recognize as separate from themselves. The important characteristic of such sexuality is not the specific body parts it involves, but the fact that it entails a movement outside the tight little island of the self. It is a movement between one reasonably complete being and another.

We do not come into the world with our sexuality full blown, nor does it suddenly descend on us sometime between our third and fifth years. It grows out of our earliest transactions with other humans, in most cases with our parents. In the beginning we do not even recognize those people as separate from ourselves. Once upon a time, the woman who gave birth to me was *home*, for lack of a better word, and comfort and sustenance. She was only the warmth and softness of her arms and the milk of her breasts. She was as much a part of me as my hands and feet, and in those days, she seemed equally subject to my desires.

In the earliest stage of development our relations with the human environment are primarily oral. An infant knows his mother as the thing he sucks and swallows and sometimes bites, as his satisfaction and occasional frustration. In early life she possesses no reality apart from that. If we define love as a movement from self to self, the infant cannot be said to love, but only to need. Born profoundly solipsistic, he only becomes less so by degrees. Most studies of the young child suggest that the recognition of the difference between self and other is extremely painful. We come to this knowledge only through hunger and rage and terror, and we fight against it every step of the way.

This discussion, simplified though it is, of the origins of adult sexuality and its difference from infantile eroticism is essential to an understanding of the mentality I call devouring. Devouring is the rarest—and I think the most frightening—way in which the Casanova approaches women. I have detected hints of this mentality in my conversations with other men and in my old letters and journals: it is what informed my insistence that my lovers make me whole; it is what drives Saul to project bits of himself indiscriminately onto his partners, and makes Fred so fearful of being swallowed in his wife's embrace. It is the remote, unconscious basis of the Casanova's endless quest for more thrills and more conquests. But devouring is only fully apparent in the most gravely disturbed individuals. It is a remnant of—or perhaps a throwback to—the primitive desires of infancy. To devour a woman is to negate her separateness, to make her, not a lover, but one's food and drink. Devouring is a way of reducing a human being to an object, to ingest that object and then dispose of it utterly. To devour the other precludes the possibility of ever telling her "I want you to be."

NO SATISFACTION

One gets no immediate sensation that there is much wrong with Anthony. If anything, he seems too normal. He has lived most of his twenty-six years in fulfillment of his parents' expectations: to get good grades in school, to hang out with the right crowd, to live at home and work hard for his father's business. It must be difficult for a boy—a man, really—Anthony's age to live with his parents. He has no complaints. As long as he keeps his sex life confined to his nights and weekends and doesn't bring his girlfriends home, he has license to do what he wants.

But when Anthony speaks at any length, you sense an undercurrent of dissatisfaction. His life has no consuming interest or central purpose. His job is just a job, the place he goes at eight in the morning and leaves at five that afternoon. His friends are just the guys that he hangs out with. He likes watching television, driving his Trans Am and getting high interchangeably: as ways to spend time, or kill it. I suspect he is often bored. It's only when the conversation turns to women that he shows any liveliness. But even here, he seems eternally frustrated. He can never seem to find the right woman; there *are* no right ones. He wants a girl who will do "outrageous" things in bed. He wants a decent girl he can take home to his parents. He gives his girlfriends so much, but they never give him what he needs. He is young and smart and good-looking, and he deserves more than he's getting. He can't get no satisfaction.

Many Casanovas lead lives of substance and accomplishment. We need only think of Ernest Hemingway or Herman Tarnower, Lord Byron or John F. Kennedy. But some of these men are plagued with a brooding sense of incompleteness, of emptiness. In extreme cases, the sense of emptiness is all-encompassing and virtually crippling. It robs all pursuits of their meaning, reduces them to mere interruptions in the course of the day. It is as pervasive and distracting as the gnawing of an empty stomach and is often experienced as a kind of hunger. And when one is truly hungry, one cannot get much out of life.

It's not all that unusual to feel incomplete: most people undergo something like it from time to time, especially during periods of depression. But for some Casanovas incompleteness is a constant, and what is missing feels like something essential. They feel not just bereft, but unfairly deprived. They voice their complaints in the language of entitlement: Anthony "deserves" more than he gets; his girlfriends never give him what he needs. In their unhappiness Casanovas often sound spoiled and cranky. But I believe that they truly feel entitled to the missing piece of themselves and that their petulance is in some ways understandable: an amputee feels he has a right to the limb he lost, and an infant who is used to being fed squawls when the breast unaccountably runs dry.

AN INFINITY OF OBJECTS

It's only in womanizing that the Casanova can satisfy this hunger. When Anthony leaves his home for the cruising circuit, he sloughs off his ennui and comes alive for the first time. His pulse speeds up. He feels vital and witty and desirable. The search for a partner invigorates him. For a man who seems so picky after the fact, he has remarkable luck in finding attractive partners: there is always *someone*, if not at the first spot, then at the one after that. How often do most men fall in love, or even in lust? Anthony seems to do it once every few weeks, virtually at first sight. "She's what I was looking for all my life," he says, moments after he has glimpsed another girl across another crowded room.

The frequency and swiftness with which Anthony falls in love suggest the same kind of projection and idealization that occur in thrill seeking. Actually it represents these processes in an exaggerated form. Any woman, it seems, can be transformed in an instant from a stranger—pretty, perhaps, and a good dancer—to the ultimate object of desire. To the devourer, she is more than desirable: she is *essential*, but essential in ways that have nothing to do with who she is. The Casanova has suddenly endowed her with all that he misses so acutely at other times. In this stranger he suddenly sees the one piece that will complete him. How can he help but want her desperately, even if he doesn't know her name? And should she reject him, it's little wonder that he is overcome by rage: she has deprived him of a vital piece of himself, a piece that he projected onto her in the first place.

Love at first sight, or the illusion of it, is not essential to devouring. Many Casanovas experience this immediate and overpowering desire without the luster of romance. They survey the nightclub as starving men look at a banquet where the dishes are so plentiful and varied that they can't choose what to eat first. "I'll be talking to this dynamite blonde," another man tells me, "but just behind her there's a brunette with hair down to her ass, and she seems to be giving me the eye. But over to *her* left there's a model with a killer, permatanned, health-club body, who's obviously bored with the guy she's talking to . . . and I get completely overwhelmed. In the end, I'll go home with somebody—she might not even be all that attractive —and all night I'll be going crazy thinking about the others I left behind."

When the haze of idealized yearning burns away, devouring seems brutal and indiscriminate. Casanova looks, wants and takes. He has no illusions about his partners; they are no more to him than Byron's "transient pieces" or Frank Sinatra's showgirls or John F. Kennedy's endless supply of disposable mistresses. I think it's no coincidence that we often encounter the devouring mind-set among the rich and gifted and powerful. Devouring is sexual consumption stripped of seductiveness or charm, and only the most privileged or charismatic men can truly get away with it. Power insulates these Casanovas from the realities of rejection. A politician or a rock star may become so accustomed to getting what he wants that he retreats further into his narcissism, into a world in which wishes— including the wish for endless sexual gratification—really are satisfied on demand and, in the process, lose the quality of wishes. David Herbert Donald's recent biography of Thomas Wolfe tells us that he believed that "any woman who did not want to go to bed with him must have something wrong with her."

TO GIVE AND TO TAKE

One expects devouring men to be selfish lovers, the kind who pin a woman down, pound away at her for a few minutes and then roll off and fall asleep. Some Casanovas do behave that way, defining the act of love as "Wham-bam-thank-you-ma'am." When a man sees a woman only as a desirable object—really as a desired part of himself—he is unlikely to consider her pleasure. As well consider whether masturbation is pleasant to the hand, he might say. Devouring has less to do with the object-oriented sexuality of adulthood than with the self-seeking oral gratification of infancy, and it is thus characterized by strong feelings of entitlement. Anthony *expects* his partners to give him many orgasms, to act out his most bizarre fantasies of possession, and when they fail to do so, he feels cheated.

But Anthony, as we have seen, also tries to "give" women "what they need," which suggests some awareness of his partners as separate beings. Yet whose needs is he satisfying? If devouring often entails the reckless pursuit of one's own satisfaction, it also sometimes means a panicky emphasis on satisfying the other. When these men climax before their girlfriends, they get angry with them and leave quickly. Their reactions, one suspects, have less to do with embarrassment than with fear. It's as though they felt that any failure to give their partners what they need would have dire consequences.

I believe that this undercurrent of fear stems from the nature of the psychic content that the devouring Casanova projects onto his women. When I say that he perceives his partners as objects, I don't necessarily mean that he sees them as inanimate. Rather, he endows them with *intention,* as well. If a woman looks at him with more than casual interest, he believes she loves him. Later, as we shall see, he believes she wants to possess him, even devour him, as he unconsciously wishes to possess and devour her. These primitive desires cannot be acknowledged. During intercourse, the devouring Casanova projects his own hungers onto the woman who lies beneath him: *she* is the ravenous, insatiable one, and if what he gives her is not enough she will be furious, as he is when circumstances are reversed. His fevered attempts to satisfy her are a magical way of propitiating his own psychic appetites and of denying the rage that always lies behind them.

Little wonder that these men are rarely satisfied in the act of love. Their eroticism is in some way disconnected from the normal genital circuit and is usually fraught with anger and dread. Like Anthony, a striking number have difficulty attaining orgasm. One man told me that this makes him a better lover, but complained that "sex for me is a problematic exercise, an attempt to see how long I can go before I get tired or fed up." The same man also periodically suffers from impotence: "Sometimes sex feels like a choice between frustration and humiliation," he said, "with an infinitesimally small point in the middle where I'm actually satisfied." When climax occurs, it yields little pleasure. Another Casanova compares his orgasm to a burp, an oddly appropriate description that betrays its oral significance. Always, even after repeated climaxes, these men feel obscurely cheated. Some psychic space inside them remains unfilled. Some hunger is still unfed. How can it ever be, if what they hunger for is really a missing piece of self?

"A MAN WHO NEEDS THAT WAY"

I'm jealous and threatened, and just terrified of the feeling because it comes from a need, a desire, whose depth is inexcusable—at least I can't excuse or tolerate it in myself. The fear and the fear of the fear are a pure, ravaging craziness that blinds and sickens me. I imagine everything and hate myself for imagining it and hate S. for instilling this madness in me just because I need her. Suddenly she's an unknown quantity, someone whose failure to call or answer the phone shocks me into spasms of jealousy. I twitch like someone strapped into the electric chair and try to convince myself that I'm sitting perfectly still while the smoke pours out of my ears. But I know I'm not and I curse myself for twitching, for doubting. Even if she were fucking every man on her crew I'd be hating myself, because I can't stand that depth of need and I can't stand myself for being a man who needs that way....
          —entry from the author's journal, November 1979

If some Casanovas are always frustrated in sex, it's partly because coitus only approximates the kind of possession they desire. In lovemaking they can enter their partners' bodies only to a limited extent and for a short period of time. Men like Anthony want more: "When I'm doing it," he tells me, "it's like I've got to push harder and harder. Sometimes it even hurts. It's like I'm trying to screw myself into her, to get *completely* inside her. Otherwise I feel like I'm outside, just floating outside her. Sometimes I want to say, 'Hey, let me in, okay?'" His true desire is to inhabit the other, to become one with her not just figuratively but literally, as though through this woman he could reenter the private space of his mother's womb. Alternatively, he seems to want to take his partner *inside himself* through oral sex, which he will practice for hours at a time. Neither way of making love is exceptional in itself: it's only his obsessiveness that marks them as attempts to deny the boundaries between self and other. In this respect, the sexuality of devouring often seems perverse, a rebellion against the laws that make each of us separate from the other.

I have described the erotic escalation of thrill seeking as a movement toward possession of the beloved. The same thing occurs to an even greater extent in devouring. Anthony wastes no time examining his feeings toward a new lover. Within moments of their first encounter, he has planned an entire future with her, a romantic campaign that races inevitably toward an idealized image of marriage. The campaign has nothing to do with getting to know this wonderful new woman: he knows her already, and wants her, and wants only to make her want him. He wants her to want him so much that she will submit to his slightest desire—fulfill it even before he asks her to. Devouring aims to sweep the other off her feet, to make her succumb to the tidal force of the Casanova's passion.

Some women find such ardor highly seductive. How deliciously romantic to find a man who will kick down your bedroom door where others meekly knock. Others, though, are properly skeptical of the Casanova's sudden attentions, and back away from him. I got the feeling that this has happened to Anthony more times than he cares to admit. To a devouring Casanova, a woman's slightest hesitation is synonymous with rejection, crushing and infuriating. "If she's going to be like that," he says of a girlfriend who asked him not to call her every night, "fuck her! I don't have time to play games." Certainly, a woman who wants to slow things down is unlikely to submit to his wishes for total possession; instead of remaining a compliant object of desire, she has committed the crime of having a will of her own.

Not surprisingly, the devouring Casanova is a jealous man. From the moment he meets her, he desires no less than his partner's undivided loyalty. He will go to dramatic lengths to get it, investing all his time, money and imagination to convince her that *he* is the best of all possible choices and to separate her from his rivals. (I can't help recalling the climax of the film *Morgan,* in which David Warner kidnaps his estranged wife from her new lover while dressed in a gorilla suit.) Should he fail, however, he is tormented by a rage and anxiety that recall the pangs of sibling rivalry or the Oedipal furies of a toddler. The object that he misses so desperately insists on belonging to someone else. There's an indignation in the Casanova's jealousy, the wrath of a man who feels that his rightful possession has been denied him. When Anthony suspects that a new lover has other boyfriends, he shadows her like a jealous husband.

TO EAT AND BE EATEN

But what if he succeeds in possessing his beloved? For some Casanovas conquest is immediately followed by boredom, as the exciting new is exposed as one more version of the disappointing old. But in devouring, the reaction is far stronger. Once conquered, a woman is not just boring, but repulsive and even frightening. Her defects leap into high relief: beneath that otherworldly glow, Casanova now sees stupidity and stretch marks. Where once she was all that is beautiful and good, now he can hardly find anything nice to say about her. Even her affection is suspect. When she calls him up, she is invading his privacy; when she asks to see him, she is making demands. When she tells him she loves him, he hears her asking him to love her back.

The violence of this revolution in attitude suggests that the devouring Casanova has imaginatively split his partner in two. When he met her, she represented the longed-for missing part of himself, the shining thing that would make him whole. From that moment on all his efforts were directed toward possessing her, so as to take this idealized fragment back into his psyche. But even after devouring her, Casanova still feels empty. His lover has failed him. Worse still, she has betrayed him. For if she is not the best thing that ever happened to him, she must by default be the worst, the embodiment of the very unease she was supposed to cure.

Everything turns inside out. Having devoured his lover, Anthony now turns her into a devourer, a predatory figure who seeks only to colonize and possess him. The thing he longed for has become the thing he fears, and instead of being the active party in this romance he is now its panicky victim. He makes excuses, he breaks dates, he ignores the ringing of his telephone. All he wants is to get this sharklike creature off his back, and if he can't do so politely he will be cruel. Anthony has said "terrible things" to women who "just wouldn't get the message" (even their ignorance was willful). Another man told me that on a date with an unwanted girlfriend, he excused himself to go to the men's room, crept out a side door and drove away, leaving her stranded in a restaurant several miles from her home.

But flight is not enough; the devouring Casanova's lover is now a malign and importuning presence inside him. Even though he has ingested her, she remains terribly alive, far more threatening in his imagination than she could ever be in real life, as the unanswered ring of the telephone is always more unnerving than the voice on the other end. To silence her demands requires nothing less than an exorcism—a violent expulsion from the canals of the psyche. The final stage of devouring is thus not hatred, but forgetting. Often enough, men like Anthony can't even recall the names of their old lovers. Thomas Wolfe, according to Donald, could look at a woman he'd coupled with barely an hour before and wonder, "Who is she?" The metaphor of devouring is now complete, as what was taken into the self so eagerly is at last flushed from memory.

Devouring often masquerades as love, or really, as love of the sentimental pop-song variety, with its instant yearning, hazy, soft-focus vision of the beloved, and relentless movement toward possession and fusion. Underneath lies a kind of perversion that stems from a fundamental confusion about the boundaries between self and other and that seeks to obliterate those differences through the sheer exercise of the Casanova's will. The devourer inhabits a universe of cracked mirrors, in which each new lover is nothing more than a fragmentary reflection of the self. He cannot see her as a separate being. He cannot love her as one adult loves another. He can only subject her to an unvarying series of psychic transformations that suggest the processes of ingestion and digestion: from a longed-for "good girl" to a "piece of meat," and finally, to a disposable "mistake," the same word we use when a child forgets its toilet training.

The singer Suzanne Vega has summarized the devouring mind-set in a single verse of terrifying accuracy:

I believe right now if I could I would swallow you whole
I would leave only bones and teeth
We could see what was underneath
And you would be free then.

THE PRISON OF METAPHOR

Metaphor is a way of lending meaning—often several layers of meaning—to reality. To Wallace Stevens a blackbird is at once a shadow, a small part of a pantomime and something that marks the edge of one of many circles. These different ways of seeing do not contradict each other; rather they give each other, and the elusive blackbird, resonance, as different notes form a chord when played at the same time. In the same way, the Casanova's unconscious metaphors often reinforce each other: at different moments he may function as a bored aesthete seeking erotic experience, a sexual adventurer racking up new conquests, a prisoner fleeing from his prison and a starving man trying to fill himself with female sustenance. The end result, though, is always the same—an unending cycle of pursuit, seduction, betrayal and abandonment.

To these metaphors we might add the part of Casanova that sees women as they are, and likes them that way, and wants nothing more than to find one he can love steadfastly and without harm. During my sexual addiction I had many woman friends. Our relationships were close and even passionate; all that was missing from them was sex, and that didn't seem such a great loss at all, given the usual consequences of my sexual liaisons. Some of these women had once been my lovers, and I was always astonished by the warmth and loyalty I felt for them once I got over the insanity of loving them. I encountered a similar division among many of the men I spoke with—a psychic split that enabled us to get along with women only until the moment we entered their bodies, at which point we—and they—suddenly became enemies. In many of us the metaphors are at war: to paraphrase Freud, where we love, we cannot like; whom we love, we cannot live with.

For the artist, metaphor is liberating: it lets him unchain things from their leaden dailiness; it lets him *play* with them. This, of course, has much to do with the fact that he consciously chooses his metaphors and is always aware that metaphor is not the same as life. Outside the field of the printed page, Wallace Stevens's blackbirds remain blackbirds. But Casanova never chose his metaphors. His visions of women, his definitions of self, grew out of his earliest experience, were in some way handed down to him by parents and culture. Nor does he fully realize that his metaphors, his ingrained ways of seeing, are not the same thing as life: to Saul a woman really *is* a source of excitement, who loses all value as soon as her thrill is gone; Howard treats his lovers exactly as though they were stakes in a game and is always startled and irritated when they protest that, no, his game is their life. Unchosen and unconscious, Casanova's metaphors are his prison. They dictate his behavior as surely as the cell limits the pacing of the convict: he walks back and forth, he walks in a circle, in spirals, he pounds the walls and rattles the bars; he still cannot get out.

PART TWO

---◆◆◆---

The Six Faces
of Casanova

THE WAYS WE MAKE A BROKEN HEART

We now have a fair idea as to how Casanova thinks and feels. But how does he act? Within the prison of metaphor different prisoners behave differently. Casanovas habitually seduce and abandon women, but the ways in which they do so vary enormously. Some make love to different women night after night and never linger long enough to breakfast with their partners of the night before. Some keep falling breathlessly in love only to fall out of it a few weeks later. Some seem happily married but cheat regularly on their wives. The fact that these men share a similarly impoverished sense of self and see women as means of the self's reparation and replenishment nevertheless allows them to pursue their compulsion in different ways, from a career of one-night stands to a long but chronically adulterous marriage.

All Casanovas, however, behave according to recognizable patterns, whose recurring traits can be summed up as follows:

•*As a rule, they are strongly drawn to women, one would have to say addictively so. They require constant sexual companionship, whether in the form of wives, girlfriends or casual partners. Deprived of such companionship, they suffer from depression and anxiety; they cannot sleep; they binge on drugs or alcohol, food or work. The pursuit and conquest of women is the central activity around which these men's lives are organized. When that activity fails or is otherwise interrupted, their lives collapse in disorder.*

•*Casanovas seem unable to form a strong attachment to any particular woman. No matter how long-lived or intense, their relationships have an air of transience and improvisation. When separated from their wives or lovers, they do not seem to suffer from genuine loss; their bereavement ends the moment they find new partners. For these men no loss is unbearable, no woman irreplaceable.*

•*Their intimate, monogamous relationships are usually short-lived.*

•*In longer relationships Casanovas are habitually unfaithful. None of the married men I interviewed has gone more than six months without an extramarital affair, and most stray far more often. To a certain extent Casanovas use infidelity both as a means of escaping their relationships and of securing them; they can only stay with women whom they periodically betray.*

•*Their relationships with women begin quickly, with an instant of physical attraction. Casanovas rarely question their passion or analyze their sexual urges before acting on them. For these men, there is no lag between desire and its fulfillment.*

•*Along with this quick sexual start-up comes a general impatience with the dynamics of courtship and an unwillingness to postpone gratification. Most Casanovas, including the most artful seducers, quickly push every encounter to a sexual conclusion. If deprived of an immediate conquest, they tend to lose interest, perhaps because they interpret female reticence as outright rejection, perhaps because the only reality women possess for them is that of sexual objects.*

•*Along with sexual impulsiveness comes sexual recklessness. Casanovas rarely take responsibility for birth control, and in an age when casual sex has come to be a high-risk activity, they seem indifferent to the dangers of sexually transmitted disease. They are careless adulterers, who take only the crudest precautions against discovery. These men seem peculiarly unaware of the consequences of desire and unable to link their behavior with its effects.*

•When Casanovas fall in love, they do so impulsively, often on the basis of the most cursory knowledge of the beloved. Their affairs usually end as abruptly as they began, with a moment of shattering disillusionment. As soon as the beloved loses her veil of otherness, the Casanova abandons her. There are no second acts in these men's romances.

•Although they enjoy sex, Casanovas approach it in an oddly mechanistic fashion. They measure satisfaction in quantitative terms, accumulating lovers like belt notches and judging each encounter by how long it lasts and how many orgasms it includes. They may also enact a kind of sexual escalation, requiring their partners to perform a succession of erotic variations, beginning with "straight" intercourse and leading to oral and anal sex, bondage and discipline, and sex with multiple partners. These variations seem to have no intrinsic attraction; their pleasure derives from their novelty. Moreover, Casanovas see sexual escalation in terms of conquest, as a series of concessions won by persistence, charm and skill. To get a girlfriend to submit to anal penetration or have sex with another woman is to win a new victory, to extend seduction to levels beyond the "first base, second base, third base, home" of the high-school locker room.

•While for most men sexual desire usually grows out of intimacy, Casanovas seem most attracted to strangers. They rarely sleep with women whom they know too well in a nonsexual context. Moreover, they quickly lose interest in their sexual partners. Among these men intimacy is inimical to sexual attraction.

•Casanovas are habitual deceivers, whose deceptiveness goes far beyond simple lying. In courtship, they assume new identities—seductive masks that allow them only a limited range of expression. They keep their genuine feelings deeply hidden from their partners, and as a result often feel lonely and misunderstood.

•Beneath their romantic ardor lies an ingrained sense of love as a set of demands and obligations. It's all right to make love to a woman, but once she loves you, Casanovas worry, all sorts of responsibilities are sure to follow. For this reason, they avoid deeper involvements and run as soon as their liaisons show signs of getting serious.

•Casanovas often have difficulty handling money, which they seem to equate with love. They are the kind of men who take their dates to chic clubs and restaurants and shower them with expen-

sive gifts. On the other hand, they may be extraordinarily tight-fisted, resentful of even the most trifling expenditures on their partners. When asked if they had ever paid for sex, many Casanovas told me that they always paid for it, a statement that suggests a deep-seated suspicion of women and an underlying view of sex as a commercial transaction.

•Unconsciously, Casanovas divide women into "good girls" and "bad girls," virgins and whores. While they are drawn to women who seem sexually expressive and uninhibited, those they take as wives or steady girlfriends are often timid and repressed, unwilling to act out their mates's elaborate erotic fantasies. It sometimes seems that these men compel the women they live with to fill the role of virgin, usually by withdrawing from them sexually. This in turn frees them to seek out whores for the erotic excitement that has vanished from the primary relationship.

•Casanovas are strongly predisposed toward alcoholism, drug addiction and other obsessive-compulsive disorders. They use mood-altering substances—or compulsive eating, gambling or overwork—in much the same way as they use women: as crutches, as avenues of escape and as tools for verifying a self that is otherwise tenuous and deficient.

We can think of these traits as symptoms, as fever, a runny nose and an upset stomach are symptoms of the flu. A single symptom means little in itself: if you wake one morning with a runny nose, chances are you just have allergies; a man can fall in love quickly or suffer from a slight virgin-whore complex without being a dyed-in-the-wool Don Juan. When we look at Casanovas, however, we see that the symptoms are both persistent and clustered. Most of us have, at least once in our lives, fallen in love at first sight; a true Casanova will do so again and again. Among married men adultery is now fairly common, but adultery takes on a different meaning when it is a weekly occurrence and when the erring husband always takes his pleasure in cheap hotel rooms, with women he has bribed with a few drinks and whom he treats with an uneasy mixture of desire and contempt. When such behavior is habitual and accompanied by other symptoms, we are in the presence of an underlying disorder of the feelings—the ravenous and fragmented personality of the Casanova.

Just as Casanovas have four characteristic motivations—thrill seeking, game playing, escaping and devouring—they also fall into six identifiable types of behavior, which I call hitters, drifters, romantics, nesters, jugglers and tomcats. These behavioral groups form a rough continuum, from men who have the briefest and most noncommittal contacts with women to those who form long and apparently durable relationships marked by chronic infidelity. They represent a spectrum of commitment, that ill-defined buzzword of the 1980s. Commitment implies a willingness to extend a relationship beyond the moment, to make—and to let one's partner make —assumptions about a shared future. One may phrase those assumptions as a marriage vow or simply as a promise to call the next day; the relationship may last a day at a time or into eternity. Thus, at one end of the scale are hitters, practitioners of the one-night stand who rarely sleep with the same woman twice and even hesitate to give out their phone numbers the morning after. From there, it's a step up to drifters, who may date their partners for a few weeks without ever committing themselves to a predictable relationship. The turbulent liaisons of the men I call romantics usually flare out after a few months; nesters may stay with their lovers for years but leave them at a moment's notice. Polygyny is the juggler's hedge against commitment: there are always at least two women in his life, and he meticulously divides his time and affection between them. Tomcats, finally, may live with their spouses for decades, but cheat on them constantly.

It would be a mistake, though, to sum up Casanovas as men who can't commit; they are also men who can't get close to the women they claim to love. I define intimacy as the ability to reveal oneself to another human being and to bear witness to that person's humanity; it calls for a basic awareness of the difference between self and other. Here, too, we see a continuum among Casanovas. Romantics and nesters, for example, seem capable of at least some degree of intimacy, and their love affairs are far more vital and emotionally expressive than the anonymous genital transactions of hitters or the silent and insular alliances of tomcats and their spouses. They may at times touch the regions of the heart. In fact, it is when their hearts are touched that romantics and nesters usually leave their partners: for these men the heart is too dangerous a territory.

How does one measure intangibles like commitment and intimacy? We can make assumptions about a man's ability to commit be seeing how long his relationships last: it was the first question I asked the men I interviewed. I also wanted to know how they formalized their relationships. For all the talk to the contrary, there's a real difference between being married and simply living together. With marriage come financial and legal obligations that may not guarantee the relationship but surely make it harder to dissolve. Living with a partner, though, also carries its share of responsibilities, from paying bills to cleaning house, that couples who live apart never face. I asked Casanovas how often they saw their lovers and under what circumstances. Did they plan their evenings together in advance? Did they ever break dates without warning? Did they integrate their relationships with the rest of their lives, introducing their partners to friends and families? Could their relationships tolerate conflict, or did they break up at the first argument? All of these things indicate the degree of energy and ego that a man is willing to invest in a woman, the strength of the bond between them.

It was harder to draw up a scale of intimacy, because intimacy itself is so much harder to define. Unlike commitment, it is not dependent on time. A romantic may reveal as much to his partner in a few weeks as a tomcat discloses in a thirty-year marriage. Intimacy is based on communication, so I asked Casanovas how much time they spent talking with their partners and what they talked about. Were any subjects off-limits? Did they discuss their sexual preferences and problems? How comfortable were they sharing their feelings? When conflicts arose, how did they deal with them? (I gave low marks in intimacy to men who claimed they never fought.) What secrets did they keep from their wives and girlfriends? How well did they know their partners, and how well did they believe their partners knew them?

What emerged from these interviews was a sort of seesaw pattern. All the men I spoke with have damaged capacities for commitment and intimacy: some are handicapped more severely than others. Those, like jugglers and tomcats, who can sustain long relationships nevertheless use infidelity and polygyny to avoid getting too close to their partners. Romantics and nesters, who generally seem more comfortable expressing their feelings, can't remain with the women they express them to. Among Casanovas each strength seems counterbalanced by a crippling weakness, which prevents them from developing the warm, equitable and lasting unions that many of us achieve and most of us yearn for.

A word of warning is called for here, lest one imagine that Casanovas conform rigidly to these behavioral patterns. On the basis of my conversations with these men, I doubt that there exists anything like a "pure" type of Casanova. Womanizers adopt—or, really, fall into—different sexual strategies in the course of a lifetime, shifting from one to another in accordance with mood and circumstance. Most of the hitters I interviewed have some steady relationship, if only with a high-school girlfriend, tucked away in their past; most nesters have at one time or another enjoyed a night of zipless sex with a stranger. In the course of my own active addiction, I went from one-night stands, to short, explosive love affairs, to a marriage that ended when I left my wife for another woman. It's only in retrospect that I realize how superficial those changes were. They affected my overall pattern of sexual compulsion no more than changing drinks affects an alcoholic. He may switch from scotch to beer and flatter himself that he has kicked his habit: he cannot admit that he still gets drunk night after night and awakens with a crushing hangover in the light of day.

CHAPTER FOUR

———— ◆•◆ ————

Hitters

THE EXAMPLE OF DON JUAN

He is the archetypal womanizer, the kind of man that mothers used to warn their daughters about in the days when daughters still listened to their mothers' advice. Even Don Juan's servant, Cataliñon, says of him:

> *"The best*
> *Way to describe you, sir, would be*
> *As a locust to whom girls are grass...*
> *Whenever you're about to arrive*
> *Towns should be warned: 'Here comes the plague*
> *Of women in a single man.'"*

In the play by Tirso de Molina, Don Juan first appears in mid-seduction, or rather, in mid-imposture: he has made love to the Duchess Isabel while disguised as her fiancé. When his identity is revealed, she cries out in shame. Her honor is gone. Subterfuge is essential to this man, as it was to Casanova, who described the ballet between the seducer and the seduced as a reciprocal dupery. In later acts, Don Juan repeats the trick of stealing into a woman's bedchamber in the guise of another man. At one point, he takes on the identity of his best friend in order to sleep with his betrothed. This pattern of disguise raises questions about the true object of Don Juan's desires: does he masquerade as other men in order to gain access to their women, or are his seductions only pretexts for the obscure delight of briefly becoming another man?

The Don practices other kinds of deception. He falsely proposes marriage to the fisherwoman Thisbe, who has saved his life, and not only abandons her but burns down her hut as he skulks away. Later, he gets another woman to sleep with him by persuading her that her fiancé has given her up. True, he possesses a native charm, an élan and nobility of bearing that sweep women off their feet. But the real secret of Don Juan's appeal to the opposite sex is his capacity for lies and subterfuge, the edged, insinuating tongue that can make his victims overlook their suspicions. He is not so much a lover as an erotic con man, whose "greatest pleasure is to trick women."

The pleasure of trickery takes precedence over sex itself. Don Juan is a coldly mannered seducer; even Thisbe calls his desire "frosty." He promises fire but delivers ice. The text of Molina's play suggests that the Don doesn't linger in the bedroom. He leaves as soon as the act is finished and never returns. For this man, passion is purely a matter of arithmetic, a relentless tallying of sexual scores. His partners feel defiled after he beds them, and Don Juan knows he has defiled them. By stripping his conquests of virtue and dignity he has injured not only them but also their fathers, brothers and lovers. Don Juan's exploits are thus acts of vengeance for God knows what distant hurt, directed against man and woman alike. And when he dies—in the stony embrace of a man he has murdered—it's as though some ancient and motiveless vendetta had finally claimed its last victim.

NICK: THE SPORTING LIFE

Incapable of commitment or intimacy, hitters are the guerrillas of the war between the sexes. They view women solely as sexual—or genital—objects and demand instant gratification of their sexual needs. They rarely date, they never enter long relationships, they do not fall in love. They are men who pursue sex in its rawest and most minimal form, with as many different partners as possible, and who avoid any subsequent involvement with the women who have satisfied them.

Nick is a litigator for a prestigious law firm in Milwaukee. He's good at his job, a hard worker who loves argument and competition. In his work he is a perfectionist; he finds it hard to accept defeat and usually blames himself when he loses a case. That's why his leisure time is so important to him. Several nights a week he undergoes a transformation. The pin-striped suit is replaced by a loosely corrugated Armani jacket and a Hawaiian shirt. He molds his hair into a style that makes him look younger than his thirty-four years and would be decidedly too rakish for his daytime life in the courtroom. Before leaving his apartment, he snorts a few lines of cocaine and downs a vodka and tonic. "I'm a little edgy before I go out," Nick says. "What I'm doing is a kind of sporting event, and I've got to be in exactly the right frame of mind to be good at it." The sporting event consists of going to a couple of bars with some friends and looking for women.

Nick thinks of himself as easygoing and nonchalant, but his search for sexual partners is ruthless. From the moment he leaves his job, everything from the clothes he wears to the drugs he takes serves a sexual end. When he enters a bar, he immediately scans it for interesting prospects, and he chooses his prospects quickly.

Some hitters approach women with blind enthusiasm, propositioning one after another until they find one who says yes. Nick's approach is delicately indirect. He tries not to sound too eager or aggressive. He often excuses himself to talk to other women nearby, making sure that his prospective partner can see him. The object is both to take off the pressure and to convey an impression of himself as a man who is safe yet attractive to her sex. "At first, it reassures her," Nick says. "And then she starts to wonder why I'm not coming on stronger. She knows I'm not some ordinary jerk, and now she's wondering if I'm interested in her. A lot of women are so used to being hit on that they're cocky; what I do is undermine that cockiness. I get women to question the idea that they're the most desirable things on earth. And then, of course, they're going to want to *prove* they are."

The goal is to make women participate in their own seduction, to turn demure, professional women into sexual aggressors. "The girls I pick up are always decent, presentable—the kind of girl who wouldn't be out of place in a good restaurant. Sometimes that's all they're good for—decoration. When you get them into the bedroom, they just lie there. What turns me on, though, is when one of these nice little girls turns into a tiger." In Nick's eyes, eagerness and generosity are what make a woman a tiger. Although he is something of a game player, he also wants women to please him, and he makes them work hard at it. The ideal encounter ends only when he and his partner are exhausted. Often, he boasts, she must beg him to stop.

Yet no matter how much Nick enjoys sex, a part of him is always detached and quietly anxious. Even before he enters the bedroom, he is planning his exit. He prefers going to the woman's home, knowing that it will be easier for him to leave. "If we're at my place, there's no polite way I know to tell her I want her to go. I don't like scenes. Keeping the evening civil is very important to me." What remains unvarying is his distaste for any encounter beyond the one-night stand. In the past ten years he has slept with more than two hundred women and rarely seen the same one twice.

THE QUEST AND ITS RITUALS

Some men find sex by accident; hitters pursue it deliberately and single-mindedly. They endow their quests with the urgency of work and indeed are often more dedicated after-hours than they are at their paying jobs. The quest is highly ritualized. It requires special vestments—a stylishly wrinkled Armani or pants too tight to wear at work but just tight enough for a nightclub. (Interestingly, many of the men's fashions of the past twenty years seem to have been designed specifically for cruising—a sort of sexual safari wear.) There are drugs and alcohol to give courage: a shot and a line or two turn anxiety into aggression, fear into what-the-hell confidence. Hitters also use drugs to augment their sexual performance, to produce strong erections and delay orgasm. Sometimes, of course, the drugs' effect is quite the opposite; they may be too drunk to complete intercourse. But some alteration of consciousness seems essential to hitting, if only to mark the boundary between the world of the ordinary and the night kingdom of desire.

Most rituals occur in consecrated space, in churches or temples or cemeteries. Hitters tend to look for women in special places. Most of the men I spoke with habitually find their partners in the same few bars or discos. One man frequents a neighborhood Laundromat. The value of these places is not just that women can be found there. They are also *familiar,* and their familiarity allays the fear that accompanies any sexual overture. A man who is turned down by a woman in his favorite hangout can always exchange a chagrined laugh with the other regulars. At least he is at home there. Although hitters prefer sex with partners they don't know, they seem to need places where they are known and the tacit reassurance of people who know them. Indeed, they are sometimes unable to approach a strange woman unless they have male friends nearby. And, because so much of the hitter's sexuality is competitive, he needs other men to witness his prowess and so validate it.

Rituals themselves often serve as filters for anxiety. The trappings of the funeral mediate the terror of death. The meticulous counting of the obsessive-compulsive wards off sexual dread. Hitters, it would seem, employ clothing, drugs and special places as talismans of success and as protection against fear. Seeking women is a fearful activity, fraught with the potential for rejection. And rejection is especially dangerous for these men. Because they have defined the purpose of the evening—and of their very lives—as sexual conquest, every failure can be a mortal blow to their self-esteem. Underlying every come-on is a confrontation with a woman who has the power to validate the self or to annihilate it. Given this primal terror, hitters need all the security their rituals can give them.

ANY WOMAN WILL DO

Whether they seek beauty, intelligence or personality in their sexual partners, hitters seem to find it within minutes, sometimes at first glance. This abrupt and superficial attraction to women is one of their basic traits, and I attribute it to two factors: the first is the overriding urgency of their sexual desire; the second is anxiety. It often seems that the first factor is only a manifestation of the second—that Casanova's lust defends him against fear. Long before he has glimpsed the woman he wants that evening, Nick is determined to find a sexual partner. Primed by alcohol and cocaine, he is aroused from the start. Most hitters perform their rituals in a similar state of love-readiness. Sometimes they call it "horniness" or "lover's nuts," but their tension isn't always or exclusively sexual. Many will simply describe themselves as "ready." They are men who want something—something that might be sex—and in a pinch almost any woman can provide it.

Their descriptions of love-readiness often remind one of the symptoms of anxiety: tautness of the muscles, dryness of the mouth, a hollow feeling in the stomach. Some hitters feel depressed immediately before embarking on a sexual quest: I suspect they genuinely are. Among these men an entire battery of emotions—fear, sadness, anger—masquerades as desire. Desire, after all, is easier to acknowledge than fear or grief; it is at once more "manly" and more easily relieved. A man who is horny can satisfy his urges by finding a woman, but what does a man do when he is sad or fearful, especially if he doesn't know why? Just as the hitter's rituals ward off the anxiety of seduction, so seduction itself may be his way of easing a discomfort that has nothing to do with lust. To approach a strange woman may be risky business, but not to approach her may be riskier still, and being rejected may be preferable to sitting with feelings he can neither tolerate nor name.

It follows, then, that the hitter *must* find his partners quickly and make whatever allowances he has to in order to classify an available woman as an attractive one. Waiting long enough to decide whether she is truly intelligent or personable may cost him a conquest and leave him no choice but to go home alone. There has to be somebody, even if the light of day exposes her as one more "coyote fuck."

THE EROTIC COMBAT ZONE

The term "coyote fuck" is significant, suggesting as it does the undercurrent of revulsion, hostility and dread that runs through every hitter's sexual transactions. When Nick sizes up a woman and subjects her to his adroit cross-examination, it's in the spirit of a man sizing up an adversary and probing her for weaknesses. Getting a woman to talk about herself is a kind of flattery, but it's also a way to learn about her without divulging much about himself. It's a sort of reconnaissance mission, while the hitter who talks about himself may be seen as waging a frontal assault: he seeks to overwhelm his opponent with a sheer volume of biographical detail. When hitters talk about themselves, as Nick rightly observes, they are usually boasting—about their jobs, their incomes or their educations. Their object is not so much to convey information as it is to impress and intimidate. Seduction, as practiced by these men, is not a fair contract, a clear-cut exchange of sexual favors. Rather, it's a kind of fraud, an attempt to gain advantage over the other through subterfuge or strength.

Why should seduction be construed as warfare? Why does it require intimidation or trickery? When Nick describes certain women as "cocky" and talks about "undermining that cockiness," he inadvertently betrays the roots of his hostility. Although he enjoys good looks, a respected profession and a decent income, he apparently still feels inferior to most of the women he meets in his nocturnal forays. Most hitters harbor similar feeings of inferiority and resentment. In their voices one hears the plaintive note of the underdog: women, as these men see them, are invariably arrogant and frigid. The hitter who approaches one of these *belles dames sans merci* is always a petitioner begging for sexual favors from someone whose natural inclination is to withhold them. Every woman, simply by virtue of being the object of desire, is automatically endowed with power—the power to deny, reject and humiliate the man who desires her.

Consciously, he may realize that she, too, is a sexual being, with appetites just as fierce and driving as his own, but his unconscious scenario is quite different. Just as all the power is concentrated on her side of the male-female transaction, all the desire is on his. Unconsciously, he sees every woman as a glacially indifferent virgin, accessible only by fraud and intimidation. It's little wonder that the greatest part of his pleasure comes from making these superior creatures take part in their own seduction and from transforming virgins, as though by magic, into sexually voracious tigers, who writhe, scream and beg for more before they finally beg for mercy. The hitter's seductions have a tidy economy: conquest erases the inequality that made it necessary in the first place. Desire becomes the great leveler.

For hitters, coitus is the climax of a power struggle, and their descriptions of sex are charged with the symbolism of power. Some of these men strive gallantly to please their partners. Others, like Nick, are chiefly concerned with their own satisfaction, and many hitters are indifferent to whether a woman comes at all. But even the most solicitous of these men seems to view sex as something that a man inflicts upon a woman. When describing an erotic episode, they are far more likely to say "I fucked her" than "we made love." While they prize women who are sexually aggressive—women who will work to satisfy them—they also dread being passive. Even when they are being fellated or are lying beneath their partners, they cling to a fantasy of control. If they are not "giving" women orgasms, they are telling women how to make them come. Sex for these men is a wrestling match that ends only when the woman cries uncle.

AFTERGLOW/AFTERMATH

But when coitus ends, the illusion of control vanishes; the old inequality surfaces once more. And with it returns the anxiety that was previously masked by the drama of seduction and the ensuing struggle. For some men the anxiety is specifically sexual, especially if they have climaxed before their partners and are unable to continue intercourse. "The problem is that so many women are greedy," one man complains. "They figure there's something the matter with you if you can't go all night." The fact that a woman can have three or four orgasms to his one and want more when he is depleted fills him with fear and anger, and he quickly projects his feelings of inadequacy onto her. The tiger has become a voracious and castrating she-shark.

My own intuition is that performance anxiety is a secondary source of discomfort for hitters, a translation of a malaise that is deeper and less easily labeled. Even men who have sexually exhausted their partners seem ill at ease once the sweat of passion has dried. Glib when talking a woman into bed with him, Nick is tongue-tied afterward, reduced to clumsy and artificial small talk. Again, he tends to deny his discomfort and project it outward: the same woman who once glowed with vitality and intelligence suddenly seems dull and shallow to him. No wonder he and so many other hitters suffer from postcoital blues. Whatever his partners are or aren't is as irrelevant after sex as it was before. Just as their personalities were overshadowed by the urgency of the erotic quest, they are now eclipsed by the private and persistent unease that every hitter carries with him. Naked, flaccid and crashing from his erotic high, he is aware of nothing so much as of his own vulnerability. And so excruciating is that awareness that he seldom realizes that the woman beside him may be just as vulnerable.

The recognition of their common vulnerability can lead two strangers to the threshold of intimacy. When we apprehend only our own, the sense of isolation can be heightened to the point of paranoia. It's startling and a little sad to see how quickly a hitter's sexual confidence evaporates, and how often it gives way to suspicion and barely stifled rage at the woman he held close to him just moments before. Nick is an expert at undermining women's "arrogance," but to his dismay he finds that immediately after sex the arrogance returns. "I hate it when someone thinks she can make emotional claims on you, just because you found her attractive enough to take her to bed. I hate it when she throws her phone number at me and expects me to give her mine. I hate it when she keeps hugging me so tightly I feel like I'm choking to death." Implicit in these charges is a confusion between intimacy and invasion and a sense of women as aggressors. In the afterglow of sex, just when he has been rocked into complacency, women start making "emotional claims," demanding time, affection and information that, no matter how trivial, suddenly seem sacred to the man who is asked to give them up. Asking a hitter for his phone number is like asking him to amputate his arm, and even a postcoital embrace can strike him as an attempt at strangulation. Sex, as these men repeatedly tell you, always has its price.

FIFTY WAYS TO LEAVE A LOVER

Yet the price is one they are unwilling to pay. Whether they are motivated by fear or by anger, hitters disengage from women soon after sex. Some men are open about their distaste for further meetings. But most, like Nick, sidestep confrontation. Often enough, they are fleeing from their own anger as well as from the women who provoke it. What anger they do feel is usually suppressed. In the afterglow, they fall silent and edge away from partners whose very touch has become offensive to them. Few hitters will spend an entire night with a woman; they are too agitated to get much sleep.

Like Nick, they tend to make excuses for leaving. A single hitter I spoke with sometimes tells his partners that he is married just to facilitate his exit. When asked about future plans, hitters offer to call at an unspecified time or to "get together real soon." They have many ways of saying good-bye.

Of all the types of Casanovas, hitters seem the least likely to examine their behavior or question its underlying motives. They do not suffer the guilt of the adulterous tomcat or the grief that sometimes descends on romantics and nesters. They may change their sexual pattern, especially as they grow older, but the change is usually based on pragmatic considerations: the competition of the singles bar doesn't favor men in their forties. When asked to explain his behavior, Nick cites a personal code of freedom and experience that resembles a mixture of *Playboy* philosophy and undergraduate existentialism, studded with appeals to "honesty" and "adventure" and "living for the moment." Underneath one hears a bottomless greed for more conquests and a panicky rage at the women he conquers:

"There are so many women out there, and they're all different. Their breasts, their vaginas, the sounds they make when they come. Why should I limit myself to just one, just because that's what she thinks I should do? Why should I give any woman that power over my life? Look," he says, his voice rising, "one day I'm going to be eighty and my last hard-on will be behind me. But I'll be able to look back and say, 'Well, at least I lived honestly. At least I didn't compromise myself. At least I had this adventure.'"

CHAPTER FIVE

———◆◆◆———

Drifters

THE EXAMPLE OF JAMES BOND

And of course he's fun, he has a lust for life. He gambles, he drinks, he has casual sex or at least falls in love for a rather limited time. But that's because he lives on the edge of life and wants to live it to the full while he's still got it.

—Timothy Dalton, on James Bond

There have always been two James Bonds. The first was Ian Fleming's fictional creation, who embodied all the fears and fantasies of the Cold War. He was not a pleasant fellow at all, this tuxedoed angel of death. The James Bond of cinema, although portrayed by four different actors, was always lighter, more cartoony. He didn't fight real Russians, just the grotesques of SPECTRE, the second cousins of Lex Luthor and Ming the Merciless. Fleming's Bond is a killing machine; the movie Bond lets his machinery do the killing and is no more frightening than the man who baby-sits ICBMs in an underground silo. He turns his necessary acts of mayhem into a joke between himself and his audience, muttering wisecracks like Popeye.

The celluloid Bond has lots of women—at least two per film. (In The Living Daylights the new 007 has only one love interest—an obvious bow to the omnipresent fear of AIDS. But the fact that Bond's sexuality has been so openly toned down is an implicit acknowledgment of his status as a male role model.) The girls have names like Pussy Galore, Kissy Suzuki and Plenty O'Toole; they represent a UN calendar of nations and skin tones and work at varied professions. But as their names suggest, they serve chiefly as sexual objects for the British superspy. Bond's appetites transcend ideology as well as nationality and race: he is as comfortable pressing the sheets with Anya Amasova, a Russian secret agent, as he is with Holly Goodhead, her CIA counterpart. For that matter, he has no qualms about sleeping with women who want to kill him. In Thunderball he escapes death by casually sweeping a treacherous lover into the path of her accomplice's bullet. 007 does not require his partners to be faithful, honest or even trustworthy: he asks only that they be willing.

And of course they are. In his sexual encounters, Bond is not so much the pursuer as the pursued. Women fall all over him. They greet him from the waters off a deserted Caribbean beach. They follow him across Europe. They lie in wait for him in a couchette on the Orient Express, clad in nothing but a black choker. In his acceptance of female desire, he is almost passive: he needn't lift a finger to arouse women beyond endurance. Those who don't fall for him at first glance (and in Bond films it's standard formula that the most important women are at first elusive, if not openly hostile) yield in due course to his heroism, physical grace and cold-blooded self-possession. Women chase Bond because he is confident enough not to chase them.

Does 007 fall in love? True, he marries twice, but one bride is cover for an assignment in Japan: we hear no more of her after the mission is over. (Was there a quiet annulment in the chambers of MI5?) The second woman is murdered on their honeymoon. He doesn't spend much time mourning her. Although he likes women, Bond never invests too much in them. When he rescues a lover from certain death, we can chalk it up to British sportsmanship and derring-do. In all other ways, Bond is reserved, and even repressed, in his relations with the opposite sex, a desultory seducer whose pulse never races, who never seems to blush or stammer. Even in the bedroom he remains in command of his feelings and responses —stirred but not shaken. His highest compliment to any woman is "good girl." Nor is he especially upset when a bedmate turns traitor. As a spy, Bond knows that betrayal goes with his territory. More important, he never ventures enough of himself to make true betrayal possible.

If 007's women make no lasting claim on his feelings, they also make no demands on his loyalty. He sleeps with many women in the course of each adventure, and every lover knows that there are others. None ever seems jealous. No woman has ever left Bond because he wouldn't make a commitment. No woman has ever left him, period. Rejection would place a serious dent in the ideal he represents. Nor does he ever really leave his women. Pussy Galore and Holly Goodhead simply vanish in the interregnum between films. The last frame catches the lovers in midclinch, whether the clinch takes place under a parachute, on board a Chinese junk or in an orbiting space capsule. We are spared the ignominy of the morning after and the sight of Bond fumbling evasively when his newest bedmate asks: "When will I see you again?" More often, Bond's partners are killed off before they can ask the question. This man is simply death on women. A recent fan book identifies an entire class of Bond girls as "victims." Some are SPECTRE agents—or the villains' mistresses—who fall for Bond and incur their masters' lethal displeasure; others are allies who pay for their involvement with their lives. This sacrifice of lovers is part of the Bond formula, as unvarying as the sacrifice of virgins in satanic rite. Bond isn't always to blame for their deaths, but these sacrifices serve a purpose, keeping this consummate womanizer free of entanglement while absolving him of the onus of walking out. Every James Bond film elaborates the fantasy of the eternally potent man whose lovers are plentiful, willing, grateful and, on top of that, always disappear on cue.

ED: ALWAYS ANOTHER CUSTOMER

If hitters are sexual predators, the men I call drifters are creatures of opportunity. They find women everywhere; they don't pursue them so much as they simply fall into bed with them and take their relationships from there. Those relationships never amount to much. In comparison with hitters, whose search for sexual partners is driven and fraught with anxiety, drifters seem relaxed and almost affectless, as though floating on a cloud of Valium. Not for them the peaks and valleys of passion and panic. They cruise through their affairs as through the flattest of landscapes. Drifters are men who need to keep their options open—the option to see other women, the option to leave when they get bored. This type of man may date one partner for a few weeks out of pure inertia, because she is there. And when he leaves, it is simply because he prefers not to continue.

By his own admission, Ed, a salesman who lives in Atlanta, isn't especially good-looking. At thirty-six, he notices that his waist is thickening even as his hair is thinning. Nor does he think of himself as a virtuoso of the bedroom. Here his modesty ends. Ed is one of those infuriating men who believes unshakably in his good fortune. And his luck with women *is* phenomenal; he has never wanted for sexual partners. "I don't have to go out of my way to find women," he says, "and I don't have the feeling that I'm conquering anyone: it's too easy; it's like waking up in the morning and finding that the sun's shining."

In the past twenty years Ed has never gone more than a month without a girlfriend. As a teenager he was so secure in his virility that he refused to go steady: that would have been too limiting. In college he dated the homecoming queen; on their nights apart other women filed through his dorm room and onto his waterbed. It was the late sixties, a time Ed still recalls fondly for its relaxed sexual ethic. "You didn't even have to take a girl out to dinner. You'd just say, 'Why don't you come over?' I remember I'd have women in the living room and when I wanted to get down, I'd just stick my hand out and reach for them without saying anything, and we'd walk into the bedroom. I didn't have to say a word—I was that confident. Success breeds success. The more you do, the better you get. And the better you get, the more they want to come back."

Today Ed meets women everywhere: in bars and restaurants, at airports, sales conferences and even on buses. He attributes his success to his impish charm and what he calls his "bad-boy attitude." Like many salesmen, he projects a breezy self-assurance, an implicit conviction of well-being that is almost hypnotically persuasive. Everything seems to be for the best in his best of all possible worlds. I imagine that women sense this in him, and want to be with him simply because he is so buoyant. Rejection leaves him undaunted. Meeting women is merely another kind of salesmanship to Ed, and he knows that for every woman who doesn't want his product, there's always another customer who will.

His approach to sex is just as easygoing. He earmarks women as sexual possibilities but doesn't insist on immediate consummation and is pleasantly surprised if one agrees to sleep with him on a first date. Usually he takes women out two or three times before expecting a sexual payoff. If nothing happens, he quickly loses interest and resents the time and money squandered.

But even women who meet Ed's sexual expectations have a hard time holding his interest. Although he presents himself as relaxed and undemanding, he has a hidden set of criteria so stringent that no woman seems able to satisfy them. He has stopped seeing women because they had slight physical imperfections, because they were too passive in bed, because they expected him to spend too much time or money on them. He has left women because they were too dull or too sharp-tempered, because they had the wrong accents or chewed gum and smoked at the same time. He has lost interest in women because they had too many roommates or lived too far away, because he had been seeing them too long and was beginning to feel bored and itchy. As Ed grows older, he sometimes feels lonely and wonders if he will ever settle down. But he quickly shrugs off his doubts. He's convinced that the right woman is out there: he just hasn't found her yet.

A LOVER ON EVERY BRANCH

What first impressed me about drifters is how easily they find women. The world is their erotic garden, with potential lovers hanging from every branch. Every drifter has tales of lucky encounters with the opposite sex—the passionate blondes whose cars break down just as they are driving past. Of course, it's hard to tell how many are exaggerated. But as a rule these men are alive to the sexual possibilities in any situation, and they have a gift for improvisation that the rest of us might envy.

In addition to this ready eye for the main chance, drifters seem gifted with endless confidence and persistence. Most strikingly, they seem virtually immune to rejection. Even after the most shattering breakups, they waste no time in finding someone new. In an average day, Ed introduces himself to a dozen women or more, on the off-chance that something will click. It's no coincidence that many of the men I classify as drifters are employed in sales: the same persuasiveness, drive and emotional resilience that enable them to find sexual partners at will make them ideally suited for that profession.

Are drifters really devoid of the insecurities that afflict other men? True, they seem extraordinarily plucky, but their unfailing confidence seems suspect. Each rejection prompts Ed to redouble his efforts: for every women who turns him down, he'll approach two more, exercising his own variant of the Pete Rose theory, and when an affair ends he dives into its sequel. Loss and rejection serve drifters as aphrodisiacs. They treat their bruised hearts and sagging egos by seeking out new partners, anesthetizing themselves with the drama of the chase, even though the chase itself may mean further losses.

For drifters, the chase is what matters: it's the act of pursuit—however lackadaisical—that eases discomfort and inflates the ego. The chase's object is secondary and relatively unimportant. When he first approaches women, Ed is indiscriminate: he will talk to any female who interests him in the slightest. It's only later that his elaborate restrictive criteria crash down and he begins to notice his partners' imperfections. Like hitters, drifters relate to women as to a vast, collective resource whose members are as faceless and interchangeable as ingots of bullion. At the onset all women are equally suited to meet their needs for sex, companionship and ego gratification. It's no coincidence that Ed refers to one of his conquests as a "total package."

SEXUAL OBJECTS, SOCIAL ASSETS

Despite our expectations of Casanovas, drifters do not view women primarily as sexual objects or treat them as such. Obviously, sexual gratification is important to them and they expect their partners to provide it. Yet Ed has often dated women whom he found to be indifferent lovers. Nor, interestingly, do these men display the sexual neediness that characterizes other Casanovas. Ed is happy to make love with a woman once in the course of a three-day weekend; he and his date will spend the rest of the time dining out, going to movies or watching television. "I like sex—don't get me wrong," he says. "But it's probably only number three on my list of priorities. In my spare time I want to shop or play tennis or whatever, and if a woman's not willing to do these things with me, no amount of sex is going to make up for it."

But if drifters don't view women as sexual objects, they definitely want them to be social assets: women are there to make them look good. The word "presentable" keeps popping up in their descriptions of what they search for in the opposite sex. Ed likes his women "to blend in well with my crowd, to be lively and intelligent and keyed in to my life-style. That's what my friends expect me to have, and that's the kind of woman I look for." When drifters drop their partners, it's often because they perceive them as social liabilities.

This curious snobbery suggests that drifters relate to women as narcissistic objects, reflections of their own idealized self-images. Having defined himself as a fun-loving man-about-town, Ed demands that his partners complement that persona. He needs women who can be paraded forth at parties, who will laugh obligingly at his jokes and excite the approval and veiled envy of his friends—women who will "go with" his tailored self-image as a white shirt and red tie go with a blue suit. The unfortunates who fail to measure up go back on the shelf.

Women rarely fare well in their relationships with drifters. While seldom cruel or actively malicious, these men seem incapable of treating women as separate beings possessed of feelings and desires. Instead they view their partners with a bland disregard, the fond indifference one might bestow on a borrowed car or lawn mower. They are often cavalier about birth control, assuming that the women they sleep with will protect themselves and not really caring if they don't.

Drifters can be charming, animated and even courtly, the kind of men who open doors and light their dates' cigarettes. Like Ed, they often spend a great deal of money taking women out. But, characteristically, they may be so busy checking coats and scanning wine lists that they can't see or listen to the women they entertain so generously. Ed recently broke up with a woman who accused him of ignoring her: "We were out on a date and I took my eyes off her while we were talking and she got mad at me. She said: 'We never really talk when we're together. We have trouble communicating.'" Underlying the drifter's courtesy and charm is a fundamental insensitivity, an inability to perceive women as anything more than bit players in the drama of his own life.

WITHOUT PASSION OR RAGE

This is a far cry from the ecstatic turbulence and heightened focus we associate with erotic love. Few drifters feel a need to spend much time alone with their partners unless they are actually having sex. They are rarely jealous or possessive. "Any woman who's got anything on the ball is going to have other guys interested in her," Ed says. "I begin to wonder about her if she's available every time I call." Occasionally drifters are involved in monogamous relationships, though rarely by choice. "I've dated one woman at a time, but it was just because the pickings were slim," Ed admits. "I was getting enough sex, but the routine got boring. Routine is the enemy of romance. You see two or three women and you've got more variety: it's as simple as that." For these men, infidelity is a nonissue, because they have never promised fidelity or asked for it. No woman ever seems worth the effort.

If drifters' relationships lack romantic passion, they are also devoid of anger. Men like Ed seem immune to extremes of feeling, and indeed seem to avoid them. Like hitters, they are loath to "make scenes," and will quickly flee any relationship that threatens to become confrontational. Ed has never fought with any of the women he dated. Even when breaking up, he veers away from conflict. "I usually just stop calling," he says. "Most women get the message. I make myself impossible to get hold of. I don't like to get nasty or leave them feeling bad. I don't like to make enemies." Drifters make their exits on tiptoe.

Yet this stealth suggests an undercurrent of rage. As we have seen in our discussion of devouring, severing relations in such fashion, without warning or farewell, is a way of annihilating the partner left behind, of punishing her for failing to meet the tyrannical demands of the ego. The drifter's relationships decay from mild interest to anger at his lover's inadequacies, and finally to a defensive boredom. He often forgets his women as soon as he stops seeing them, as though even their memory has become distasteful. Having ingested his partners, he now transforms them into waste, which is promptly flushed into the sewers of the unconscious.

The process has severe consequences. After the drifter has banished his partner from his life and psyche, his anger often turns inward; he falls into the cottony paralysis of depression. Indeed, I sometimes had the impression that beneath their self-confidence and apparent indifference to loss, drifters are perpetually depressed. Their charm lacks warmth or spontaneity, and their self-confidence, on closer inspection, seems forced. And the energy with which these men pursue women provides only a brief reprieve from a fundamental listlessness: when they are without women for any length of time, men like Ed stay home, stare dully at the television screen and eat and drink more than is good for them. For drifters, women are only distractions, incapable of truly arousing them or of engaging their hearts and spirits. Even as they lie beside their lovers, they remain solitary and detached. Having smothered anger and denied grief, they have also deprived themselves of anything remotely resembling passion. Unable to mourn what they lose, they cannot enjoy what they have.

On some level Ed seems to recognize this. The pleasures of bachelorhood are wearing thin. He gets dissatisfied more quickly, not only with his partners' shortcomings but with his own dissatisfaction as well: "They say that if you haven't loved, you haven't lived. I'm thirty-six, and there are times I think I've never lived at all."

CHAPTER SIX

---◆◆---

Romantics

THE EXAMPLE OF ARNIE BECKER

As played by Corbin Bernsen, Arnie Becker of "L.A. Law" is a divided man. Half-WASP, half-Jewish, he has the tanned, sun-blond and slightly debauched good looks of an aging surfer and the haimish, fidgety manner of a nice boy who's eager to please and impress. In conference with his divorce clients, most of whom seem to be female, he combines compassion and rapacity. When these women list their husbands' sins, Arnie nods like a sympathetic confessor. When they cry, his eyes moisten. Yet he never loses sight of his main purpose, which is to take the bastards on the other side for everything they have. Becker's predatory streak sometimes appears to grow out of a sense of chivalry: he feels so sorry for his clients that he has to avenge them. He can turn even a no-fault divorce into a bloodbath. No sooner has a woman told him that she wants to go easy on her husband than Becker, his features crimped in reluctance and gentlemanly distaste, slides her the photographic evidence of the man's adultery.

The genius of the Arnie Becker character is that he is guilty of every infraction for which he crucifies his clients' spouses. His courtroom savagery is penance for his own sexual caddishness, the schizoid zeal of a backsliding convert. In a law firm that seethes with erotic tension, Becker is the womanizer par excellence, naturally, even uncontrollably, seductive. His husky voice is always pitched in a romantic invitation. His eyes plead. His great success as a divorce lawyer stems from his ability to give every conference the conspiratorial heat of an assignation. His great charm is that he rarely seems calculated. When he falls into bed with yet another woman, it's because he just can't help himself.

Part of this, of course, is Becker's shtick. He knows how to play his vulnerability for maximum effect. Underneath, though, is a shrewd, self-congratulatory sense of what a woman will fall for and a lawyer's delight in intrigue. At a party with a superbly coiffed consort, he sidles over to another woman and whispers into her ear: "I'll see you as soon as I dump her." Then he glides serenely, guiltlessly back, drops his date off at home and an hour later is undressing the second girl in her apartment. Both women seem fully aware that Arnie is playing games with them. But because he has made them partners in his duplicity, they have no qualms about being two-timed: chances are he will dump the other girl, too. With some women—the younger, flightier ones—Arnie is an unashamed rake. His manipulations are harmless precisely because they are so expected, like a magician's sleight of hand. Arnie's women mind his trickery no more than people watching the Amazing Kreskin mind having handkerchiefs plucked from their ears.

But beneath the trickery lies a second layer of vulnerability, one that's genuine and unfeigned. All too often, Arnie Becker falls in love. Usually it's with a client, a thirtyish or fortyish woman who seems to have been especially ill-treated by her husband. What impels him into these affairs seems to be his gallantry, a protective urge run amok. But the flip side of his desire to protect is an ache to be protected. It's no coincidence that the women he falls for are older than the ones he fools around with. They hold out the promise, not just of passion, but of nurturance. The irony is that Becker's love affairs so often end up badly, with hurt feelings on both sides. Sometimes, these bruised madonnas scare him away with the yawning depth of their needs: this divorce lawyer seems never to have learned that the newly divorced are as desperate as the newly orphaned. And sometimes, Becker himself is a victim, as in the two-part episode in which he was made a sexual slave by a devotee of bondage and discipline. The saving grace of this man is that the seducer in him shares space with a schlemiel.

Telling insight into movie and television characters is sometimes provided by the actors who play them. A recent article on Corbin Bernsen characterizes him as "a shy phallocrat, a sophisticated naif. He will describe himself, solemnly, as a one-woman man, then extol the joys of bachelorhood, and then ache for a soul-mate." After telling the reporter that he longs for true love and prefers mastur-bation to one-night stands, Bernsen goes on to complain, "Can you believe this perverse timing? I finally get into this sort of privileged position and here's AIDS! Sometimes I think it's some perverse joke on me....At least I got to know ten or fifteen years of the good life."

ALAN: "LOVE IS AN ARENA OF ACHIEVEMENT"

Lacking the cynicism of hitters or the fatal diffidence of drifters, romantics are, at first glance, the most appealing of Casanovas, the ones who most resemble the dramatic and tormented dream figures of the Gothic novel. Although they are passionate lovers, they are not in this game for sex alone. For these men sex is a pathway to the heart, a key to intimacies greater than those of the bedroom. What they seek—and offer to their partners—is nothing less than total emotional involvement, ecstatic, frictionless and, in its exclusion of the outside world, almost trancelike. Romantics envision a love without quarrels or tedium, a love in which man and women are perpetually aroused and never scold each other for leaving the toi-let seat up or burning the toast. When, usually within two weeks to six months, that vision collapses—when erections don't always last all night and not every orgasm shakes the earth, when the toast *is* burnt, the toilet seat left up and both partners plenty irritated about it—they leave, heartbroken and embittered, as though they themselves had been seduced and abandoned.

The first thing that Alan (he has anglicized it from Alain) tells you about himself is that he is rich, with a high-level position in a Boston bank and a prodigious trust fund. Actually, the word he uses is "viable," a term that connotes not just wealth but success, refinement, good looks and erotic savoir faire. Viability is a trait he seeks in women, too. "The women I let into my life are always viable— that is to say, they're articulate, they're well-dressed, they're classy. They know how to handle wealth. They know how to move in wealthy circles. I could—and have—fucked women who weren't viable," he admits. "But I could never fall in love with one who wasn't."

To Alan love is supremely important. "Love is an arena of achievement, like your career or your finances or your home. It's a place where you prove your quality. I'm twenty-eight years old and I hold a position of authority that most men don't even aspire to until they're in their mid-thirties. I have as much money as I could possibly want. I have a house on Beacon Hill that I'm proud of. It's only in the arena of love that I feel there's still something substantial yet to achieve. I devote the kind of effort to it that other men devote to their careers. And, frankly, I think I'm good at it."

Although he first had sex while still in high school, Alan didn't fall in love until he had graduated from college. "By then I found that casual sex was already played out for me. I knew I could do sex. I'm orally inclined, and I can give a woman many, many powerful orgasms—quality orgasms—before I even enter her. And I can prolong my own performance by doing multiplication tables inside my head or staring at the clock. But I wanted something more. I wanted a chance to reveal myself, and you can't really reveal yourself to someone who's just a piece of ass. She isn't going to understand you, if you're at all sensitive or complex, which is what I was and still am."

When he went to France to work in a bank belonging to his French mother's family, Alan was already in a state of love-readiness, filled with a nebulous desire that as yet had no object. He found her shortly. Catherine was the daughter of some family friends. She was beautiful, wealthy and French, the distillation of a thousand romantic fantasies. Alan was aroused by her immediately but beset by a worry and indecision that were new to him. In the past he had taken his sex appeal for granted, had expected women to fall into his hands like ripe fruit. Catherine, though, seemed remote and inaccessibly lovely. He was surprised when she agreed to see him at all and astonished when their first encounter took them into the bedroom. Their lovemaking was extraordinarily satisfying.

By the next morning, he knew he was in love with her. "I didn't want to leave her, couldn't stand the thought of being separated from her. In college I'd always been amused by guys who let their romantic involvements shoot their grades to hell. I'd never had any trouble detaching from whomever I'd spent the night with and making my classes the next day. But if Catherine hadn't had to go to work, I wouldn't have been able to tear myself out of her bed. I'd known her for all of twenty-four hours, and already I was sending out bilingual wedding announcements. I remember that when I finally got up the nerve to call her, I was fibrillating. I was so frightened that she wouldn't find me as viable as I found her."

But she did. Their love affair had the silvery glamour of a 1930s musical: hours of exquisite lovemaking, perfect dinners in out-of-the-way restaurants, carriage rides in the Bois de Boulogne, and long bedroom conversations in which Alan, aided by cognac and champagne, unveiled himself to another human being for the first time in his life: "I'd always felt fairly lonely, partly because I came from a cold and uncommunicative family and partly because I knew I was different from other people. Suddenly I didn't feel lonely anymore. My God, here at last was this woman who understood me and appreciated me!"

But after two months Alan fell from his state of grace. Although he spoke French and Catherine, English, he was suddenly aware of the language barrier between them; it kept her from laughing at his jokes and turned the most casual conversation into a rarefied *discours*. Catherine struck him as too serious, and he got bored with being serious all the time. He found himself becoming uncommunicative and impatient with her. It was he who had first brought up the possibility of marriage, but he now cringed whenever she mentioned it. One night he broke a date with her to go drinking by himself, picked up a girl in a rough district and took her home with him. "The sex was strictly ordinary. For Christ's sake, the girl was a piece of meat to me! But the next night making love with Catherine was just as ordinary. Worse than ordinary, because it had been fantastic once. I knew I had made a terrible mistake, and I told her. It was the only decent thing to do."

If I've recounted Alan's abortive affair in such detail, it's because he has repeated it, with minor variations, dozens of times since then. Following a binge of embittered promiscuity, he found another girl who, like Catherine, seemed eminently viable at first but finally disappointed him as cruelly as her predecessor. Back in the States, he romanced graduate students, professionals and the daughters and sisters of friends and colleagues. All were attractive and educated. And all of them at first seemed hard to get. Each liaison began at a peak of excitement and apparent intimacy only to end abruptly in disillusionment. At first, Alan felt that these exalted creatures suddenly had intolerable blemishes. Lately, though, he has come to feel that he is the source of his own disillusionment: "I can't kid myself anymore that all these girls had some horrible defect that they hid from me. Over and over, I just lost interest. And suddenly I knew that it wasn't Catherine or Helen or any of the rest of them. It was me."

THE DRAMATIZED SELF

What are the origins of this idyllic—and utterly impracticable—kind of love? Among romantics it seems to stem from a highly dramatized vision of the self. Like Alan, they see themselves as special, set apart from other men by their passion, intelligence and emotional depth. The romantic sense of self has its literary antecedents in the poetry of Byron and Shelley and its cultural roots in the rise of bourgeois individualism, which dislocated men and women from the familiar matrixes of class, country and religion. Romantics, its modern inheritors, are solitaries, acutely self-conscious and painfully attuned to the differences between themselves and those around them.

This vision of the self represents narcissism at its most isolating. It permits Alan to imagine himself as a Byronic hero, but it also condemns him to solitude, to a sense of being always unappreciated and misunderstood. "I was a lonely child," he recalls, and many romantics have similar memories. The question is whether they were lonely because they were special or whether the feeling of specialness arose as a comforting explanation for their loneliness, a private myth that warmed them against the chill of their early environment. But even more so than other Casanovas, romantics tend to be loners, without close friends of either sex or a deep connection to their families. For them the true love object is the self, which commands so much attention and solicitude that all other relationships are eclipsed.

It's natural for these lonely men to seek companionship. But more than companionship, they seek validation of their uniqueness. Above all, they want to be understood, *appreciated*. Other men, after all, are attractive and successful, but only Alan is Alan. He craves recognition of that solitary, deeply buried gem of self, the cluster of traits and perceptions that is the source of his uniqueness. Where hitters look for nothing more than a quick sexual fix and drifters search for complaisant social ornaments, romantics desire women who will bear witness to their individuality while assuaging its accompanying loneliness. Like the French essayist Michel Leiris, the romantic longs for a lover "tender as a mistress, sweet as a mother, who would share my pains and my joys, driving away the harsh suffering that gnaws at my heart, warding off the melancholy boredom of my mind with one glance of her clear eyes, or with a single long kiss from her cool mouth. Yes, I would be understood at last."

JUDITH: THE LOVER AS ANIMAL

Only special women can truly understand these special men, and romantics are thus necessarily more selective lovers than hitters or drifters. This is not to say that they bide their time chastely until the right woman comes along: not for them the amorous codes of the medieval troubadors. Before he met Catherine, Alan was sexually promiscuous. And until recently, when the specter of AIDS made him more cautious, he mourned each blighted love affair with a flurry of casual sex, sleeping with up to ten different women in a month. Lord Byron, the archetypal romantic, similarly divided women into idealized virgins and anonymous "animals." While they wait anxiously for love to find them, romantics, like other Casanovas, make do with lust.

As the term "animals" suggests, romantics view their casual partners with contempt. To Alan a pickup from Revere, a blue-collar suburb of Boston, can never be viable. An encounter with one of these coarse, disposable creatures requires a separate terminology: "There's a difference between fucking and making love. I've probably fucked a hundred women; I've made love to no more than a dozen." The scorn that romantics feel for these women is often touched with racism or class prejudice, as though only women from a "lower" ethnic or economic stratum were fair game for a one-night stand.

The sexual animal represents one pole of the romantic's split view of femininity—his unconscious sense of women as embodiments of primitive appetite. Not surprisingly, his contempt for his casual partners is tinged with dread. Alan now avoids one-night stands for fear of sexually transmitted disease. He seems oblivious to the notion that he could just as easily be infected by a woman from a "good" family or a lofty profession, as though these attributes provided a shield against spirochetes or the AIDS virus. If the romantic sees his anonymous conquests as animals, we must always remember that some animals are dangerous. Michel Leiris associates such women with the biblical archetype of Judith, the warrior-prostitute who seduced the Assyrian general Holofernes in order to lop off his head—"Judith, placid and already seeming to ignore the bearded ball she holds like a phallic glans she could have sundered merely by pressing her legs together when Holofernes' floodgates opened; or which, an ogress at the height of her madness, she might have cut from the powerful member...with a sudden snap of her teeth."

Sex with a Judith is rarely satisfying to romantics. At best they feel that they are wasting themselves in impersonal rutting—in Alan's terminology, in "fucking" as opposed to "lovemaking." At worst they feel constantly threatened by sickness and exploitation —even by symbolic murder or castration. During the drought between love affairs, they are sad and anxious. "I've always had trouble sleeping—actually sleeping—with women I don't care for," Alan says. "I toss and turn. When they touch me, I recoil as though I'd been assaulted. There've been so many nights when I'd look down at whoever was lying next to me and think how terribly, terribly sad it was. I'd think, here's this woman hugging me as though there were something real between us, and the fact is we hardly know each other's names. I'd look at her, and all I could think of was when, oh when, was I going to find someone I could love?"

"I NEVER COULD LOVE BUT THAT WHICH LOVES"

Gnawed by loneliness and sexual disgust, Alan can't go long without a passionate involvement with a worthy partner. But what must a woman possess for a man like Alan to find her worthy? Beauty, though a prerequisite, is not enough for romantics. The women they love must be available and sexually exciting, but they are suspicious of those who seem *too* free: "There's something wrong with a woman who just wants to get laid for the sake of getting laid," Alan says. "There has to be some sort of magic involved, some sense of wonder." Wealth, breeding, intelligence and sensitivity are all desirable traits, but no one quality is sufficient. Ultimately, romantics view love as a mystical process, one that centers around that elusive ingredient—"viability," or, sometimes, "magic" or "glow."

Love usually depends on a chemistry that is not wholly quantifiable. We fall in love for reasons we can never quite explain. Romantics would seem to be no exception to the love-blind general populace. Yet their love affairs have certain recurring characteristics that distinguish them from those of other men. They fall in love hastily. There is none of the slow growing-together that characterizes companionate love, no hesitation or indecision, no weighing of the partner's qualities or tortuous sifting of their own motives. Love falls on these men like a safe dropped from a tenth-floor window.

It is not, however, love at first sight. For the romantic, love doesn't begin with a glance across a crowded room: it begins in bed. He needs to know his partner sexually before he loves her, in keeping with the old formula: among men, sex sometimes leads to intimacy; among women, intimacy sometimes leads to sex. Needless to say, the first night of lovemaking must be successful. An episode of impotence or premature ejaculation is guaranteed to nip a romantic's passion in the bud, for how can he fall in love with someone who has witnessed his humiliation? The beloved should be avid but not voracious, which might make him feel too threatened. She should, in Alan's words, "lose herself" in his embrace. Almost as a rule, the romantic falls in love with women who are less experienced than he is. In this preference, he echoes Casanova himself, who proclaimed that "the union of beauty, intelligence and innocence has always swayed me." Little wonder that this man, so erotically jaded and uptight, is drawn to his opposite, to a virgin whom he can initiate into the art of love and whose spontaneity will make up for his own rigidity.

By the same token, romantics are rarely the first to fall in love. They only pursue women whom they sense are willing to be pursued. "I don't think I've ever told a girl I loved her unless I was sure she wasn't going to tell me to get lost," Alan says. "On some level, I've got to know that she wants me as much as I want her." Romantics thrive on challenge, taking special pleasure, for instance, in seeing women whom they suspect have other boyfriends, but they shy away from hopeless competition. "I know that down the road I'll convince her that I'm the only one for her," Alan continues, "and if I can't, I'll just say screw it, and shut myself off. I could never put up with being someone's piece on the side." In love as in sex, these men demand reciprocity, an equity of feeling, an equilibrium of risk. "I never could love but that which loves," wrote Lord Byron. "My attachment always increases in due proportion to the return it meets with."

Although he is always ready for love and longs constantly for sharing and understanding, the romantic is fundamentally cautious, unwilling to take the risk of loving someone who might not love him just as much. He can fall in love only with a woman whose innocence distinguishes her from the hardened, predatory figure of Judith, with one whose vulnerability encourages him to give up some of his stultifying self-control and experience something like passion. Only when a woman seems willing to appreciate his hidden self can he let that self emerge. The intensity of his feelings has much to do with the degree to which they have been bottled up: the ecstasy he feels in the arms of a new lover is the ecstasy of relief. For a few hours, weeks or months, this self-conscious seducer forgets himself. In mid-seduction he allows himself to be seduced, like some overly polished actor who disappears in his role only when he sees that his audience is moved to tears.

LUCRETIA: THE LOVER AS ANGEL

Apart from weeping, the audience need do nothing. For all the requirements he places on his lovers, Alan seems oddly indifferent to their personalities. From his accounts of his affairs, one never learns much about his partners' individual characteristics, the little things that made them unique and lovable. All the emphasis is on *his* actions, feelings and performance: the ways he made them come, the places he took them, the gifts he bought for them. The women themselves are gradually effaced from these narratives, transformed into luminous screens of desire onto which the romantic projects his own frustrated yearnings for intimacy, his obsession with perfection and his fantasies of effortless union.

All of us tend to endow the people we love with the traits we find desirable. Romantics carry this tendency to an extreme, transforming real women into imaginary—almost hallucinatory—constructs of desire. The words they use to describe their lovers suggest a feminine paradigm: "sweetness," "patience," "faithfulness," "sensitivity." They might be talking about saints or Breck girls; they might be talking about their mothers. They rarely describe their partners as temperamental, cunning or seductive—those, after all, are Judith's traits. These angelic creatures may be rare in real life—one suspects that they're too good to be true—but romantics have the power and the overwhelming inclination to invent them, if not from clay, then from real women and the projected fragments of their own unconscious.

Why is it necessary for these men to idealize their love objects instead of taking them as they are? Casanova believed that it was "the delicacy and power of idealization which alone justifies the excesses of passion." And in one of his letters, Byron noted that "a true voluptuary will never abandon his mind to the grossness of reality. It is by exalting the earthly, the material, the *physique* of our pleasures, by veiling these ideas, by forgetting them altogether, or, at least, never naming them hardly to one's self, that we alone can prevent them from disgusting." In this context we might recall Alan's distinction between fucking and making love and his distress when he found the boundary between them suddenly blurring: "It had been fantastic once and now it was just stick-it-in-and-pull-it-out." Among romantics it would seem that the fascination with sex disguises a puritanical horror that can only be fended off through euphemism and projection: "fucking" must be called "lovemaking"; the woman one fucks must be turned into the angelic creature one makes love to.

If romantics only fuck bestial whores or Judiths, the women they make love to are virgins. It might be better still to describe them, as Michel Leiris does, as "Lucretias," after the Roman matron whose chastity led to her rape and self-martyrdom. "The image of Lucrèce in tears after being raped by her brother-in-law, the soldier Sextus Tarquin, is...ideally suited to affect me," Leiris writes. "I cannot conceive of love save in torment and tears; nothing moves or attracts me so much as a woman weeping." The archetype is particularly useful, evoking as it does chastity and martyrdom, two ideas that figure prominently in romantics' relations with the opposite sex. Chastity represents the exalted, rarefied sexuality that they seek in their partners, sex as an otherworldly initiation rather than a transaction between equals. And martyrdom is all too often an apt description of the penalties that romantics exact from the women who love them.

LUCRETIA: THE LOVER AS MARTYR

This is not to say that romantics are sadists, though there *is* a strong element of vengeful hostility in their relations with women. It's rather that the role of Lucretia is so demanding that few women can fill it. She must be chaste yet passionate, attractive to other men yet faithful to her lover, vulnerable yet strong, nurturing yet not so motherly that she makes her partner seem childish by comparison. Above all, she must love—or at least appear to love—unconditionally, which to romantics means not only understanding them, but admiring them as well. To attempt such a tortuous juggling of opposites is in itself an act of martyrdom. It's all the more difficult because Lucretia is an unconscious image in the romantic's psychic gallery. How can any woman become what her partner wants when he is not even aware that he wants it?

Romantics are constantly testing their women to see how well they correspond to this ideal. Testing is not unusual in love relationships. Most men and women have an underlying vision of an ideal partner, one that is largely unconscious but that nonetheless helps determine their choice of love object. Before we fall in love we test and evaluate, measuring a real person against the ideal: courtship is not only the act of making ourselves beloved, it is the act of determining whether the other is worth loving. But romantics, as we have seen, fall in love quickly, with any woman who loosely approximates the Lucretia archetype. They do their testing after the fact, in a form so veiled that they are scarcely conscious of it.

Part of that testing takes place in bed. Lucretia should be both chaste and sexually submissive, and these men often subject their lovers to a series of erotic variations, from "straight" intercourse, say, to fellatio, anal sex and light bondage and discipline. "If a woman really loves you," one romantic told me, "she'll go anywhere you want to take her sexually—*anywhere*." A true Lucretia can never be the initiator of such routines. Her job is to *follow* her partner's lead, to surrender meekly to his sexual whims.

Romantics are also emotional taskmasters who plumb the limits of their lovers' patience and devotion. Alan has left women because they failed to appreciate his sense of humor, because they disagreed with him "too aggressively" over a book or film, because they asked for too much of his time, because they overlooked things he had done for them and because they were not available whenever he wanted them. This passionate lover has a hidden list of expectations: to sustain his love, his women must flatter him, share his opinions, accept his absence or inattention, yet be ceaselessly there for him. His apparent generosity of feeling disguises an intensely judgmental streak that demands nothing less than perfection and cannot tolerate or forgive any lapse from it.

What is most insidious about this testing is that it goes on in secret, in the clicking machinery of the romantic's unconscious. His conscious definition of love brooks no reservations or second thoughts. "When I fall in love, I give myself totally to a woman. There's no holding back," Alan says. He can't recall ever having criticized one of his lovers until he was actually breaking up with her. To hold back in any way, to take the slightest notice of a partner's shortcomings constitutes nothing less than a betrayal of love itself. Thus, all judgment of the beloved must be repressed, confined to a gulag of the psyche. On the surface, the romantic courts at a constant fever pitch in which, as Alan says, "No moment is ever wasted and every encounter is pure magic." Indeed, his love affairs may owe much of their urgency to his fierce repression of his doubts about the women he loves. For this man, doubt is so charged with anxiety that its faintest stirring prompts a frenzy of compensatory activity whose purpose is not only to reassure the beloved but to lull the self, the original and primary object of seduction. In love with love itself, he cannot tolerate any diminution of his feelings: he must be rapturously in love twenty-four hours a day.

To judge the lover, to doubt her in any way, is terrifying to him because it awakens severe doubts about himself. When speaking with Alan, I often had the impression that beneath his operatic passions lay an emotional deadness. Or perhaps it would be better to say that I sensed in him a *fear* of being emotionally dead. Like so many other romantics—like myself—he recalls feeling unloved as a child. And although the man now tells himself that he was simply misunderstood by his insensitive parents, the child must have believed that he was unloved because he was unlovable. In the confusion of those years, he may also have feared that *he* did not, could not, love. This was the great dread of my own childhood; I remember the pangs I felt whenever my mother told me that I was too selfish to love, and the terrible need I felt to prove that yes, I could, in the hope that she would then love me back.

The fears of childhood persist in the adult. The romantic is a man who keeps pinching himself to prove that he is not dead, who bombards himself with sensation to show that he can feel and to assure himself that the other will feel for him. The problem is that his regime of emotional excess makes littler, gentler feelings inadequate. The quiet moments after lovemaking, the brief, affectionate glance over the pages of the Sunday paper, are so anticlimactic that he cannot recognize them as varieties of love. Certainly, he cannot permit himself those moments of honest doubt that exist in most healthy relationships. To love less than blindly is, for the romantic, not to love at all. Worse still, it means that his lover might harbor similar doubts and withdraw her love from him at any moment. He can only trust his feelings—and hers—as long as they are in overdrive.

The romantic defines love in absolute terms because any lesser and more realistic definition forces him—as it forces all of us—to confront the possibility that love may not last forever. When most of us love, it's with the implicit recognition that our feelings occasionally waver. We come home some days and our hearts fail to leap in the presence of our beloved: we go on loving. We fight, and we go on. We hurt each other's feelings more times than we can count, and we go on. In the midst of disappointment and self-doubt, we go on, in the fragile assumption that those we love will keep on loving us until further notice, and because this is still the best thing we know. For all their apparent self-assurance, men like Alan know no such certainty. Any doubt about the lover, any interruption of desire sounds for them with the leaden finality of a death knell. If this Lucretia is less than perfect, she cannot be Lucretia. If they love less than unconditionally, they cannot love at all.

Such fears are too unnerving to be acknowledged consciously. But sooner or later romantics realize that their partners are not perfect Lucretias. After weeks or months of denial, the testing, judging unconscious delivers its verdict. Typically the realization descends on them suddenly and with shattering impact: Alan was fatally disillusioned with Catherine in the act of making love to her. And, because they have previously ignored their partners' defects, they often feel that they have been deceived by them, so that disillusionment is compounded by a sense of betrayal. These men do not fall out of love so much as they are thrust from it, into a harshly lit room in which the lover's slightest defect becomes a deformity.

Romantics begin their affairs by endowing women with all the virtues of an immaculate femininity. When the romance ends, they quickly divest their lovers of the qualities they once valued in them. In his disillusionment, Alan saw Catherine as boring, sheltered and selfish—"an emotional parasite." Her foreignness, which had once been so attractive to him, now struck him as affected. Today, years after the breakup with his first love, he still finds it hard to say anything charitable about her. When speaking of subsequent girlfriends and fiancées—for he has been engaged three times—the most he can manage is remorse: "They were nice, naive women who were desperate to find a mate before their biological clocks ran down. And what they got was me." Lucretia, the serene and unconditionally loving paragon, has given way to Lucretia the victim, a denuded husk who inspires nothing but pity.

HEARTBREAKERS WITH BROKEN HEARTS

The unconscious projection with which the love affair began now continues in a different form. Romantics, as we have seen, are enormously dependent men, who expect their partners to love them worshipfully and unconditionally and their relationships to deliver them from pain. When they fall out of love, they are all too likely to project those thwarted needs onto those they leave. Alan begins his relationships wanting to spend every available moment with his lovers and resenting even the intrusion of work; he ends them fleeing from demands—both real and imaginary—on his time and affection. "Even the ones who seem independent are incredibly needy," he complains. "No matter what kind of commitment you make, they always want more, and eventually you end up feeling strangled." For these men, falling out of love is not a simple negation of the other, but an orgy of anger, guilt and fear. Where hitters avoid even the pretense of commitment and drifters never truly engage with the women they sleep with, romantics invest a great deal of energy in their relationships and endow them with great drama. For Alan the breakup can be just as charged as the first kiss. Often, it includes a tearful confrontation, in which he accuses his partner of being too demanding while scourging himself for being too neurotic to sustain the relationship any longer. For weeks afterward, he is consumed by remorse and fantasies of punishment from the woman he has left.

Guilt is an integral part of the romantic's scenario of love. The guilt of separation induces in him a rapture fully as intense as the rapture of infatuation. The romantic, after all, is addicted to feeling, and the value that women hold for him lies in their power to evoke extremes of emotion that are otherwise beyond him. He sees them not as individual human beings, but as archetypal embodiments of desire, bliss, pity and dread. He defines his relationships with them as so many heightened emotional states. Every affair carries for him both the promise of unconditional acceptance and the threat of exposure and rejection. The fact that to realize the promise he must incur the risk makes true union impossible for him, but creates a delicious suspense: will this woman accept him as he is? Will he finally be able to bare his soul to her? And if he does, will he be able to keep on loving her or will he lose interest as he so often has before?

These questions are not the stuff of true drama, but of melodrama, of "Dynasty" and "Days of Our Lives." The theater of a real relationship, with its finely nuanced characters and its endlessly complex unfolding and intertwining of separate lives, is beyond him. He is comfortable only with the rush of sudden infatuation, the ecstasy of the bedroom and the heartache of the big breakup. He recognizes women only in the simplified roles of Judith and Lucretia, the slut and the saint, and can only imagine himself as a doomed Byronic hero, a heartbreaker with a broken heart. "I have a horror of becoming a cliché," Alan says, "and I can see myself turning into one if I go on like this. My friends already joke about me. One month I'm with this girl, the next month I'm alone, and the month after that I'm involved with someone else. Each time I tell myself: this one is the real thing. But I'm beginning to wonder whether I'll ever find her. Or whether maybe it's me who's not real."

CHAPTER SEVEN

———◄•►———

Nesters

THE EXAMPLE OF ERNEST HEMINGWAY

Ernest Hemingway met Hadley Richardson when he was twenty-one. She was a big, sporty girl eight years his senior, with a lively sense of humor and a man's capacity for liquor. The moment he saw her, he later told his brother, "I knew she was the girl I was going to marry." The premonition filled him with happiness and dread. While he courted Hadley, he also pursued other women, dutifully informing her of each flirtation. Some part of him equated marriage with death, and in the aftermath of a visit with his fiancée he wrote a bleak poem that included the lines: "Love curdles in the city. Love sours in the hot whispering from the pavements. Love grows old." Sensing his misgivings, Hadley asked him if he wanted to break the engagement. Hemingway said nothing. They married in August of 1921 and shortly afterward set off for Paris. "The world's a jail," Hadley told him, "and we're going to break it together."

For a time they were happy. They lived like affluent gypsies, Hadley running the household while her husband wrote and traveled through Europe on assignment as a wire-service reporter. She joined in his enthusiasms for skiing, fishing and, later, bullfighting. But Hadley committed some unpardonable sins. First, she lost Hemingway's manuscripts, a catastrophic blow that sent him into a drunken and blackhearted depression. Then she had a baby. Although Hemingway was a proud father, he resented his son's claim on his time and attention, the limitations on his wife's mobility. He was, he complained, too young to be a father. As the years passed and his reputation grew, he spent more and more time away from her. He carried on a blatant flirtation with Duff Twysden, who inspired his portrait of Lady Brett Ashley, and then had an affair with a wealthy American named Pauline Pfeiffer. In 1926, he separated from Hadley, saluting her as "the best and truest and loveliest person I have ever known." A few months later he married Pauline.

Supported by Hemingway's increased book sales and by contributions from his new bride's uncle, the couple lived in Europe, Key West and Cuba. Pauline gave him two more sons and, like Hadley before her, did everything she could to be a perfect companion to him, traveling with him on hunting and fishing trips while fobbing off the children on her sister. Yet this marriage, too, gradually deteriorated. After the birth of Gregory, his third son, Hemingway had a brief liaison with a disturbed young woman named Jane Mason, which ended with her attempted suicide. Pauline tried desperately to win her husband back, but even after his affair with Jane ended, he continued to drift away from her. Still, he would not leave Pauline until he had found her successor, the journalist Martha Gellhorn.

This third marriage and the one that followed it, to Mary Welsh, were scarred from the first by conflict. Hemingway was abusive to both women and flirted openly with others. He seemed determined to turn both Martha and Mary into female versions of himself, yet was furious with their successes. He did not like women competing with him. Visiting Martha in Europe in 1944, he calmly preempted her press credentials so he could cover the Allied invasion of Nor-

mandy in her stead. During his last marriage, he was more his wife's patient than her husband, ravaged as he was by the physical and emotional consequences of alcoholism. When he left Mary in 1961, it was not for another woman. On July 2, he took a shotgun from the storeroom of their house in Ketchum, Idaho, and blew off his head. His last words to her, the night before, had been "Good night, my kitten."

In those final years, Hemingway seemed increasingly aware of his role in his marital breakups. The bitch women of The Sun Also Rises *and "The Short Happy Life of Francis Macomber" give way to a succession of warped, lonely men who crave affection yet are incapable of giving it in return. In one of his later stories, "The Strange Country," a newly married writer engages in a bitter soliloquy while driving with his worshipful young bride up the spine of Florida: "You really can start it all over now. You really can. Please don't be silly, another part of him said. You really can, he said to himself. You can be just as good a guy as she thinks you are and as you are at this moment. There is such a thing as starting it all over and you've been given a chance to and you can do it and you will do it.* Will you make all the promises again?"

DEREK: "IT WITHERS ON THE VINE"

To speak with some Casanovas—with hitters or romantics, for example—is to know immediately and unequivocally that you are in the presence of a pathology. There is no other way to describe their driven appetites or paranoid vision of the opposite sex. The men I call nesters are different. They seem to seek deep and lasting unions, with women whom they not only love but like and respect. Their relationships often last for some time and extend to arenas beyond the bedroom. They want companionship as well as romance and sexual excitement from real women and not from idealized saints or degraded sluts. Serious, often shy, yet quick to respond to any woman who interests them, nesters begin their affairs on a note of high promise: often they are the ones who make the first appeal for commitment. Yet once they have married or set up housekeeping with their partners, they gradually withdraw from them, becoming increasingly taciturn, hostile and remote. Such relationships end either in the woman's total alienation or with the man's announcement that the affair is over. Nesters may leave suddenly, walking out one evening for a pack of cigarettes and never coming back. But just as often their departures are anticlimactic, like the death of a loved one after a long illness.

Derek, forty-two, is a film editor who lives in Los Angeles. He's an unusually tall, soft-spoken man who seems to have been shoved around by life, from place to place and from woman to woman. He is at once resigned to this state of affairs and depressed by it. "I have few interests—movies, music and swimming—and I seem to enjoy those things most when I'm by myself. I work hard, but I'm basically a profound underachiever. I often think that's been the main impediment in my relationships. I can be an effervescent conversationalist and very attentive in the courtship phase and will do anything to get attention. But I can never sustain it, and after a couple months I undergo a sort of Jekyll-Hyde transformation. I go from being a charming, attentive lover to the kind of person who goes on reading the newspaper while you're trying to tell him something important. That's not the kind of person who functions well in a romantic relationship."

Awkward as a teenager, Derek didn't lose his virginity until he was nineteen. His first lover was the wife of one of his college instructors. When their affair became public, Derek was forced to leave school. When he tried to break with her, his lover began harassing him. "She'd cry, call me up, show up at my parents' house. I knew that she was older and that she'd been the one to start things, but I felt like I was the user, the betrayer."

In the year that followed he supported himself by doing odd jobs and then met a girl his own age, began sleeping with her and after four months married her. "I'd gotten her pregnant and she'd had an abortion, but I still had a sense of responsibility toward her— maybe more than I would have had if she'd actually gone on and had the baby. Marriage sounded like a good idea. We were going to join a commune, travel around the country, just live on love. But it doesn't really work that way. After a year the sex wore out, and there were tensions about money. There'd be four or five days in a row where we hardly spoke to each other. Most times we solved our problems by falling into bed, and that would be it until the next problem came up. It went on like that for two years: if we hadn't gotten married, it would have withered on the vine after six months."

Since then Derek has lived with four more women, for anywhere from five months to three years. All the relationships began suddenly: "We'd date a couple of times, she'd come over one night, and then she'd never leave." The women were all different—a student at his film school, a fellow editor, a chef and a sculptor—but in all his relationships Derek found himself gradually losing interest, retreating into his work and into his solitary routines at home. "My last girlfriend would make an effort to draw me out of my shell and get me to talk about what I was feeling instead of just moping around and sulking. The problem was that so much of the time I didn't *know* what I was feeling, or just didn't want to face it." Again and again, his affairs have succumbed to entropy, a slow draining away of tenderness and enthusiasm. "I think that a good, enduring relationship must be like a comfortable old shoe," he says, "the kind of thing where you wake up one morning and realize, 'Yeah, this is working.' That's never happened to me. Instead, I get so used to my girlfriends' routines that I feel like I've got a Walkman around my ears that plays the same two tapes over and over. I start to feel suffocated. It might take a few months, it might take a few years, but eventually it withers on the vine and I'm looking for a way out."

THE CAUTIOUS CASANOVA

Unlike most Casanovas, nesters are not reckless sexual predators. For them sex is just one part of a full relationship, enjoyable but nowhere near so compulsively charged as it is for hitters, drifters or romantics. Derek sometimes betrays a wistful longing for what he calls "the Cinderella date: the girl who comes over and spends six hours in bed with you and then turns into a six-pack and a pizza." At the same time, though, he dislikes "just seeing a woman once for a couple of hours of wham-bam-thank-you-ma'am. I've done it, but I always felt guilty and vaguely used afterward."

Nesters treat sex as a medium of communication, a way of learning more about the women they find attractive. Indeed, when Derek talks about sex, it's often as a kind of conversation, "I'm attracted to women by the way they speak, by their way with words," he says. "The initial stage of any relationship is conversation, *then* comes the physical." In their fantasies, nesters long for much more than the perfect 10 or the ultimate sexual object: they want soul mates, women who will share their thoughts and ideas and join them for long walks and conversations over late-night coffee.

But for a man who so prizes the art of conversation, Derek is shy, a trait shared by most of the nesters I spoke with. Like Derek, who is self-conscious about his height and his pockmarked complexion, they often feel that there is something wrong with them, some physical or emotional defect that will keep women from liking them. The shyness and its underlying insecurities are not always immediately apparent. Ernest Hemingway, for example, was outwardly brash to the point of arrogance yet riddled by doubts about his masculinity, an introvert in extrovert's clothing.

The nester's shyness makes him oddly passive in his relations with the other sex. Far from being a polished seducer, gifted with an endless repertoire of come-ons, he often has difficulty asking women out, and it's harder still for him to ask for sex. He can do so only after the reassurance of several encounters and getting clear evidence of his dates' interest in him. Sometimes, he can make a pass only when drunk or stoned. Even then, he may be reluctant to make a direct overture. (Both Hadley and Pauline had to actively pursue Hemingway, who at first returned their enthusiasm with uncharacteristic passivity.) More often than not, the nester describes sex as something that *just happens*. Derek's accounts of his romantic encounters are circumspect and even vague, as though he couldn't recall exactly what happened between the threshold of the bedroom and the bed. "One thing led to another" is a recurring phrase in his erotic narratives.

SHEETS MADE OF FLYPAPER

For nesters, sex often carries a burden of dread and guilt. Derek grew up with the idea that sex had consequences. In the small New England town where he spent his teens, too many of his friends' affairs ended in pregnancy, early marriage and aborted hopes. "Sex," he remembers his father telling him, "is a horror show." Not every nester grew up with these attitudes, but as a rule they are acutely, even anachronistically, aware that sex has ramifications and entanglements, both physical and emotional. They are far more likely to use prophylactics than are hitters, drifters or romantics. They are far more likely to see sex as a step toward responsibility— the beginning of something and not just an end in itself.

Not the least of their fears is that sex, no matter how casual, will drag them willy-nilly into relationships of unwanted duration and complexity. Earlier I noted that hitters see every sexual partner as a secret manhunter, whose early compliance masks a ravenous hunger for commitment. Nesters share an understated and more realistic version of the same view. "The women I'm seeing now are older, and they're conscious of the ticking of their biological clocks," says Derek. "They're a bit more desperate, a bit more grabby. Really and truly, they're shopping in the husband market. There are too many women who are looking for Mr. Wonderful, someone with whom they can settle down and start grinding out the kids. That's not what I want from my life." Few nesters truly believe that women enjoy sex for its own sake; rather, they view sex as the ploy that women use to secure affection and commitment, as a medium of exchange in the age-old haggling between the genders. It's little wonder that men like Derek are cautious when sliding between the sheets; they are always afraid that they will turn out to be made of flypaper.

In both hitters and nesters this fear arises from the unconscious male dread of entrapment and castration. In their imaginations a woman's postcoital embrace is equated with the crushing grip of an iron maiden. Affection becomes suffocation. Commitment is a form of emasculation, in which a virile man is reduced to a passive "Mr. Wonderful," a hapless instrument for making babies. Hitters deal with their fear by fleeing as soon as the sexual encounter is finished, as though they were stealing a treasure from the cave of an ogress. But nesters stay. Often enough, they stay because they genuinely like their partners and look forward to seeing more of them. But, once they have slept with a new woman, nesters also feel vaguely, helplessly responsible to her, as Derek felt toward the older woman who first seduced him. In this respect, their worst fears become self-fulfilling: dreading responsibility, they nonetheless keep on assuming it, even for women they are just beginning to know.

THE MASQUERADE OF COMMITMENT

Although they fear entanglement, nesters are also driven by a great need for security and warmth. Like romantics, they are often lonely men. Derek has few real friends and sees his family only on rare occasions. He prides himself on having transcended his provincial origins, but he misses "the nebulous, family kind of warmth" that his parents and married friends enjoy. Beneath his cool demeanor is a nostalgic yearning for the vanished comforts of the hearth. It is this idyllic state—whether remembered or merely imagined—that nesters seek to re-create in their relationships with women. Their longing for security is at least as great as their terror of entrapment and, for a time at least, appears to overcome it.

Unfortunately, the truce that these men make with their demons rarely lasts. At first, the sexual excitement and sudden intimacy of a new relationship give Derek the sense of living in a state of grace. But even then he's haunted by premonitions of failure. Indeed, many nesters suffer from a peculiar fatalism about love, an overwhelming conviction of its transience. Where most people see love in terms of a progression, an ascending curve of intimacy and commitment, these men envision their love affairs as an inevitable decline: they start out in full bloom and gradually wither on the vine.

The healthiest response would be to delay serious involvement and avoid promises about the future. Yet nesters, once they have begun sexual relations, quickly plunge into a deeper commitment. Within a few months—and sometimes weeks—of sleeping with a new partner, Derek is living with her. Rather than restrain him, his premonitions seem to drive him forward, as though he were trying to wring every ounce of pleasure from the liaison before it withered. I believe that the urgency with which nesters pursue relationships they don't really believe in springs partly from a fear of rejection ("If I don't love her enough, how can she love me?") and partly from a kind of magical thinking, a wishful assumption that acting as if something is true can make it so. Derek himself acknowledges the wishful element in his affairs: "When I look back at the women I left, I realize that I never loved them in the first place. I was pretending that I did, or whipping myself into a frenzy where I briefly believed I did. I never actually fell in love: it's more that at a certain point I said, 'What the hell. The sex is good. I enjoy talking with this woman. I can stand being with her. Let's just do it.' "

Like so many romantics, nesters are intolerant of uncertainty, unable to face their ambivalence head-on. No matter how divided they may actually feel, they embark on their affairs with a masquerade of enthusiasm, whose true intent is less to deceive their lovers than it is to assuage their own doubts. The tension between their genuine need for affection and companionship and their fear of actually attaining them leads them to assume a spurious new identity, a narcissistic mask. Derek in love is a new man: the new Derek is neat where the old Derek was slovenly, outgoing where the old one was withdrawn. The new Derek listens attentively to his girlfriend where the old one was happier reading the newspaper in an empty kitchen. He gives every sign of wanting a deeper and firmer bond with his partner, while the old Derek wonders uneasily what he is getting into.

This charade is not a conscious deception. The nester may be thoroughly convinced by his own behavior and believe that for once he really is falling in love, as Hemingway's fictional alter ego believes that he really *can* start over. If the nester sometimes detects false notes in his performance, he blames them on nervousness or his eagerness to please his partner. Because of his overwhelming fear of rejection, he may be especially loath to do or say anything that a woman might find hurtful: it is too early in the game to risk a confrontation. And quite often, the nester is completely unaware of the disparity between his outward warmth and his inner ambivalence.

OVERTURES TO ENTRAPMENT

So women can scarcely be blamed for taking nesters at face value and for responding to their displays of affection and commitment in kind. Why behave any differently toward an attractive man who, unlike so many other men, seems to want to get closer? Yet such behavior often has an alarming effect on nesters, who are so deeply suspicious of women and so sensitive to the least intrusion into their lives. They are quick to interpret every affectionate gesture as a veiled appeal, to see every request as a demand and to cringe inwardly whenever the future comes up as a topic of conversation. To Derek, all such occasions are overtures to entrapment: "I'm seeing a woman now who's plainly looking for someone to monopolize. I've gone out with her for three weeks, and if we eat at the same place twice, the next time we're out she'll say, 'Oh, let's go to *our* place!' She's already making the assumption that we're a bona fide couple."

What's at work here is more than a simple distrust of women; at times Derek's suspicions seem almost paranoid in their intensity. He cannot believe that women respect his desire for autonomy, and he refuses to believe any woman who expresses a similar desire of her own. A woman who claims to be independent is only lying in order to trap him. One characteristic of paranoid thinking is projection: the strangers who are "out to get" the paranoiac are convenient scapegoats for his own unconscious rage. Nesters, too, seem to project—yet what they project is their dependency, the trait with which they invariably endow women. Yearning for security, for regular companionship and a shared home, they nevertheless deny their needs, perhaps because to admit them would be to face the possibility that they may not be met. Wanting something is no guarantee of getting it, these men might say; sometimes it is safer to want nothing. In addition, dependency seems inimical to our traditional notions of maleness. We expect men to enjoy their freedom and shun commitment, and any man who wants a woman too badly diminishes himself. "Every woman should marry—and no man," Disraeli said, and marriage is still perceived as something that women want. Bridegrooms, in the meanwhile, joke about being fitted with the ball and chain. When our dependency is felt to be shameful, it is natural to deny it and to seek others as scapegoats—especially the women we need so desperately. Nesters are hardly immune to this very human tendency, and their view of women as clinging and manipulative stems, at least in part, from a projection of their own unacceptable desires.

THE FORBIDDEN ZONE

No matter how intrusive they find their partners becoming, nesters rarely express their fears or resentments. To do so as the relationship progresses is even harder than in the earlier phases. "Once I've been around a woman for any length of time," Derek says, "I very often can't speak my real feelings. Once the relationship's started, women have a stake in you, expectations about where this thing will go." Once more, Derek's vision of commitment as imprisonment or castration is self-fulfilling: now that he is involved with a woman, he cannot be honest with her. Instead, he is forced to perpetuate a masquerade of enthusiasm even as his misgivings increase, to go on yielding when every instinct tells him to rebel. For nesters, romantic involvement carries a burden of eternal and dishonest compliance. To love women is to lose themselves.

We cannot speak our true feelings without sometimes hurting others or risking a hurtful response from them. Such conflict is especially fearful to nesters, who will go to extraordinary lengths to avoid it. "I'm a profound procrastinator," says Derek. "I always did my term papers at absolutely the last minute. If I have a date coming up two weeks from now and know I won't be able to make it, I'll put off the unpleasantness of breaking it until it's far worse because I'm doing it at the last minute."

For the nester, confronting a lover carries a twofold risk. She might reject him, and for such a shy man rejection is nothing less than annihilation. And he himself might get angry, perhaps *too* angry, losing his self-control and even his sanity. Many nesters, therefore, express their anger only when intoxicated, in a sudden, volcanic outburst that sometimes escalates into violence. In those cases, all the fears about anger and its consequences are fulfilled. Even to fantasize about such an outburst is terrifying. Safer, then, to shun anger altogether, to turn conflict into a forbidden zone and leave all roads that might lead to it untraveled.

But those roads are fearfully interconnected: to avoid conflict eventually means avoiding anything that might provoke it. Passion, which touches so closely on rage, must be replaced by neutral routine. "When you live with someone, you lose all sexual spontaneity," Derek laments. "The spark just dies." Intimate conversation must give way to small talk as the topics that really matter are increasingly fraught with resentment. Ultimately, the loved one herself becomes suspect, for the mere sight of her now raises a host of unspoken irritations. Nesters frequently experience their repressed anger as boredom—Derek's sensation of being stuck with "a Walkman over my ears that plays the same two tapes over and over"—for boredom is at once safer than true anger and annihilates its object more completely: a person you are angry with still commands your interest; a person who bores you is only in the way. In time, the nester's dread of conflict contaminates every aspect of his relationship, smothering all its vitality beneath a blanket of the noncommittal and the inoffensive.

THE VANISHING LOVER

For men like Derek the only way out of this self-created wasteland is withdrawal. Physically, the nester spends more time away from his partner. Work, the most acceptable avenue of escape, takes on exaggerated importance. Other friendships may become especially consuming and demand all of his attention. When contact with his partner is unavoidable, the nester withdraws. He stops speaking to her or restricts his speech to the blandest commonplaces: the weather and that night's menu take on overwhelming importance. In bed, he replaces spontaneous ardor with a work-manlike sexual performance whose primary purpose is to keep up the fiction that nothing has changed. He may fantasize about other, more desirable partners and begins, almost unconsciously, to search for replacements for the woman who has become no more than an obligation to him. Slowly, imperceptibly, he is vanishing from the relationship.

Although he withdraws chiefly out of repressed anger, the nester may also experience guilt and panic as he detaches from his lover. Unable to acknowledge his disaffection, he often feels that external forces—an emotional form of continental drift—are pulling him and his lover apart. He may project his own indifference onto her and start questioning her love for him. Frequently, he feels unworthy of the love he receives, recoiling in guilt from any gesture of tenderness or warmth: "I hate it when a woman I'm no longer attracted to gives me a present," Derek says. "I feel that accepting it is only going to mean some new obligation. I want to tell her 'You're wasting your money. You're wasting your time.'" Even as he falls out of love, he attempts to deny it. Rather than face his difficulty in sustaining commitments, the nester finds it safer to blame his partners or the machinations of an impersonal fate for making commitment impossible.

Women often end up cooperating in this withdrawal, particularly if they too fear confrontation. The relationship may degenerate into long, sullen silences punctuated by irritable sniping or, more peaceably, into a grown-up version of parallel play, with both partners occupying themselves in separate friendships and private pursuits. Because the bond between the nester and his partner is based on avoidance, any challenge to their fragile détente is likely to shatter it. A dispute over an unpaid bill or a quarrel over domestic chores can escalate into a climactic fight. A simple question may open a floodgate of resentments which, after months or years of silence, are now unpalatably and irremediably bitter. There may be a "final" discussion, a "final" confrontation, but it is final in name only: it ends things in the same way that pulling the plug of a life-support system may be said to "kill" someone in a terminal coma. Whether the nester's relationship ends with a bang or a whimper, it has usually died long before, enduring only in a half-life of wishful thinking and routine.

Although he often feels guilty during the final months of a relationship, Derek seems relieved when it is over. There are times when he feels that he has been liberated from "a daily unpleasantness" and restored to his true, ungregarious self, the man who enjoys vacationing alone and dining on TV dinners and doughnuts. "I sometimes think that I'm meant to be alone. My marriage was a stupid romantic notion, and the few times I've considered remarrying have been brief moments of hallucination. An ideal marriage for me would be one where I lived on the fifth floor of my apartment building and my wife lived on the third; we could get together a few nights a week. I do sometimes miss stability and family warmth. But the only times I really regret it are those cold nights when I come home from work to an empty apartment, and there's nothing to do but have a cigarette, watch some TV and go to sleep."

There is something inexpressibly sad in Derek's resignation, for of all Casanovas nesters seem the ones with the greatest potential for making a genuine peace with the opposite sex. Unlike hitters, drifters and romantics, they have a true hunger for connectedness, for the warmth and tenderness that exist only in the friction between two human beings. Although they are fearful of entrapment and are all too likely to see women as its embodiments, they are also capable of recognizing them as members of the same species and of understanding their needs, even when they cannot meet them. If other Casanovas are blind, nesters at least seem to have one functioning eye, endowed with the clarity of hindsight.

The great stumbling block in their search for a common bond with women is the fear that in turn engenders a crippling syndrome of dishonesty and evasion. Their fear of loss strikes them dumb and compels them to keep their misgivings to themselves; in time, it makes them choose avoidance over confrontation, even when confrontation might save the relationship. During courtship, the diffidence of nesters gives them some charm; later on, that same diffidence becomes a fatal passivity. Often painfully aware of the path that must be taken if they are to love women, they remain terrified of traveling it, and instead wander off at the same point again and again. "It's very difficult to break your program," Derek says. "The same fuckups you were making when you were fourteen and fifteen are the ones you're going to make for the rest of your life. You just learn to sit back and read the warning signals: 'Uh-oh, I'm starting to do it again. Let's see if I can straighten it out.' And of course I never do."

CHAPTER EIGHT

———◆———

Jugglers

THE EXAMPLE OF HERMAN TARNOWER

You have been what you very carefully set out to be, Hi—the most important thing in my life, the most important human in my life, and that will never change. You keep me in control by threatening me with banishment—an easy threat which you know I couldn't live with—and so I stay home alone while you make love to someone who has almost totally destroyed me.
                                    —Jean Harris, letter to Herman Tarnower

Dr. Herman Tarnower was an unlikely homme fatal. Bald, elderly, he resembled a cross between a vulture and a grocery-store owner. *He was more scholar than swinger, the kind of man, his lover said, "who reads Herodotus for fun." He had made his reputation tending to the hearts of wealthy patients; he had made a fortune telling millions of readers—most of them women—what to eat. His book,* The Complete Scarsdale Medical Diet, *was a best-seller. On its proceeds, he lived with a peculiar combination of extravagance and meanness. The doctor was both a fitness freak and a gourmet. His house in Westchester County, New York, was expensive but cramped. He lavished his mistresses with jewelry and took them on trips to the Caribbean and the Far East, but he wouldn't go out of his way to visit them. If he possessed charm and erudition, he seemed utterly lacking in tenderness or even a basic empathy with his lovers' needs: he gave out affection by the gram, as though it were fattening.*

Tarnower met Jean Harris in 1967. She had little money, but a formidable intellect and social savoir faire. He wrote and called her regularly. In May of that year he gave her a $35,000 diamond ring and asked her to marry him. Shortly afterward he changed his mind: "It was better that we didn't get married," he told her later. "I didn't want to worry about what retirement home your mother was in, and I didn't want to watch you die of cancer, and I didn't want you to play nursemaid to me." But he continued to see her; Harris became a frequent guest in his home and his regular companion on trips abroad. "He did all the right things, and I was very much in love with him by then, and it was too late. It was seeing Hi that mattered," she recalled.

Hi had always had other women, and Jean took his infidelities in stride, assuming that she would always be the first woman in his life—the hostess at his dinner parties, the collaborator on his books. In 1977, though, her assumptions were shattered. While on a trip with Tarnower, she found him reading a letter from another woman, who evidently knew his itinerary. She also saw that the doctor's cuff links were engraved with the name Lynne. Lynne Tryforos was more than a passing fling. She was in her thirties, nineteen years younger than Harris and thirty-two years younger than her lover. She had left her husband for him. In due course she became his nurse and secretary, and when Jean moved to Virginia to become headmistress of the Madeira School, Lynne supplanted her as the doctor's chief guest. She made up buttons that said "Superdoctor" and scattered them through his house like rose petals. She had her daughters send him Father's Day cards.

But this was not a simple case of one woman replacing another.

Tarnower wouldn't give up Jean entirely, and indeed he imposed a perverse parity on his mistresses, alternating visits from Tryforos with visits from Harris, vacations with one woman with vacations with the other. Both women had clothes in his closets. Both served him not just as bedmates but as amanuenses: if Mrs. Harris disparagingly referred to her rival as a "girl Friday," she could hardly deny that she herself was editing her lover's newest "masterpiece" while he went off to a dinner party: he acknowledged her assistance with a check for $4,000. In his will the doctor left both women almost identical bequests—$200,000 for Lynne Tryforos and $220,000 for Mrs. Harris.

In late 1979 and early 1980 the tension between the two women, and between Mrs. Harris and Dr. Tarnower, reached a critical point. A mysterious caller kept phoning Jean at her home. Jean in turn kept calling her rival: Lynne's phone number was unlisted but Jean's anonymous caller had given it to her. Someone sent Jean a copy of Tarnower's will, with her name scratched out of it. On a visit to the doctor's house she found that her clothes had been slashed and smeared with excrement. Tarnower accused Jean of harassing Lynne, of harassing his friends for an invitation to a testimonial dinner to which he had failed to ask her. His neglect of her was growing, and she found herself begging for his time, his affection, for the pills that she now needed in order to keep up her duties while her spirit was disintegrating: her lover had become her pusher. On March 10, 1980, she drove from Virginia to Westchester with a loaded gun, intending, she later claimed, to kill herself at Tarnower's house. She found him in his bedroom. According to Harris, he told her, "Get out of here. You're crazy." Then he tried to take the gun from her. She shot him three times; the doctor was dead before he reached the hospital. Later, in police custody, she wondered "how something so ugly and sad could have happened between two people who didn't argue even, except over the use of the subjunctive."

WAYNE: "THE KEY . . . IS HAVING THEM WANT TO GIVE TO YOU"

Casanovas' relationships can range from the ephemeral couplings of hitters to the long and superficially stable arrangements of nesters. Like nesters, jugglers often sustain long relationships, but those relationships are far from stable and are never monogamous. Jugglers are true polygynists, who have at least two women in their lives at any one time. In keeping with their name, they preserve a scrupulous equilibrium among their relationships, dividing their time and affection equally between partners—two or more lovers or a wife and mistress. They may see their lovers on alternating nights or weekends, commute daily between a wife and mistress or, in some instances, draw both partners into a ménage à trois like the one described in Jean Rhys's *Quartet*. Jugglers do not perform these balancing acts in secrecy: they need an audience, and their partners are usually made acutely and painfully aware of each other's existence. What drives these men is not an excess of desire or an inability to find one woman to meet all their needs. Their sexual legerdemain is motivated by an obsession with control and a mortal terror of attachment. To love one woman at a time is beyond their capacity: they can only portion out their hearts to rival supplicants, each of whom serves as a counterweight to the others.

Wayne, a thirty-seven-year-old business consultant, lives with his girlfriend Dana in her apartment in Miami. He is a tenaciously, even belligerently, independent man—the kind who insists on rephrasing your questions in his own terms before he answers them—and he dislikes this arrangement, though their living quarters are comfortable and Dana doesn't complain when he sees other women.

Wayne was married once, twelve years ago. He came from a conventional Irish-Catholic home and at twenty-five, he felt it was time to settle down. "We went to New York for our honeymoon," he says. "We drove there and back, and just as I saw the skyline, I had this flash, a little voice in my head saying, 'This is a terrible mistake.'" The marriage lasted three years. It was his last attempt at a committed relationship, and Wayne describes it as one would describe a brush with death.

Since then, Wayne has had a chorus line of lovers. He began cheating on his wife two months after their wedding and, in addition to countless casual partners, soon had taken a mistress, Janine, whom he saw weekly. He continued to date her after his marriage dissolved, but kept up his pattern of infidelity. As Janine became Wayne's unofficial "wife," the woman who shared his bed most nights and accompanied him to most social functions, Nadia became his alternate mistress. He saw her every Thursday and Saturday, took her to expensive restaurants and picked up part of her rent and living expenses—including the bills for the psychiatrist she saw to treat her frustration at being "the other woman." When

Janine finally became too possessive, Wayne stopped calling her and found Dana, while continuing to see Nadia. On a few occasions he persuaded both women to join him in an erotic threesome. Shortly after the last of these ménages à trois, Nadia had a nervous breakdown and refused to see Wayne anymore: "She was guilt-tripping me, saying that making it with another woman had flipped her out, but the fact is nobody ever held a gun to her head. I'm not the kind of man who pressures women into anything: I don't go where I'm not wanted, and I don't beg for what I want. The key to most women is having them want to give to you. The more they get to know you, the more they're going to want to give to you. Which means whatever you want it to."

Dana is the most recent of Wayne's "mainstays." He has been seeing her for almost a year, through the final months of his relationship with Nadia, and he seems fairly happy with her: "Dana's okay. She gives me everything I want. She'll be bisexual, she'll find other partners for me. She's got a nice VCR and a microwave—I bought both of them for her. The best thing about her is that she's not pressuring me for a long-term commitment. She isn't always asking me where this thing will go, which is what the others all ended up doing. Right now, I'm satisfied seeing just her and having a few extracurricular activities, women I see two or three times until I'm tired of them. There's no question in my mind that Dana loves me: every one of my mainstays has loved me. Do I question my ability to love her? No. I have no doubts about my ability. What I question is my *desire*, my desire to love."

"YOU DON'T FALL IN LOVE WITH A DOG"

Like many jugglers, Wayne is constantly on the make. Last year he slept with thirty different women, and he spends only two or three nights alone in an average month. Most of his encounters are brief: "I'll meet a woman someplace—through work, at a pub or a restaurant—and ask her out. The first date is obviously exploratory. The second date is still getting to know her, and that's usually when it becomes sexual. The third date is usually the most comfortable, but that's as far as most of these things go." Like Wayne, other jugglers enjoy an abundance of casual sexual partners, women they see once or twice and then quietly discard.

In this respect, jugglers resemble drifters, whose relations with women are similarly brief and superficial. Like drifters, they approach women with few prior expectations; as Wayne puts it, "I'm not looking for anything more than some laughs and—to be crass about it—a good lay." Usually, they are satisfied with what they get, and once satisfied they back out of their relationships with a minimum of fuss. When I asked Wayne how he broke off most of his affairs, he was quick to correct me. "I don't break off anything. I *discontinue.* I stop calling them after the third date. If they phone me and ask if I want to get together again, I tell them I'll have to call them back. When I don't, it's a pretty good indication that I'm not interested in continuing."

Unlike drifters, though, jugglers are clear about their reasons for keeping relationships short. "Women usually get too intimate around the third date. They'll suggest making plans—'By the way, why don't we do such and such next Saturday?' Something as simple as that can make the warning flags go right up." Although Wayne uses the word "intimate," his primary fear seems to be commitment, with its constricting schedules and sticky assumptions about the future, even a future that is only a weekend away. Although they crave sexual variety, most jugglers share this antipathy to commitment. Thus, they place limits on every liaison, assigning them—sometimes unconsciously—an automatic cutoff point and ending things as soon as they reach it.

Nevertheless, one or two of their encounters will evolve into a longer involvement, which may last anywhere from a few months to several years. It seems to happen spontaneously, without a deliberate effort on the part of the juggler or his lover. Sometimes, Wayne simply continues seeing women after three dates. Other jugglers drift into longer relationships with women who work in the same office or exercise at the same health club, ascribing their choice of partners to sheer convenience. Their affairs, as they describe them, are always accidents, begun with the fatalistic shrug, "As well her as another."

The distinction between choosing relationships and falling into them is one that many jugglers make, and it is yet another indication of their fear of attachment, a fear so pervasive that it muffles desire and negates choice. A juggler will rarely admit that he wants a particular woman, certainly not that he wants her more than others. He sees his affairs as weightless and inconsequential; he starts them casually and walks away from them without regret. "Have I loved somebody?" Wayne says. "Oh, sure. Have I been *in love* with her? Good question. You can love a dog, but you don't fall in love with a dog. You can have affection for a lady, you can have emotion, you can feel protective. But you can live without her."

THE SEDUCTIVE REFLEX

Yet at first jugglers appear anything but diffident. Although Wayne has never "decided" to cultivate a relationship with one particular woman, he often invests great effort in his seductions—calling women often, treating them to extravagant evenings out, making sure that sex is both emotionally and physically satisfying. A heavy drinker who also uses amphetamines and cocaine, he attributes much of his charm to the drugs he takes: "The truth is that I'm very shy, but when I'm loaded I come on very strong. When I'm high I can tune in to what a woman's needs are—if she's intelligent, I appeal to her intellect. If she's looking for warmth, I come on very warm."

Some jugglers are compulsively seductive, unable to pursue women at anything less than white heat. "At first I saw Carol as just a fling," one man recalls. "I figured I'd call her, see if we could get together, have some fun. She was very leery of me. For some reason, that drove me crazy and suddenly, though I still had no intention of getting serious, I would have done anything to get her into bed with me. I started calling her up two, three times a day. And she asked me, 'Why are you hounding me like this? I know you're married, and you're running around with somebody else. What do you want from me?' I started crying, babbling some kind of bullshit—the thing was I *knew* it was bullshit even as I said it, but I was also genuinely affected on some level. But it worked. An hour later, we were in bed together." Jugglers seem gifted—or perhaps afflicted—with a seductive reflex, an intuitive sense of the quickest, most effective route to a woman's heart. Like other reflexes, it functions automatically, unchecked by morals or pragmatism, and it is triggered by the slightest stimulus. Put one of these men in a room with a woman and he lights up, even if he is only thinking about what he'll have for lunch.

A LITTLE EDGE OF DOMINANCE

When a man who wants no commitment behaves like a passionate suitor, he gives off a set of mixed messages, a simultaneous flashing of red and green lights. While Wayne has never lied about his distaste for binding relationships, he expresses it in a mumbled aside: "Usually, the first night we're together, I'll say something like, 'Oh, I was married once. I wouldn't do that again.' You don't have to come out and say, 'I'm not going to have a long-term relationship with you,' but the implication is there." Other jugglers have begged their partners to stay with them, only to drop them a week later, while one man displayed intense jealousy about a woman he was regularly cheating on. Such mixed messages may be conscious ploys or spontaneous reflections of deep ambivalence, but they are an essential part of these men's seductive technique, a way of luring women forward even as they push them away.

Most women eventually tire of these routines. And only certain types of women are likely to fall for them in the first place. The factors that make "lady-killers' ladies" susceptible to jugglers, or for that matter to any Casanova, will be discussed at length in a later section. For the time being, it's enough to say that jugglers gravitate toward women whom they can easily manipulate—women who are younger, poorer and often a little naive, women whose loneliness and lack of self-esteem make them easy game: "I need to have that little edge of mental dominance," Wayne says. "I control women by knowing what their need is—stability, comfort, reassurance, whatever—and then making them think I can supply it. They begin to think that I really understand them, that I can make their loneliness go away. That I'll support them, be there for them. After that, they're willing to do anything for me."

True control requires more than a perception of weakness. Jugglers are adept at exploiting their partners' vulnerabilities, at widening the hairline cracks of inequality until they become a gaping chasm. Knowledge comes easily to them: they are good listeners with a gift for articulating a woman's implicit desires in explicit form. They also have a chameleon-like ability to become whatever they sense their partners want. If a woman craves reliability in a man, a juggler will be absolutely punctual for dates. If he senses a need for intimacy, he will appear extraordinarily open: he is not above using tears as a seductive tool. Like nesters, jugglers often begin relationships by adopting a new identity, one that's charming, outgoing, considerate —the answer to a woman's unvoiced prayers.

But Wayne's dance of courtship is a cha-cha-cha in which every two steps forward are followed by one step back. Even as he is persuading women that he will meet their needs, he is warning them not to expect fidelity or commitment. Every phone call ends with a muttered demurral; every gift might as well come with a card that reads, "Don't get too close to me." Another juggler may make extravagant promises while behaving ambivalently: he shows up late, breaks every third appointment or somehow allows his partner to glimpse the other names in his datebook. One man I spoke with asked a girlfriend to bring him some aspirin from his bathroom medicine cabinet: the aspirin was stored next to another woman's diaphragm. Consciously or unconsciously, jugglers use such double messages adroitly. Instead of canceling each other out, the dual messages have a resonance that's at once baffling and seductive. Every promise is coupled with an implicit challenge, a challenge that some women find irresistible.

Secrecy and selective disclosure are integral parts of the juggler's manipulative repertoire. Skilled as he is at drawing women out and at reading the emotional information coded in every utterance, he is even better at withholding information about himself and revealing only those aspects of himself he wishes his partner to see. "Women don't see me as I really am," Wayne says. "They see me as they want to see me—and as I want them to see me." The projection of a stylized persona requires unceasing vigilance: the juggler is guarded even in the afterglow. "After making love, I'll talk about anything," Wayne says. "Anything from 'Do you want a peanut-butter sandwich?' to 'What do you think of that movie we saw on TV?'" He almost never discusses his feelings, his childhood or his family. He is always acutely aware of the image he presents to his partners and takes great pains to control it. Even when jugglers appear quite open, they are more likely to be engaging in public relations than in genuine communication.

THE ISSUE OF POLYGYNY

One thing jugglers don't keep hidden is the presence of other women in their lives. Candidly and proudly polygynous, these men rarely use words like "cheating" or "infidelity" to describe their multiple affairs. Polygyny, they will tell you, is their right, an honest expression of their natures that only the most foolish and petty woman would object to. Of course, polygyny is also a useful safety valve for men who fear intimacy and commitment. An abundance of sexual choice makes it possible to see women regularly for years without feeling bound to them, for the amount of time, attention and emotional currency they can invest in any lover is automatically limited. No relationship ever becomes too tedious or constricting when they can commute back and forth between women as though between country and city houses. Nor need they worry that they will reveal too much of themselves to any one partner: they can get away with telling the same stories and the same jokes a lot longer if the audiences keep changing. Finally, polygyny greatly reduces the risk of rejection, providing jugglers with a reassuring safety net of sexual alternatives: "I don't like breaking up with a mainstay unless I've got a backup relationship," Wayne says. "But then, I've always had at least one backup."

Polygyny acquires another meaning—really, a whole nest of meanings—when it is openly acknowledged. It is no longer just a mechanism of avoidance, but a communication between the juggler and his partners. For the juggler polygyny is not just a safety valve, but a boast, a bargaining chip and an instrument of emotional blackmail. Each affair influences the other, corrects the other, exerts on it a complementary gravity and spin. When a juggler tells a woman that he has other lovers—and no intention of dropping them—he is conveying several messages. He declares that he is independent and will not be bound in the nets of commitment. When one of Wayne's lovers, for example, began asking too many questions about the future, he would spend more time with her competitor and conduct his extracurricular activities more blatantly. "You have to let women know that no amount of manipulation is going to keep you from doing what you have to do," he says defiantly. There's a perverse and rather childish element in this statement that characterizes much of the juggler's infidelity. Independence is a critical issue only for those who are unsure of it, and anyone who has raised a child will recognize the constant and belligerent assertion of autonomy as a hallmark of the terrible twos.

By making polygyny an issue in their relationships, jugglers turn their lovers into rivals. This is a convenient way of diverting anger, for their partners are far more likely to vent their resentments on shadowy competitors than on the men they sleep with and need. The "other woman" is a handy scapegoat, and jugglers seem implicitly aware of it. Women who have been involved with these men often learn a great deal about their counterparts, and what they learn influences them in extraordinary ways: out of fear and jealousy, a woman may do what she wouldn't do for love. "When I learned that Mitch was seeing someone else, I asked him what she was like," one woman told me. "I didn't really expect an answer. But he told me. In intimate detail. He told me that she was slender and had gorgeous breasts. He told me everything that she did in bed, I mean *everything*. I really wanted to say, 'Stop! I can't stand hearing all this!' And then, of course, I found myself trying to be just like *her*. I went on a crash diet and lost fifteen pounds. I started wearing push-up bras. I let Mitch take me anally, which was excruciating, but *she* let him do it, so of course I did, too. It was only after we broke up that I realized how completely he'd had me wrapped around his finger."

When a rival is held up as a positive example, she can become an object of emulation. But jugglers also use the rival as a negative example; when they complain to one woman about another, the effect is not just to reassure her but to warn her of the consequences should she imitate her counterpart's behavior: the mistakes of one woman serve as veiled threats to the other. It's discomfiting to realize that someone can be goaded into changing her appearance and sexual habits out of such primitive motives, but jealousy, envy and fear are, after all, the soil into which most advertising casts its seeds. We are less likely to buy a particular car or soda or laundry soap because we think the product is good than because we envy the man behind the wheel of the Porsche, aspire to the lean flanks of the Tab drinker or fear that a lesser brand of detergent will leave us with dingy collars. Like the best admen, jugglers are adept at finding their target market and manipulating it. A key part of their pitch is the "other woman," who serves both as scapegoat and role model—a symbolic "Ms. Jones" whom their partners will do anything to keep up with.

THE ALLURE OF THE THREESOME

Not uncommonly, jugglers try to draw two lovers into a ménage à trois, usually for occasional sessions of group sex. The idea of group sex can become an obsession for them. Its appeal is manifold. On the one hand, the ménage à trois is another—perhaps the climactic

—instance of the control the juggler wields over the women in his life, a way of pushing a lover through the barriers of morals and aesthetics and into a realm where the sole determinant is the juggler's will. Can there be any greater proof of mastery? Beyond it lies only the kind of total enthrallment envisioned by the Marquis de Sade and practiced by Charles Manson. For a man who is comfortable with women only when he is certain of his dominance, making a woman perform an act that she finds repugnant is the headiest reassurance. Whatever guilt he once felt from straying outside their relationship is now banished; his lover has gone from merely countenancing his transgressions to participating in them.

By steering his partners into ménages à trois, the juggler can also indulge any unacknowledged homosexual fantasies of his own while assuaging the anxiety such fantasies arouse in him. It's far safer to project his homosexual inclinations onto two women than it is to act them out with another man. In this regard, we note that Wayne has urged all of his mistresses to take male lovers. Perhaps he's only trying to allay his guilt by getting his partners to join him in infidelity. But he may also be attempting to satisfy his own homoerotic impulses vicariously through a female surrogate. Several jugglers I interviewed maintained simultaneous relationships with male and female lovers (and Herman Tarnower was rumored to have liaisons with men). For those men who balk at actively expressing homosexual leanings, the ménage à trois is a symbolic substitute, a masque in which the players' genders are conveniently transposed.

But the final layer of meaning in the juggler's obsession with sexual triads—and really, in his entire program of control—is his desire for a total, global and unconditional expression of love, a love that approaches the adoration that he knew in infancy. Although he enjoys watching two women making love to each other, his greatest pleasure comes from being the center of their combined attention. Doubly caressed, doubly mouthed, doubly enfolded, the juggler enjoys the overpowering sensations of a baby coddled by two indulgent parents or a fetus drifting in the womb. This pleasure is as much emotional as it is physical: Wayne calls the ménage à trois "a total giving of love." Even if he has had to cajole and bully his partners into taking part in this three-way act, the juggler sees it as evidence of a devotion that transcends squeamishness and scruples, a devotion whose intensity and group nature evoke comparisons with worship.

"GIVE ME EVERYTHING"

The ménage à trois is only a particularly dramatic expression of the obsessions that underlie all of the juggler's behavior. The first of these is the perpetual, and perpetually aborted, quest for love. It may seem strange to say that a man who doubts his desire to love is actually searching for it, but by "love" I mean something quite different from the feelings of tenderness, magnanimity and esteem that most of us call by that name. What the juggler seeks is not a mutual exchange of feeling, but a one-sided outpouring that sets no conditions on its object. It condones the juggler's infidelity; it endures in his absences; it does not wane when he is cruel or uncommunicative. Such love is total and enveloping, exalting the beloved and annihilating the lover, negating her tastes, her morals and even her instinct for self-preservation. "I want women to give me everything," Wayne says. "I want them to withhold nothing."

One ordinarily encounters such love only in the transactions between worshiper and deity and mother and child. The juggler's lack, or denial, of guilt often seems infantile, as does the egocentric pleasure he takes in ménages à trois. And there is something profoundly retrogressive about his desire for ceaseless, unconditional affection. "If I want them to cook dinner for me, they'll cook dinner," Wayne says of his lovers. "If I want them to do my laundry, they'll do the laundry. If I want to have sex, they're going to have sex with me." Leaving out the sex, his expectations of women are exactly what small boys expect from their mothers. And if we accept the notion that, early on, the bond between mother and child is in fact sexual, there is little that distinguishes Wayne's desire to possess his partners from the infant's desire to possess its mother.

The problem with that primitive bond is that it works two ways: if the child possesses his mother, he is also possessed by her. If he enjoys her total, self-abnegating attention, he is also totally subject to her will. It's easy to see how such mutual possession and annihilation inform our ideas of romantic love, which is often described as a kind of engulfment: "The crisis of engulfment can come from a wound, but also from a fusion: we die together from loving each other ... a closed death of the shared grave." For the juggler, though, the ideas of fusion and powerlessness are particularly terrifying. However much he may desire to possess his lover, he cannot tolerate the idea of being similarly possessed. That prospect is a fatal threat to his masculinity, to his sense of himself as a grown man. He will do anything to ward it off.

A recent book on men who avoid commitment argues that the fear of commitment is a form of claustrophobia. I believe that the juggler's fear of commitment arises, rather, from a deeper and more primal fear of engulfment and fusion. He is quite capable of sustaining long relationships so long as he can maintain a sense of control. The struggle for dominance, with its ceaseless manipulation and testing of the beloved, is both a struggle for unconditional adoration and a defense against the threat of engulfment that is always implicit in such love. The mental rape that the juggler inflicts on his partners is a means of extorting what few women give of their free will—not, at any rate, to a grown man. At the same time, his manipulation of women reassures him that he is not passively *receiving* love, but *taking* it through a forceful exercise of cunning and strength. For the juggler, control is both a way of recapturing the state of infantile grace and of denying its infantile nature.

The obsession with control informs every aspect of the juggler's interactions with women. It underlies his mixed messages, his polygyny and his constant playing of one woman against others. In order to control women, he must control himself: every utterance must be cleared beforehand with an internal censor and every bit of information he gives his partner checked for its coherence with the big picture. Like nesters and drifters, the juggler cannot afford the luxury of anger: "I don't think I've ever been in a shouting match with a lady," Wayne declares. "If they lose control, well, that's beautiful because now *you* have it." What Wayne overlooks is that he must control himself as much as he does his lovers. In his obsession with dominance, he has become a kind of democratic despot who shares the same chains as the tyrannized.

As conscienceless as jugglers often seem, it's possible to see them as prisoners of an arid, self-imposed hell. They have pushed the game of sexual manipulation to the point where it has become forced labor, devoid of spontaneity or play. They often complain of being exhausted, and in truth their labor *is* exhausting: on the few occasions that I was seriously involved with two women at a time, I recall being constantly on the edge of nervous collapse. Nor is it surprising that these men are often bored, as one is bound to be when one has reduced one's partners to adoring subjects. Finally, jugglers often suffer from an unappeasable insecurity, for sooner or later, their relationships tend to crumble under the weight of the demands they place on them: of all Casanovas, jugglers are the ones whose partners are most likely to leave them.

Like romantics, jugglers must live with a paradox of their own creation. These men can never know whether their partners' love is freely given or merely extorted, and whether their partners love them or the image they have projected so laboriously: "I used to feel lonely, like there was a part of me that no woman understood," Wayne admits. "Now, I don't give a damn. Either a woman takes me for what I am or she doesn't take me at all. Women don't necessarily love me more because I can control them, but they respect me more and women cannot love someone they don't respect. I'm not necessarily looking for love. I'm not looking for love at all."

CHAPTER NINE

———◆–◆———

Tomcats

THE EXAMPLE OF FRANK SINATRA

Frank Sinatra married Nancy Barbato in 1939. He was still struggling for recognition, and in the early years of their marriage most of their money went to further his career. Later, after his vault to stardom, he treated Nancy lavishly, buying her two palatial houses and a fortune in clothes and jewelry. Long before that, however, he had begun sleeping with other women, from high-school girls to movie stars. Few of them meant anything to him. When he'd come to Hollywood, he had made a list of the famous beauties he wanted to sleep with and he calmly checked off each new conquest as he came to her. Gentlemanly and even courtly before sex with

*these women, he could be brutal afterward, tossing his partners
aside like used tissues.*

*His extramarital activities were ceaseless and, with fame, in-
creasingly publicized. With each new liaison heralded in the pages
of* Variety *and* Hollywood Reporter, *it was useless for Sinatra to
bother covering them up. For a long time Nancy managed to reconcile herself to Frank's infidelity, reminding friends that, no matter
how many women he had, she was still the one he came home to. In
1951 Frank divorced Nancy in order to marry Ava Gardner, his lat-
est and most consuming paramour. Yet his first marriage had a curious afterlife. After his divorce from Gardner, Frank continued to
turn to his first wife for companionship and consolation. It seemed
natural to his cronies that when Frank was bored, confused or
lonely, he would call up Nancy.*

SAM: "I HAD ALL THESE GOOD INTENTIONS"

Incessantly and sometimes flagrantly unfaithful yet paradoxically devoted to spouse and home, tomcats are the most common
and generally the least glamorous of Casanovas. We deplore them
for trampling on the marriage vows and for inflicting countless betrayals on their partners, whom we typically see as silent and long-
suffering. We sometimes wink at their exploits, as we wink at dirty
jokes, and envy their license and apparent lack of moral inhibitions.
"How do they get away with it?" we wonder. Unlike hitters, whose
promiscuity is affectless and basically solitary, tomcats seem to
enjoy the best of both worlds—sexual variety and the comforts of
domesticity—without suffering the guilt that is one of the chief
consequences of a double life.

Tomcats are men who have little apparent difficulty with the outward trappings of commitment. They marry and may stay with one
partner for life. They pay their bills and taxes. They father children.
At the same time, they seem prey to irreconcilable conflicts about
being, as the old saw puts it, "confined for life in an institution,"
and are constantly testing the institution's limits. They are chronically unfaithful, with many different partners. It's important to distinguish tomcats from one-time or crisis adulterers, who vastly
outnumber them: they do not succumb to a grand, illicit passion or
go on a brief binge of womanizing while in the throes of midlife
crisis. Most of them began as something else—as hitters, drifters or

romantics—before they married. Many have been married and divorced several times without giving up their extrarelational activities. For tomcats, infidelity is part of a sexual pattern that began long before marriage and is likely to continue even if marriage ends. Of all Casanovas, they most clearly seem to suffer from an addictive disorder, one that rages even amid the security of marriage and the ashes of divorce.

Sam, forty-three, is a middle-level executive in the San Francisco office of a national insurance company. He has the air of someone who is used to more power than his position carries, and he often tells women that he is a senior officer in his firm. His first marriage ended when his wife discovered that he was being unfaithful to her. "I was glad to be finished with it," Sam admits, "because my first wife really hated sex. She had no interest at all in oral sex, which I like very much. Her attitude was, 'You want me to touch you *where!?*' It wasn't as though I had immoral or abnormal desires."

After four years of renewed bachelorhood, during which he had brief sexual encounters with dozens of different women, Sam remarried. He describes Elaine, his second wife, as "a wonderful person, my confidante, my best friend. She takes care of the house. She takes care of the kids. She does everything that the good American wife is supposed to do." But Elaine too seems unequal to the demands of his libido: "She's just not a very sexual person. Her idea of sex is more of a physical holding, a caring, being caressed kind of thing. She wants the physical closeness, which I like, too—don't get me wrong. But I also really enjoy intercourse, I enjoy it a lot, and my wife really doesn't all that much. During our first seven years of marriage, we averaged sex only once every two weeks."

Sam needs, or feels he needs, more than this, and he has been pursuing sex outside his marriage since shortly after the wedding. For the first few years, he favored the anonymous, one-night encounters he was familiar with from earlier on. He went to bars or clubs three nights a week, connected with someone and then had sex with her at her apartment or, occasionally, in a parked car. After a while the physical and emotional costs of this regime caught up with him: "I began to feel that it was all sort of hollow and sordid. It wasn't just that I wanted intercourse. I wanted conversation, warmth, understanding, and you don't get that in a one-night stand. Also, I was starting to worry about bringing something back home—at that time it was herpes, before the whole AIDS thing started."

At present Sam dates two women who work in his office. He sees each of them at least once a week and sometimes over the weekends, telling his wife that he has to travel for business. Neither mistress knows about the other, and one doesn't even know that he is married. In addition there are four other women whom he meets every few weeks for an evening of casual sex. He doesn't see either of his girlfriends as casual: he claims to care deeply about them.

Of course, he has cared about other women, too. He once came very close to leaving his wife for another coworker. "But in the end," he recalls, "I just ran back home. I was like some little kid who's tried to run away and suddenly realizes that he doesn't know how to cross the street. I had all these good intentions of changing, of being a faithful husband, et cetera, et cetera. But after two weeks, they just went up in smoke. I called up the girlfriend again. It's always like that. I don't know what I'm doing anymore. Maybe I'm neurotic. Or maybe I just like to get laid."

Crass and sentimental, guilt-ridden and insouciant, Sam embodies the contradictory modes of thought and behavior that characterize tomcats. In many ways, he resembles other Casanovas. Like a hitter, he has had impersonal sex with dozens of different partners. Like a romantic, he has sought something more, and occasionally found it in short, idealized love affairs. Like a juggler, he uses love affairs as counterweights, balancing one against the other with instinctive deftness. He's a versatile adulterer, who has both casual lovers and "steady" girlfriends, who sometimes lies about his marital status and sometimes tells the truth. He is a manipulator who himself often feels overwhelmed by sexual and romantic compulsions. He is a cautious man who nevertheless takes appalling risks with his marriage and career. Enjoying his relationship with his wife and the ordered life he shares with her, he still seems driven to jeopardize them: "There's a part of me that likes living on the edge of danger," Sam says. "I'm not sure that I want to stay married. I've been torn and I'm torn now—between leaving my marriage and staying in it. Sometimes I think I'm just waiting for something to push me over the edge."

EVERYTHING A WIFE IS NOT

For tomcats, infidelity seems to serve an economy of desire. Something is lacking at home, they tell you. Sex, warmth, communication—their wives simply won't, or can't, provide it. And so, their rationale goes, they are forced to look elsewhere. Like romantics, Sam seeks fulfillment from specialists. For quick, uncomplicated and affectless sex, he turns to Judiths. For intimacy, understanding and the security of a longer relationship, he turns to Lucretias. I saw the same pattern among several other men I spoke with, who presented themselves as so many discriminating consumers, combing the markets for whatever was missing from their domestic larders.

But these canny shoppers are perpetually dissatisfied. Sex with a Judith, no matter how casual in its contemplation and performance, has a hidden price tag, an aftertaste of puritanical guilt and dread. Those women, envisioned as little more than disembodied mouths, breasts and vulvas, carry with them the risks of madness and infection, blackmail and entrapment. In John Cheever's story "The Five-Forty-Eight," a lonely woman who invites her boss up to her room for an evening of sex ends up stalking him with a gun. For tomcats, infidelity is unconsciously tainted, and the taint extends to those who collaborate in it. Unwilling to take responsibility for their adulterous impulses, they project their desires onto the women who fulfill them, turning their partners into temptresses, the Eves who hand them the fatal apple. When a tomcat has sex with a Judith, what occurs is less a mutual giving and taking of pleasure than a mutual degradation, in which each partner becomes the other's "piece," a gobbet of flesh to be drained and cast aside. The anxiety that tomcats project onto their one-night stands is the sinner's dread of punishment: we should not forget that Judith, the warrior-whore, is a distant cousin of the Furies, the hideous avengers of Greco-Roman mythology.

Gnawed by unconscious guilt yet uncapable of fidelity, tomcats need to elevate their illicit desires and endow them with the sweet limpidity of romantic yearning. In Sam's affairs with Lucretias, sexual excitement takes second place: his long-term partners are usually less experienced than he is and, like Alan, he savors the role of their erotic tutor. The Lucretia is not a slut, but a font of virtue, at least at the onset of the relationship. Sam's description of the women he finds most attractive these days—"articulate, intelligent, dynamic and successful"—reflects his own idealized self-image and suggests that what he and his girlfriends do on their nights together is more like networking than lovemaking. Idealization is at its peak while the affair is still unconsummated, as poignant as a schoolboy's crush. One man told me of a liaison that began with a woman kissing his hand in gratitude after he had slapped her out of a hysterical crying jag, a gesture that might have been lifted from Cecil B. De Mille or Erich von Stroheim. Tears, a blow, a kiss: "nothing moves or attracts me so much as a woman weeping."

Where Judith supplies the tomcat with a quick sexual fix, Lucretia's appeal has much to do with *duration*—the affection she gives him is lasting, uncritical and unwavering over time. She is, the tomcat tells you, understanding and supernaturally patient, grateful for her lover's weekly visit, willing to wait forever on the off chance that he may one day leave his wife, willing to abide with him even if he never does. In many ways tomcats see this woman as a perfected version of their wives, more generous, more tolerant and more appreciative of any attention that comes her way. Better still, Lucretia takes the part of an ideal mother, the refuge from job and home, the shoulder to lean on, the bosom to weep on. Like Judith, she is everything a wife is not.

But Lucretia must be tested. Tomcats, like romantics, place grave burdens on their lovers' devotion. In his long-term affairs, Sam prescribes rules as rigorous as any imposed on a fairy-tale princess: "She's got to understand that she can't call me at home. If we work together, she can't get too intimate during office hours. And she's got to realize that we can get together only one or two nights a week, max."

Few women can stand up to such testing. No matter how patient and uncomplaining they may be, the tomcat's Lucretias eventually make demands—or are perceived to do so. "If I let myself get attached to a woman and keep seeing her, I begin to feel that I'm choking," Sam says. "She starts trying to hold me too tight, wanting to see me more. And I just can't accept the pressure that puts on me." Whether those pressures are real or imaginary, tomcats always flee from them, terminating their affairs outright or replacing their old lovers with new ones.

GOOD MOTHERS, BAD MOTHERS

Both Judith and Lucretia are imaginary constructs, originating in the tomcat's unconscious and imposed on women who are usually unaware that they are acting out predetermined roles. The role of Lucretia is especially unstable: if she starts out as a virgin, she is soon transformed into a dutiful and unconditionally loving surrogate wife or mother. Ultimately, she undergoes a further transformation in the tomcat's unconscious and becomes a bad wife/mother, who makes continual demands on her rebellious husband/son.

The origins of these splits and transformations are manifold, arising from the tomcat's cultural milieu and from the circumstances of his early childhood. According to John Money, the division of women into whores and virgins is a legacy of the Mediterranean beginnings of Western civilization. In the city-states of the ancient Middle East, the system of slavery was as much sexual as economic. Just as the wealthy profited from the labor of many men, they also enjoyed the sexual and child-rearing services of many women, and the greater a man's wealth and power, the more wives and concubines he could keep in his harem. Of course, there had to be an alternative for the common masses: if the wealthy reveled in the exclusive attentions of their concubines, the poor had to share whores. "The whorehouse, the public harem, is the counterpart of the seraglio, the private harem," Money says. "The institution of the double standard is complete. Women are either whores or madonnas." Although the double standard dates back to pre-Christian times, it has been enshrined in Christian mores and seems especially pervasive in Catholic societies, where every wife is a de facto madonna and unattached women are still sometimes treated like whores.

This is not to say that our culture directs every husband to be unfaithful; its injunctions against infidelity are just as strong. Sam's adultery, with its compulsive repetitions and incestuous overtones, seems to spring from a more primitive, unconscious source. The psychoanalyst Melanie Klein theorized that the infant cannot tolerate the fact that the same mother will sometimes offer nourishment and sometimes withhold it. How can the woman who evokes so much love and gratitude also arouse such frustration and rage? And what will become of her if he gets too angry with her? What will become of *him*, who is dependent on her for his very life? Klein believed that the infant resolves this ambiguity and wards off the unpleasant feelings it engenders by splitting the mother into two parts. The "good mother" becomes his first object of desire; the "bad mother" is projected outward, so that she cannot contaminate or threaten his image of the loving and nourishing good mother.

All this happens very early in life—according to Klein, within the child's first year. Ordinarily, he grows up to reconcile those primitive images into the complex inner portrait of a real person. But sometimes, especially in conditions like pathological narcissism and borderline disorder, the image of the mother remains split. The adult still carries within him the imaginary constructs of infancy. When he falls in love, it is always with an idealized good mother, and his love is always accompanied by impulses of hatred that must be projected elsewhere. This scenario seems a remarkably accurate description of the way in which tomcats alternately romanticize and devalue their extramarital partners.

THE WITHHOLDING WIFE

The way in which tomcats perceive their mistresses mirrors their attitude toward their wives, who inspire in them extremes of great love and corrosive hatred, dependence and fear. They turn to their wives for emotional nourishment and often feel deep tenderness and affection for the women they compulsively betray. For all his ambivalence about marriage, Sam plainly adores Elaine and believes that she "does everything that the good American wife is supposed to do." Implicit in this phrase is the idea of stereotypical perfection—of perfect "wifeliness." One receives from these men an anachronistic impression of a legion of dutiful and attentive women who keep spotless homes, cook wholesome meals and raise cheerful and obedient children.

Strength, duty and industry—these are attributes of a good mother, and the affection that tomcats feel for their wives is more filial than conjugal, lacking a strong erotic component. They often complain that their wives are uninterested in sex or unwilling to experiment sexually. If we are to believe them, these are the women who preferred cuddling to the dreaded "act" in response to Dear Abby's famous survey. This may reflect the tomcat's penchant for women who are sexually timid or repressed. But they also seem to actively desexualize their spouses, denying them the erotic power they bestow so liberally on their lovers, and especially on their one-night stands: "With my wife," Sam says, "I don't have that same drive, that same urgency. It makes me feel guilty. Why can't I get the same pleasure out of loving her that I get from other women?" Sexual desire often wanes in the course of a long marriage, but the decline is almost inevitable when the wife fills a maternal function:

in such a union the act of love becomes an act of incest. Because they need their wives to play the role of the good mother, tomcats symbolically rob them of their sexuality—and rob themselves of the sexual satisfaction that other men find in marriage.

Few tomcats acknowledge their role in the desexualization of the marriage: the blame is almost always placed on their wives, whom they stigmatize as too prudish, too passive or, most damningly, as just not sexy enough. Thus, those good mothers are transformed into bad ones. No matter how well they run their households, no matter how loyally they support their husbands, they appear to withhold love in the only form that tomcats recognize. Withholding is a recurring metaphor in their descriptions of their wives. When they don't withhold sex, they withhold affection, understanding or—in two-career marriages—money. Even tomcats' complaints of boredom are tinged with accusation, as though their spouses were maliciously depriving them of some essential stimulus. Alongside the image of the dutiful and supportive mother, or partially obscured beneath it, like an underpainting beneath a Renaissance canvas, lies its inverse, a flint-hearted monster, the bad mother of the eternally dry breast.

But even the good mother is a problematic figure for these men. Like romantics and jugglers, tomcats need ceaseless, unconditional love—the kind of love only a mother can provide. But such love may have fearful consequences: mother might suck her little boy back into her womb. It is safer for tomcats to see their wives as adversaries, for if they let themselves become too close to their spouses they risk losing themselves, as Fred fears he has lost himself to his wife: "If I climax, she climaxes. If I don't climax, she can't. Sometimes I don't know if I'm screwing or masturbating."

In their marriages, tomcats are at constant pains to assert their separateness and control, to establish boundaries that their wives cannot transgress. One method is to retreat from intimacy: these men tend to be secretive, keeping secrets from their wives simply to have something they can call exclusively their own. The other method, of course, is infidelity, which for tomcats is both a search for affection and validation and a flight from mothers who both deprive them and threaten to devour them. As compulsive as this flight is, it is also largely symbolic. Few tomcats actually leave their wives of their own free will. When a tomcat's marriage dissolves, it's often because his spouse cannot tolerate his cheating any longer.

THE COLLUSIVE MARRIAGE

Because his extramarital affairs are gestures of autonomy and need, the tomcat usually wants his wife to know about them. Given his compulsiveness, it would probably be impossible for him to keep them hidden. Often, he "advertises" his transgressions in much the same way that jugglers do. Not surprisingly, the tomcat's philandering frequently surfaces at times when he feels especially close to his wife. Shortly after his fifth wedding anniversary, one man I spoke with brought a woman back to his apartment for the first time, only to have his wife return in the middle of the act. Any event that seems to lessen the tomcat's emotional distance from his wife is likely to be followed by a blatant infidelity, a sexual declaration of independence.

Behind such behavior lies not only defiance but guilt. Unlike many Casanovas, tomcats suffer from overt conflicts about their sexual behavior. They feel guilty for violating their marriage vows and for betraying women to whom they are genuinely attached. They probably experience a vestige of the original guilt that children feel at separating from their mothers. Guilt is a pervasive, gnawing presence in these men's lives, requiring constant justification, rationalization and denial. Some tomcats try to get their spouses to condone their infidelity and even urge them to have affairs themselves. Especially during the liberated 1970s, many experimented with open marriages and swinging. The guilt that afflicts these men is all the more striking because it does not—cannot—curb their infidelity. Indeed, it often exacerbates it, creating an endless spiral of betrayal, remorse and belligerent defiance, which in turn necessitates further acts of adultery.

The ways in which women respond to their husbands' recurring infidelities—and to Casanovas in general—will be discussed at length in the fourth section of this book. For the time being, we can say that tomcats' marriages are generally collusive, with both partners perpetuating the adulterous cycle. This collusion takes three primary forms: denial, policing and appeasement, which will be familiar to anyone who has encountered them in alcoholic and addictive families. Denial is characterized by a fearful avoidance of the issue of infidelity. Tomcats will often go to extraordinary lengths to preserve a facade of normalcy, enlisting friends and co-workers in their cover-ups. Their wives often come from homes where one parent was an alcoholic or drug addict. They may have been childhood victims of physical or sexual abuse, and they are already experienced at ignoring painful realities. Between the betrayer and the betrayed lies an atmosphere of silence and unrelieved tension, the prelude to a thunderstorm that never breaks. The pattern is best summed up by one woman who finally divorced her husband after lengthy counseling: "I could never bear to face the fact that Ed was cheating on me. I still haven't figured out why I was so afraid to confront him. He wasn't a violent man; I even think he was a little scared of me. But my father was violent, and I suppose I figured that Ed would lash out at me in the same way that he had. For years we had this routine where I'd ask him where he was going at night, and he'd say, 'Out,' and I'd just say, 'Oh.' Only 'Oh.' It took years before I stopped pretending to be asleep when he came home. I used to go through his laundry, and if I found a woman's phone number or a stained handkerchief, I'd just throw it in the trash, out of sight. That was my little rebellion—throwing his handkerchiefs away instead of washing them for him. Every so often he'd tell me he was out of handkerchiefs, and I'd go to the store and buy him some new ones."

It is far more common for a tomcat's wife to monitor and confront his infidelity in the hope that she can somehow force him to give it up. The problem with policing is that it constitutes an objection rather than a correction, while placing the tomcat and his wife in much the same relation as an incorrigible criminal and the cop who keeps arresting him. The women who practice it are rarely prepared to divorce their husbands, and consciously or unconsciously their men know it. The confrontations may actually impel them to philander more blatantly rather than appear to give in to external pressure. For both partners, pride becomes the issue of paramount importance: the wife objects to being "treated like dirt"; her husband refuses to be "pussy-whipped." Thus policing degenerates into an empty ritual of threat, counterthreat and accusation, in which each partner goes through the motions of preserving his or her dignity while the infidelity goes on unchecked.

One of the most painful aspects of a tomcat's marriage is the sense of helplessness it instills in both partners. The tomcat cannot stop being unfaithful. His wife can neither force him to change nor bring herself to leave him. Sometimes, then, she tries to change herself. Appeasement is the last defense against powerlessness. In it, the responsibility for infidelity shifts from the tomcat to his wife, who comes to feel that if only she were sexier, more supportive or more understanding, her husband would at last be faithful. The tomcat, of course, is all too happy to support this fiction, which at once absolves him of blame and holds out the possibility of redemption: maybe his wife *can* change enough that he won't feel the need to cheat. Appeasement underlies the philosophy of the "total woman," which urges women to make themselves over in the image of their husbands' sexual fantasies, to become both wife and Other Woman. Indeed, it seems to be the prevailing notion behind all the recent books and programs that teach women how to anticipate and satisfy the needs of difficult men. From *The Total Woman* to *Women Men Love, Women Men Leave*, authorities have taught wives how to swing with their men, how to listen to them, nourish them, validate and put up with them—how to do everything, in short, but identify their own desires and satisfy them appropriately.

There are other patterns of complicity between tomcats and their spouses. In some marriages the wife seems to accept her husband's infidelity, chiding him for his escapades as she might for blowing ten dollars at a card game. Such acceptance often resembles another mask of denial. There is no question that it *is* possible to live with a spouse's continual infidelity. The question is always whether one *wants* to live with it. That question is one that husbands and wives must answer for themselves, according to their feelings, their values and, in the plague years of the 1980s, their recognition of the risks that attend all nonmonogamous sexuality.

What should be clear from this discussion is how resistant a collusive marriage is to change—as resistant as the tomcat himself. In a collusion based on denial, the tomcat goes on philandering while his wife continues to avoid the evidence of his behavior. Each evasion breeds another, and the original pain of infidelity is compounded by a widening rift of silence, anxiety and suppressed anger. Policing only reinforces the incestuous nature of the relationship between the betrayed wife and the betraying husband: the one is all the more clearly a scolding and domineering bad mother, the other all too obviously a bad boy, whose only avenue to manhood is to flout the mother's restrictions. Appeasement may temporarily alleviate the tomcat's guilt, but it subjects his wife to the impossible strain of becoming a different woman, with no guarantee that the transformation will pay off. An appeasing wife may spend a lifetime molding herself into the kind of lover her husband wants—or thinks he wants—without ever satisfying his desires, for he will never want just one woman. The complicity between tomcats and their spouses produces a closed system that is probably more durable than many healthy marriages. If infidelity is a bid for freedom, collusion only widens the prison walls, enclosing the jailer along with the jailed.

THE FEAR IS A BLOW TO THE HEART

In tomcats, too, we see the true force and persistence of the Casanova complex. These men often come to marriage in flight from old patterns of promiscuity or inconstancy only to find that their drives are as tyrannical as ever. Perhaps crueler, for compulsion is now joined with the sense of having violated a vow and the knowledge that they are injuring women they love. Of all Casanovas, tomcats are the most likely to try to change their behavior, but their attempts are usually as effective as the New Year's resolutions of an alcoholic. They may go from one-night stands to longer extramarital relationships or try to assuage their guilt by "domesticating" infidelity through swinging and wife swapping. Some tomcats may convince themselves that their problems originate with their wives and disappear as soon as they find new, more sympathetic partners: they only find new mothers to replace the ones they fled. The tomcat's dichotomy of good and bad mothers is as inescapable as the juggler's obsession with unconditional love or the hitter's quest for a zipless fuck. It is the form his sickness takes. It is the baggage that remains with him even when he has stowed the last of his possessions in the drawers and closets of a new home where a new wife waits for him.

"I'm trying to change," Sam says. "I'm in therapy to try to change the way I am. I know I have a problem, but on some level I still like it, and how do you change a problem that you like? I still like the things that I do; I just don't like the way I am. I don't have the self-discipline. I have all these good intentions about my marriage and my wife, but I have no goddamned self-discipline. If I see a woman walking down the street...It's the sense of newness. Why can't I get past that? I just literally can't give up looking for the new thing, fantasizing about the new thing, lusting after the new thing. I don't know how long I can go on like this. I'm getting old. How long can I still interest them? A great fear I have is that one day I'm going to end up alone. And that fear is like a blow to the heart."

PART THREE

The Making of
the Casanova

CHAPTER TEN

"Trying to Make Someone Love Me": The Family of the Womanizer

THE EXAMPLE OF LORD BYRON

...I have been all my life trying to make someone love me.
—Lord Byron

George Gordon, the sixth Lord Byron, was born with a clubfoot in 1788, in virtual poverty. His father was an incessant gambler and philanderer. He had married for money and once he had exhausted his wife's inheritance, he abandoned her and their young son. His attitude toward his family is captured in a letter he wrote to his sister in 1791, when George was three: "...[Mrs. Byron] is very amiable at a distance; but I defy you and all the Apostles to live with her for two months, for, if any body could live with her, it was me....For my son, I am happy to hear he is well; but for his walking, 'tis impossible, as he is club-footed."

Byron's mother, Catherine Gordon, was a plain, awkward woman who never recovered from her infatuation with her husband and never forgave his cavalier treatment of her. Her son became the vessel for her thwarted, wildly demonstrative love and her vicarious anger at the husband who had left her. She cared for him devotedly but also scolded him for his lameness; she alternately indulged and smothered him. The child was stubborn and strong-willed; she accused him of heartlessness. Throughout his youth he was embarrassed by her emotional and often angry outbursts and took great pains to distance himself from her.

Although his father was absent from Byron's life, he was constantly held up as a negative example to his son, who as far as Mrs. Gordon was concerned was distressingly like him. In later years Byron recalled that "my mother, when she was in a rage with me ...used to say, 'Ah, you little dog, you are a Byron all over; you are as bad as your father.'" Was it heredity or this maternal indoctrination that made Byron, in his turn, a spendthrift and a womanizer? How much of his later character can we attribute to his seduction at age nine by a family maidservant? What is clear is that Byron grew up without a real male presence in his life and with a mother who loved him narcissistically—as a surrogate and scapegoat for her absent husband and a convenient object of longing and rage. His deformity was at once a source of attention and a focus of shame. His mother's oscillating behavior and her frequent comparisons of the son to the father imparted two messages to the young Byron: that men were cruel, irresponsible creatures who hurt women, and that women continued to love them anyway.

The Casanova complex is more than a way of acting. It is a disorder of the feelings characterized by the compulsive—one should say addictive—pursuit and abandonment of women or by symbolic flight through infidelity and multiple relationships. The men afflicted with it define their relations with women chiefly in sexual terms and place an obsessive emphasis on sexual frequency, variety and performance. Often they also suffer from parallel addictions to drugs, alcohol, work or gambling. Emotionally, they exhibit diminished capacities for intimacy and commitment, which seem to stem respectively from deep-seated feelings of worthlessness and impotence. Among Casanovas—especially among romantics, nesters and jugglers—we see a split between "true" and "false" personalities, the one fearful and dependent, the other confident and seductive. Frequently, they have difficulty expressing anger and instead act it out in the sexual arena. Casanovas appear to relate to women not as separate, autonomous beings, but only as narcissistic objects, sources of ego gratification and refuges from psychic unrest. For these men, women and sex serve the same function as drugs or alcohol, providing a high that is at once exhilarating and numbing. Thus women are both exalted and vengefully degraded and are perceived, sometimes simultaneously, sometimes alternately, as virgins and whores, Lucretias and Judiths, good mothers and bad mothers. Casanovas respond to these different archetypes by oscillating between engagement and detachment, romanticism and cynicism, pursuit and abandonment.

What follows is my attempt to trace the causes of this disorder in the childhoods of Casanovas. The attempt is more an educated hypothesis than a thorough, scientific model: I am not a psychiatrist or psychoanalyst, after all, only one of the afflicted, and my perceptions will differ from a medical professional's in the same way that the memoirs of a Russian exile will differ from a study by a Sovietologist. Nor can any single explanation successfully encompass all Casanovas. Some are more damaged than others, and their conditions range from ordinary neurosis to pathological narcissism and borderline personality disorder. It further seems to me that traditional Freudian psychology can provide only a partial explanation for the ways in which people think and act. As a disorder that closely resembles addiction, the Casanova complex may also have a hereditary or physiological component; as yet we have no way of knowing whether some people are genetically or chemically "pre-disposed" toward womanizing. Still another misgiving I have is that psychology often seems overly deterministic in its attribution of adult behavior to childhood factors—to assume that because our parents did x, y and z we are bound to like wearing ladies' dresses, spend ourselves into hopeless debt or flee from our lovers the moment we rise from their beds. Little allowance is made for the fact that people from remarkably similar backgrounds may take remarkably different directions in life and even sometimes escape from final sentences of neurosis and worse. If we are indeed condemned to illness, there is no denying that some of us choose health. The reasons for this choice remain mysterious.

The following case histories and the interpretation that follows them, then, are descriptive rather than prescriptive—road signs and not maps.

ED

We are already familiar with Ed from the chapter on drifters. At thirty-six, he has never enjoyed a relationship that lasted longer than five months. He has never fallen in love, nor has he mourned a single one of the many women he has left. Outwardly cheerful and unshakably self-confident, he often betrays an undercurrent of depression. After years of sexual adventuring, he is beginning to worry that he will spend the rest of his life alone.

Ed's parents were middle-class and of Scotch, Irish and German descent. He was born in Detroit, where his father owned a small business. Ed was their first child. He was followed two years later by a sister. Because he was an older son and gifted with a quick mind and a sunny disposition, he was pampered by both parents, placed in private schools and showered with gifts. His parents had grown up during the Depression, and they had a terror of poverty and deprivation. They overfed both children; Ed was chubby until he entered college.

Ed describes his parents' marriage as close and affectionate. His father, a large bearlike man whose body was covered with coarse hair, was the unquestioned head of household during Ed's childhood. Although he worked long hours—often till ten at night—he also supervised the family's finances and his children's education. He and his wife appear to have enjoyed a vigorous sex life; Ed recalls overhearing the sounds of their lovemaking from the time he was very little. "When I was four," he remembers, "I found one of my old man's condoms in a bedroom drawer. I asked him, 'Daddy, what are those?' 'Oh, that's a balloon,' he said. I didn't know what a condom was until I was fifteen, the first time I slept with a girl." Ed's father inspired in him both adoration and fear, for he was a stern disciplinarian and his temper was easily roused: he spanked the children for small transgressions. When Ed was fifteen, his father thrashed him for coming home late from a date with a girl.

Ed's mother was clearly overshadowed by this powerful and vital man. When Ed was little, she relegated all decisions about the children's upbringing to her husband. If Ed misbehaved, she would call her husband at work and ask him what to do: usually, punishment was deferred until he came home. She could not or would not help the children with their homework; early on Ed and his sister learned to call their father for assistance. When Ed was six his father's business folded. Ed knew nothing about it at the time, for the bankruptcy was not discussed and his family maintained its former standard of living. But under the strain of financial uncertainty, his mother suffered a nervous breakdown. She spent the next year in her bedroom, heavily sedated, while the children were cared for by nursemaids and baby-sitters.

To support his family Ed's father started a new business—a small chain of motels in Atlanta. For the next five years, he spent most of his time in Georgia, returning only for brief visits or summoning his wife and children during the summer months. Although his parents' relationship remained close, Ed's mother was now thrust into a position of unaccustomed responsibility. By Ed's account, she became a zealous and attentive mother, "the kind who'd call up your schoolteacher to see why she'd given you a C. Her problem was she didn't know how to deal with a boy, especially because I was an athletic, smart-assed kid. She wouldn't let me go out and play ball without sticking some Band-Aids in my pocket. I remember once I was fighting with this kid—I was winning, too—and she stepped in and broke it up because she was scared I'd get hurt." At the same time, though, she treated him as a confidant and companion—the man of the family. "It was a privilege," he says, "but it was also a hassle sometimes, because she'd go from treating me like a little boy to treating me like a man."

When Ed was twelve he moved to Georgia with his mother and sister. The family was now reunited, but he had entered a period of adolescent rebellion. "I started fighting with both of them. My dad was pissed off because my grades went down. He was always telling me that I had to make something of myself. And then, when I started messing with girls—I was chubby, but I was tall and good-looking and girls went after me right away—my mom was all worried. She was scared that I'd 'waste myself' on the wrong girl. The moment she knew I was seeing someone she'd say, 'She's not good enough for you.' Who would have been?" His adolescence was thus marked by loud and bitter quarrels with both parents, which came to an end when his father died of a heart attack when Ed was sixteen. He had to postpone college for three years while his father's affairs were settled. Even then his mother remained shattered by her husband's death. She died two years later, when Ed was in his junior year of college.

ERIC

Eric is a forty-eight-year-old mathematician employed by a Silicon Valley computer firm. He has been married and divorced and has two children whom he rarely sees. Up until three years ago he was a member of an Asian religious sect and lived for a time in a communal village, where he was part of a group marriage that comprised seven members. He now lives with a woman he met at the commune but has another regular partner with whom he spends weekends. Periodically, he sleeps with other women, whom he meets through a vast, informal network of coreligionists and science-fiction buffs. He considers his sexuality an extension of his New Age spiritual and political values and eschews monogamy on the same principle that he refuses to vote: "It would be buying into the system." He is haunted by fears of aging and of "exhausting" his sexual options. Bored and irritated with both of his present lovers, he nevertheless dreads reentering what he calls "the market." He believes that his appearance (he is some thirty pounds overweight) and unconventional views will drive most women away and fears that he won't find it easy to meet new, untried partners within his small community of interest.

Eric remembers little of his early childhood. He grew up in a small city in Texas, the youngest child—the only son—of a sometime insurance agent and a devoutly religious housewife. He had three sisters. Through most of his childhood the family lived on the edge of poverty; his alcoholic father was frequently unemployed.

Even when he was working, most of his wages went to pay off old debts; Eric lived in a succession of rented houses that "were always teetering on the edge of decay."

As the only son, Eric enjoyed special attention during his early childhood: "My mother tells me I was the favorite." However, as he grew older he turned into a studious, withdrawn and physically uncoordinated child, a constant affront to a father who expected his son to be outgoing and rough-and-tumble. He frequently called Eric a sissy and a misfit and exposed him to the ridicule of his drinking companions as well. "I remember him coming home from the bar with a bunch of his friends one afternoon—I must have been around six—and demanding that I play catch with him. Now I couldn't throw a ball at all competently, and he knew it. He threw me the ball and somehow I caught it, but when I tried to throw it back—well, it was pitiful. They all started laughing, and he said something like, 'See, I told you, the kid throws worse than a girl.'"

When Eric's father was drinking, he was often violent. He attacked everyone in the family, but Eric believes that he bore the brunt of the assaults. During the beatings, his mother's response was to pray loudly without intervening. Afterward she would tend to Eric's injuries, tell him to forgive his father and make him kneel with her in prayer. When he expressed anger, she told him that he was being sinful—a true Christian didn't harbor wrath. She admonished Eric to follow her example of piety and forbearance, to consider her own trials and the faith with which she met them. Eric attributes his present unconventional beliefs to his early sense that his mother's Christianity was hollow and ineffectual: "It was always Jesus this, Jesus that, but Jesus didn't keep my father from beating the shit out of me. And He didn't comfort me afterward. The conclusion I came to quite early on was that Jesus was a hoax or that He was utterly indifferent to what His children did to each other."

When Eric was sixteen his father deserted the family. They moved to Kansas to live with his mother's relatives. Although he was relieved to be free of his father's abuse, Eric found the climate of unrelieved piety unbearable and left home soon afterward, enlisting in the army and then attending college on a veteran's loan. He is still bitter about his childhood and has virtually no contact with his family. "My mother sees me as a heathen, and I suppose that's what I am," he says. "The fact that I'm divorced is bad enough. God knows what she'd say if she knew what I've been doing since then."

SAUL

I first discussed Saul as an example of the thrill-seeking mentality that is so common among Casanovas. He is also a romantic, whose relationships with women are brief and volatile, beginning on a note of exaltation and ending in boredom and resentment. Like most romantics, he is a perfectionist. He expects his women to be eternally compliant, beautiful and responsive; he expects himself to be always suave and virile. Any lapse from those ideals fills him with anxiety and bitterness. At thirty-six, he has lived with many attractive women but has yet to stay with one for more than six months. Like Ed, he worries that he will never know a permanent attachment and will spend his old age alone.

Although he gives off an air of cultivated chic, Saul grew up in drab surroundings, in the warrens of Levittown, New York. He is the younger son of immigrant Jews—his parents had immigrated to the United States from Poland. His father was a jeweler, his mother a housewife. During our interview, Saul seemed embarrassed by his childhood and origins. He hated the house he grew up in, which was indistinguishable from the houses around it. He disliked having to share a room with his older brother. He was humiliated by his parents' heavy accents and provincial manners and by his father's religious orthodoxy. His father had wanted him to be a rabbi, a notion he dismissed as "ridiculous." One can see in him that seriocomic and peculiarly Jewish self-hatred that afflicts so many protagonists in the novels of Philip Roth.

Saul describes his parents' marriage as loveless. He can't recall ever seeing them hug or kiss. When I asked him if he could imagine them having sex, he laughed. "Absolutely not. I must be Jesus Christ, or else I was adopted. They never had sexual relations, I am convinced of that." His father worked long hours, partly, Saul believes, in order to escape from his wife's nagging, which was the only interaction between them. "Otherwise," Saul says, "they were like two strangers. They hardly talked to each other." He was not surprised that they divorced when he was fourteen.

Throughout his childhood Saul was alternately neglected and subjected to intense parental pressure. His father was gone all week except for Saturdays, when he took the boys to synagogue, the only activity Saul remembers sharing with him. His mother was over-protective, obsessed with her children's health, cleanliness and school grades. When she was happy with Saul, she praised him immoderately, calling him her "prince." When she was angry with him, she accused him of being cruel and selfish. She often complained to him about his father's shortcomings as husband and wage earner. "The message I got from my mother," Saul says, "was that my father was a total nonentity—a nebbish."

By the time he was fourteen, Saul was an internal exile from this regime. His parents' divorce gave him a liberty he hadn't had before. He stopped going to synagogue and no longer listened to his mother. "I just completely tuned her out." Sex became his principal avenue of escape. He had learned about it when he was nine, from his peers, and he now began pursuing sexual experience with the furtive intensity of someone tunneling out of a cell: "Necking, petting, groping—I did whatever I could with whoever I could find. The first time I went all the way I was seventeen. This friend of mine had a girlfriend. She had to be totally in love with him or a total idiot, because he exploited the hell out of her: you know, 'If you love me, you'll screw my friends.' There were three of us in a row. We were down at the beach, and she was inside a cabana and we took turns at her—in and out, no foreplay. I felt disgusted afterward."

Today Saul still seems to be rebelling against the strictures of his childhood. He rarely sees his parents. His mother wants him to marry and settle down, but the few times he introduced women to her, he was all too aware of her disapproval. "She wants me to marry a nice, plain Jewish girl who'll give her grandchildren, and I keep bringing her these shikses. She doesn't seem too disappointed when I tell her that we've broken up." Saul's brother, his only sibling, is also a Casanova, divorced for the second time at the age of thirty-nine. "He's even worse than I am," Saul says. "His ambition is to get blown by every girl in Miami." In part Saul feels that his sexuality is a reaction to his parents' loveless marriage and their Victorian values: "I look at my folks and all I see is duty, duty, duty. No tenderness, no passion, just duty. You get married, you make babies, you go to work and you bring home the bacon—really, I should say the corned beef—and your wife complains that you're never around and tells your kids you're a nebbish. That's not what I want from my life. Even loneliness has got to be better than that."

IMITATIONS OF CHILDHOOD

As different as these short biographies are, they have several features in common: what unites them is not so much individual incidents—the assaults of a drunken father or a mother's nervous
breakdown—as a general pattern of parental absence, neglect, in-
consistency and manipulation. I found the same factors in the
childhoods of nearly every Casanova I interviewed, regardless of
age, race, class, religion or geographical origin. As a rule these men
came from dysfunctional families, in which one or both parents
were either absent or inadequate. Their mothers were often ineffectual care-givers: during Ed's early childhood, his mother relied on
her husband to make the smallest decisions about his upbringing;
Eric's mother failed to protect him from his father's drunken rages
and couldn't even console him afterward. The care they gave their
sons was often oppressive, characterized by nagging and overpro-
tectiveness. Indeed, the love these men experienced in childhood
was often tainted by maternal narcissism: their mothers loved
them not as separate beings, but as extensions of themselves and as
vehicles of their own psychic dramas. When her husband went
away to start a new business, Ed's mother turned to him to fill the
vacuum. Saul's mother seems to have had similar expectations of
her younger son; she enlisted him as her ally in a guerrilla war
against her husband and, in her moments of tenderness, elevated
him to the status of an adored prince. By insisting that her battered
son pray with her after his father's beatings and forbidding him the
legitimate options of rage and mourning, Eric's mother forced him
to conform to her own rigid value system, one that might be appropriate for an adult but could scarcely address the incoherent suffering of a young child. The messages these mothers gave their sons
often seem wildly inconsistent. Were they good or bad, loved or despised? Were they to act like boys or like men? These Casanovas, in
effect, grew up without a sure sense of being loved and valued and
with schizoid notions of their place as children and individuals.

And there was little consolation in the love of their fathers: *they*
were absent, either physically or emotionally, during their sons'
critical years. Ed's father was away on business during much of his
childhood. Saul's father fled the house long before his wife divorced
him and had little interaction with his sons outside their Sabbath

outings. They often saw their fathers as weak and ineffectual; their mothers reinforced that impression by making them party to their marital grievances. How can you respect a man who your mother tells you is a nebbish? Often the father was not only inadequate but threatening, a physical and emotional terrorist. A high proportion were alcoholics, workaholics or compulsive gamblers, which made them unpredictable as well as inaccessible. The Casanovas I interviewed had not only grown up in a maternal void; they had grown up without adequate male figures on which to model themselves. The result was a barren imitation of childhood, in which love was confused with possessiveness, authority with violence and parental guidance with absurd rigidity or neglect.

FROM FUSION TO SEPARATENESS

To better understand the ramifications of this type of upbringing, we should consider the normal scenario of childhood. Before birth and in early infancy, every child enjoys a utopian fusion with his mother, whose body both contains and nourishes him. Even after birth, the baby experiences the connection between his mother and himself as a self-contained, symbiotic unit. In the narcissistic fantasy world of infancy, he is both the nurturer and the nurtured, all-powerful, pansexual and immortal. The universal tragedy of childhood lies in the necessity of leaving this Eden and gradually confronting one's separateness and powerlessness, the hard facts of gender and mortality. This process usually takes a lifetime; it entails a constant tension and mediation between conflicting drives— the desire for oneness and the need for separateness, the yearning for eternal childhood and the struggle for autonomous adulthood.

It has taken three generations of psychologists and psychoanalysts to help us realize how tortuous this process really is. To the infant, each new discovery of his limitations is a source of rage, terror and shame. At different stages in his development he dreams of possessing the mother and of devouring her, fears destroying her and being annihilated by her. Later on—between the ages of three and five, according to Freudian psychoanalysts—the male child's desire for union with his mother takes on sexual connotations and is accompanied by fear of castration by a vengeful father. Even more shatteringly, he comes to realize that he cannot fill his father's procreative role. No matter how loving and protective his parents may be, growing up is a series of brutal shocks, as though he were being kicked out of Eden over and over again.

According to orthodox psychoanalysts, the child's first buffer against his sense of isolation and dependency is the fantasy of omnipotent fusion, in which he sees his mother as an extension of himself and her ministration to him as evidence of his control: her breast is there for him, he imagines, because it is *part* of him, even *one* with him. We have seen how the child later deals with the inconsistencies in his mother's care by imaginatively splitting her in two, projecting the bad mother outward and incorporating the good one into his internal psychic repertory. His good mother is now inside him, in the safe house of his psyche, and when she leaves the room he can comfort himself by saying "Mommy." Much the same thing helps the boy resolve his Oedipal competition with his father: if his own little penis is unequal to the task of giving his mother a baby, he can magically assimilate his father's, providing himself with an internal model of masculine power and efficacy with which to identify. Competition turns to emulation. In the ideal course of development, the child eventually reconciles his first fantasies and mental images with perceptions of his real parents. He comes to acknowledge his separateness from his mother and his dependence on her care. Although he may still harbor an internal image of her as omnipotent and eternally nurturing, he comes to realize that his real mother is both good and bad—not so good as he had once imagined, not so awful as he had once feared. He continues to imitate his father even as he realizes that he is still a little boy. In time—and this is true for all of us, regardless of gender—he learns to be mother and father to himself.

What is remarkable about this whole process is that the child does most of the work himself. Apart from protection, love and nurturance, the role of the parents consists largely of giving him the necessary encouragement to do it. They must give him the models that he will eventually incorporate into his inner world and help him come to terms with his separateness and dependence. Often they must give him the language he needs to voice the fear, rage and grief that his discoveries cause him, and make those feelings safe enough for him to acknowledge and accept. Perhaps most important, they must be able to stand back as he grows away from them, to love him not only as a helpless infant but as a grown-up in the making. Reflecting the biases of his society, the psychologist D. W. Winnicott described this job as "good-enough mothering," which he summed up as "meet[ing] the omnipotence of the infant and to some extent mak[ing] sense of it."

HIS MAJESTY, KING BABY

Unfortunately, the mothering that most Casanovas received was not good enough. We can trace a large part of their disturbance to deficiencies or breakdowns in their early interactions with their mothers. At first glance, many of these men seem to have been recipients of maternal care that was *too good*—theatrically solicitous, overbearing and almost sexual in its intensity. Ed's mother was obsessed with his health and went to embarrassing extremes to protect him from physical injury; in his father's absence he became her cherished companion and confidant. Saul, too, had dethroned his father in his mother's esteem and become her little prince. The mothers of Casanovas seem to have had an unusual and highly exclusive identification with their sons: they were not only their offspring, but their fulfillment, bandages for their psychic wounds and hapless stand-ins for missing husbands and their own mothers and fathers. As one observer of this configuration notes: "One sometimes has the impression that there was no project in the parents' minds with regard to the child's future independence and adult sexual life."

The sons reacted to the inflated esteem in which their mothers held them in two ways. On the one hand, they perceived their mothers' narcissistic love as a kind of hunger, a desire to smother and devour. Often—and especially when their fathers were absent —these boys formed an unconscious image of women as insatiable voids which it was their hopeless task to fill. They never truly achieved the separation that is one of the milestones of childhood; instead, their sense of their personal boundaries remained blurred, and they were never quite sure where they began and their mothers ended. We can see the residue of these beliefs in the adult Casanova's fears of castration and entrapment by the opposite sex, in his fantasy that every woman expects him to be a perpetually erect fucking machine or a submissive "Mr. Wonderful." Their uneasy sense of boundaries is echoed in Fred's confusion as to whether he is making love to his wife or himself. For these men, every interaction with women conjures up the specter of engulfment by mothers who loved them hungrily and narcissistically—as extensions of themselves.

At the same time, Casanovas never quite relinquish the omnipotent and grandiose self-images of infancy. They continue to see themselves as what they were told they were: beautiful, special and even vitally important to their mothers' well-being. This inflated self-image was at one time a defense against the threat of annihilation: the only protection against an omnipotent and omnipresent parent is to become omnipotent oneself. In adulthood, such grandiosity can come across as self-confidence or thinly veiled conceit. It is what informs Ed's belief that he can pick up women effortlessly and Alan's fantasy of secret specialness. Casanovas are men who never acknowledged their limitations. In their innermost imaginations they remain "His Majesty, King Baby," the centers of their mothers' universe and the objects of their idolatrous love.

TRUE AND FALSE SELVES

It's tempting to see these Casanovas as having been spoiled by excessive love. But on closer examination, the love they knew as children turns out to have been painfully inconsistent. As solicitous as their mothers were of their physical well-being, they were oddly callous when it came to emotional needs. Like Ed's mother, they often seemed unsure of how to care for their sons. More disturbingly, these women placed rigid conditions on their love and could be hostile and rejecting when their sons failed to live up to their lofty expectations. When these women did not devour their sons, they abandoned them, exiling them from the vital field of their attention and approval.

According to D. W. Winnicott, such ambivalent care may produce a split in the child's ego. One self, the "false" one, is compliant and often prematurely independent: it is the facade with which the child meets the unrealistic demands of his parents. The other self, the "true" one, retreats inward. Because the child only gets approval when he is quiet and well-behaved, it is the false self with which he increasingly identifies. But as an adult, the Casanova is likely to feel empty and unreal and to suffer from a gnawing sense that some part of him remains unrecognized and unfed. He may believe that women only perceive his false self, but feel compelled to keep his true self hidden. He may fear that his partners love him only for his ability to satisfy them sexually or indulge their romantic yearnings. Yet he dare not drop this facade, for he feels that the facade is what makes him lovable. His true self—helpless, needy and angry—was rejected years ago and he lacks the courage, and often the ability, to find and expose it again. The inflated self-image of the Casanova turns out to be merely that, a thin, hyperextended membrane enclosing a core of unloved, unlovable self.

Most children eventually learn to assimilate their mothers' nurturing aspects, to become mothers to themselves. These cloven personalities never manage it; their real mothers were not truly nurturing to begin with. If Casanovas' false selves are confident and independent, their true selves are fearful and ravenous for comfort and validation. They will continue to seek nurturance—and even a sense of personal completion—from mother substitutes long after childhood has passed. The desperation that underlies this quest is usually disguised. Their grandiose egos forbid even the semblance of dependency, and their unconscious image of the mother as cannibal makes it dangerous to come too close to the object of desire: the only time Ed ever longed for a particular woman—his high-school girlfriend—was when she was safely on vacation in another state. Forced to adopt a facade of self-sufficiency and equating their own needs with the prospect of annihilation by needy mothers, Casanovas pursue gratification in secret while masquerading as indefatigable givers of love and sexual pleasure.

THE LOVER AS DRUG

A peculiarity of the Casanova's search is that its true end is not the mother, but a transitional object that offers an illusion of maternal nurturance. Transitional objects, such as baby blankets, dolls or stuffed animals, play a crucial role in the child's growth into an autonomous being. These objects become his first substitute for the absent mother; the child's ability to comfort himself with his woolen blanket stands in for the time when he will be able to comfort himself with an internal image of the mother. Transitional objects are also the first things that he actually controls and manipulates, and as such they provide him with the first real evidence of his power over the external environment. We have all noticed how dependent a young child is on a threadbare blanket or a battered teddy bear: that same dependence characterizes all those who have been stuck in the transitional phase—drug addicts, alcoholics and Casanovas. The allure of those comforting, tranquilizing objects is the same allure that alcohol has for the alcoholic and heroin for the addict. They not only hold out the promise of longed-for nurturance, they offer these men a sense of completion—of authenticity—that they otherwise lack. The problem, of course, is that a baby blanket—or a bag of heroin—is not a mother's breast: it provides only an illusion of sustenance, an illusion that vanishes as soon as the blanket is out of sight or the drug has passed through the bloodstream. Lacking the true ability to nurture themselves and possessing only the most fragile sense of personal identity, men like Ed, Eric and Saul must seek their transitional objects again and again or suffer the panic and despair of abandoned children.

It comes as no surprise that so many Casanovas also have drug or alcohol problems or use work or gambling to maintain psychic equilibrium. But for these men, *the primary drug is women.* They seek out new sexual partners compulsively, sometimes to the endangerment of health, careers and other relationships. Their objects of desire inspire in them the same love-hate that drugs inspire in the addict. In the initial pickup or courtship stages, women are longed-for good mothers, simultaneously promising excitement and relief. Within a few months, weeks or hours, though, those same women turn into repulsive, castrating bad mothers: they cannot satisfy their lovers, only drain them. Afterward Casanovas berate themselves for giving in to the brute summons of their glands ("Ven der putz shteht, ligt der sechel in drerd"), or regret what Derek calls yet one more "idiotic romantic notion." They promise themselves never to do it again. They may unconsciously seek punishment from their wives or girlfriends and make the same promises to them: "Honey, it's the last time—I *swear* it is." The endless cycle of longing, loathing and guilt will be familiar to anyone who has known alcoholism or addiction or lived with someone who suffers from them. In each case, the true drama is the frustrated quest for a maternal nurturance and validation that can never be recaptured because it was never experienced in the first place.

Although Casanovas are powerless over their sexual compulsions, the particular form of their addiction gives them a seductive illusion of power. To be a Casanova is to conquer and manipulate women, to *act on* them. What a relief to those who in childhood felt colonized and invaded by omnipotent mothers and still fear being subjugated as adults! Every time these men seduce women, they turn them into drugs—inanimate objects that can be ingested and then disposed of. Those presences, so distant, alluring and terrifyingly alive, are now things, like the toys and baby blankets that gave these men their first sense of mastery years before. The problem is that their partners refuse to stay inanimate: Saul's models keep demonstrating their pathetic and disturbing individuality; Ed's girlfriends sooner or later develop very human faults. They are no longer good drugs. Searching for reassuring, controllable mother substitutes, these men always find the devouring bad mothers of their early childhood, reborn again and again in different guises.

SONS WITHOUT FATHERS

The one-parent family, usually headed by a woman, is increasingly common in America. While it is harder for a single parent to raise children unassisted, there is no evidence that a woman cannot successfully take on roles that were once exclusively identified with fathers: breadwinning, protection and socialization. But in the psychic realm, and especially in regard to male children, a father performs two essential and intertwined functions. He acts as a separation between the boy and his mother and provides him with his earliest definition of what it is to be a man. Most of the men I interviewed grew up in households where the father was physically absent, emotionally distant or actually threatening. While they were adequately nourished and in due course learned to play with other children, they had no refuge from the invasive attentions of their mothers and, later, no effective male model to call their own.

All children at some point see their mothers as omnipotent and devouring. Without a father's mediating presence, this perception is likely to persist. For boys, the lack of a paternal barrier can heighten the fear of engulfment by the mother's womb. If father is gone, who else is there to fill that bottomless void, and how can a little boy hope to do so? In the father's absence, boys sometimes end up identifying excessively with their mothers. This identification conjures up not only the loss of self but the loss of gender. Many Casanovas fear being unmanned by their wives and lovers—not just castrated, but *feminized*. It is this fear that accounts for Saul's

195—

revulsion at the sight of his girlfriends' lingerie hanging in his bathroom and for Wayne's obsession with mastering his sexual partners.

To ward off this fear, Casanovas must deny their mothers' power while casting off all that is feminine within themselves. While they often display superficial insight into women (a result of their early identification with their mothers and one of the chief reasons for their romantic prowess), their attitude toward them is informed less by empathy than by triumphant contempt. Ed describes women as "packages"; Eric disparages his partners for thinking irrationally and acting "hyperemotionally." If these men see women as weak, passive, emotional and dependent, they categorically reject such traits within themselves. Instead, they cling to an ego-ideal that is strong, active, cool and self-sufficient—macho or hypermasculine. Behind such rigidity one detects a secret horror of the feminine. Indeed, one reason these men are forever in flight from their partners is their fear of being somehow "contaminated" by their femininity, of being feminized through sheer proximity.

To deny one's femininity also means denying an entire range of feelings. Neither Ed nor Eric has ever experienced more than a flicker of grief at the breakup of an affair; Ed has turned anger into a taboo and associates it with powerlessness and loss of control. In extreme cases, Casanovas seem to confuse one emotion with another: hurt with anger, anxiety and sadness with sexual desire. A child who is forbidden to express certain feelings will be unable to do so as an adult. And, if those feelings are further associated with a dreaded femininity, the grown Casanova will not only deny them, but cast them vigorously outside himself. In their relationships with women, these men observe a strict economy, allowing themselves to do and feel only what is "manly" while assigning all that is soft, irrational—in a word, "feminine" —to their partners.

THE INVENTION OF MANHOOD

Such defensive and caricatured masculinity points to a shaky identification with what is genuinely masculine. And, indeed, for these men there were no proper masculine role models. Not only were their fathers away much of the time, they were far from exemplary. How could Eric ever identify with the father who beat him during his drunken rages and humiliated him when he was sober? How could Saul model himself after an ineffectual nebbish? Lacking comforting images of manhood and terrified of fusing with their mothers, they had to invent their own masculinity. They did so in much the same way that Frankenstein built his monster, taking scraps of their fathers, pieces of other men and perhaps bits of the heroes of the pop culture of their youth: in Ed one detects a little of the cocky style of Jack Nicholson, while Saul, with his romantic posturings and *langueurs*, seems to have patterned himself on Leslie Howard and Roxy Music's Bryan Ferry. But above all these men defined themselves in opposition to their mothers, paring away anything that smacked of the feminine—tenderness, vulnerability, "weakness." The problem is that this masculine Frankenstein is a fragile thing, in imminent danger of falling apart at the slightest shock. It must be guarded constantly and shored up with repeated conquests.

When a boy constructs a psychic image of his father, its earliest and central feature is the phallus, which is not only a sexual organ but an archetype of strength, order and masculine procreative power. Those attributes are markedly absent from the masculinity of Casanovas. Instead, they seem to have a split image of the phallus. One image is vengeful and sadistic—the penis as hook or battering ram. It is what gives rise to the aggressive and sometimes cruel nature of these men's sexuality and to their tendency to treat women as disposable objects. Having patched together their maleness instead of acquiring it organically, Casanovas are left with an incomplete facsimile of manhood, cruel but not creative, powerful but not truly potent.

What is missing is the idea of the phallus as an instrument of union and fertility. Its absence is as wounding as the lack of an image of a nurturing mother, and it becomes the object of a search that is just as desperate as the search for maternal stand-ins. When Casanovas search for sexual partners they are seeking some token of their own maleness. The same search is said to underly the cruising of sexually compulsive homosexuals, and it's not surprising that a number of these men are sexually ambivalent. What is sought can be supplied by partners of either gender. What is desired is not love, nor even sexual gratification per se, but rather the sense of being filled, nurtured and made real. The only way these divided beings can feel like men is to do what "real men" are supposed to do: seduce women.

THE LOVER AS FETISH

But just as the drug-woman provides only a momentary comfort, so the phallus-woman offers only a brief illusion of masculinity. The seductions must be repeated again and again. To the scenario of addiction, we must add the scenario of fetishism, in which women serve a function akin to leather and lingerie. In classical psychoanalysis, fetishism is seen as phobia turned inside out, a way of warding off a paralyzing fear of castration by the father or engulfment by the mother. The fetish is less an object of desire than a defense against dread, and Casanovas display all the characteristic attitudes of the fetishist: their initial fascination with their sexual partners quickly turns into revulsion and sometimes seems intermingled with it; they often feel overwhelmed by their desires, bewitched by women or enslaved by their own genitals. At the same time, they are driven to prove their mastery over their lovers, to manipulate them verbally and exhaust them sexually. Like many fetishists, Casanovas often portray themselves as erotic pioneers who act out the drives that more timid men repress. Theirs is the excitement of men inventing their sexuality from scratch and the mixed fear and exaltation of children delving into the forbidden. Theirs is the skittish and obsessive dance of men flirting with their deepest fears.

In the Museum of Science in Boston I once saw an exhibit in which a small iron ball was suspended in air exactly halfway between two oppositely charged magnets: it was the tension between their charges that held the ball aloft, afloat in its own field of space. In an "ideal" family the child grows up in the field between his mother and father, identifying first with one and then with the other, but eventually growing away from both of them. With their intrusive mothers and absent or ineffectual fathers, Casanovas are in the same position as balls stuck to one magnet. As human beings, they have the will to separate but to do so requires constant effort —a compulsive and endlessly repeated struggle to master and escape the image of a devouring mother and to take on the power and authority of a missing father. Ultimately, the Casanova's struggle is as empty as the addict's search for the endless high or the fetishist's pursuit of the perfect object of desire: there is a bottomless pit in his psychic center that no lover can ever fill.

CHAPTER ELEVEN

—◆—

The Culture of the
Libertine

TWO SCENARIOS FROM THE AUTHOR'S CHILDHOOD

*1. I am ten or eleven years old and watching one of the early
James Bond films—it might be* Goldfinger *or* Dr. No. *It was long
ago; I can barely remember the plot. There is a superweapon, and a
grotesquely disfigured supervillain who plans to unleash it on the
world. And there's Bond himself, that unflappable killer who gives
mayhem the gloss of a one-man tango. What stands out is the hardware—gleaming, manta-shaped cars that fire heat-seeking rockets*

from beneath their headlights, exploding attaché cases and of course Bond's oddly delicate-looking pistol—and the women. There are many women, all as burnished and aerodynamically perfect as Bond's Ferrari. Sometimes he turns from making love to one of them to dispatch a thug lurking in the bedroom closet. Sometimes he dispatches one of them, when she turns out to be on the wrong side. There is no room for sentiment in his treatment of these creatures. He mourns them no more than he would a car wrecked in a high-speed chase; he has no difficulty replacing either. For James Bond, neither women nor hardware are true objects of desire. They are more like accoutrements of virility: that is what you need to be a man. For the rest of the year all I read were James Bond books, discreetly packaged in fake leather slip-on covers.

2.   I am roughly the same age and at home, watching an episode of "Bewitched." Who would even try to summarize its plot? Darin brings his crusty boss home for dinner, but Samantha nearly ruins the evening with one of her misfired spells. Instead of scalloping the potatoes, she turns the living room and everyone in it upside down, or turns the boss's wife into a chicken. Of course, she restores order as easily as she subverted it. One twitch of her adorable nose and the room is right side up, the chicken turned back into a wife. No one is any the worse for wear, and Samantha has an explanation for everything: she was trying out a new style of interior decorating or doing homework for her hypnosis class. What persists in my memory are the characters of Samantha and Darin. Even before she gave birth to little Tabitha, there was something maternal about Samantha: she wasn't heavy, but her bosom had a pillowy substance to it that carried the promise of repose, and like a mother who has gotten used to her three-year-old's wall paintings, she always seemed undismayed by the chaotic results of her spells. If she was occasionally maladroit, the speed with which she set things right removed any impression of incompetence. How could anyone so powerful be incompetent? As Darin, though, Dick York had the mournful sheepishness of a boy forced to wear a good suit. His ears stuck out beneath his crew cut. His voice was as hysterically overpitched as George Bush's. And in moments of distress, he had a way of calling his wife "Honeee" that made the word sound an awful lot like "Mommy."

It should be clear by now that the Casanova complex is neither a "life-style"—something that one chooses as one would a new house or wardrobe—nor a moral lapse; rather it is a compulsive disorder that bears striking parallels to alcoholism and drug addiction. Like those diseases, it seems to be linked to narcissistic disturbances in early childhood and is accompanied by a false sense of self, at once grandiose and frail, and by a ravenous hunger for affirmation and nurturance. Like alcoholism and addiction, the Casanova complex can have drastic consequences, from broken marriages to death by AIDS. In the last years of the 1980s, as casual sex becomes increasingly a contradiction in terms, the Casanova complex may finally be recognized as a genuine pathology whose victims, like Fred, are all too willing to "fuck away" their lives, and the lives of their partners as well.

If this disorder has long been masked it is because, like alcoholism, it fits so neatly into a broader cultural context. In the United States, for example, alcohol is readily available and heavily advertised. Drinking is an almost universal activity, a standard ritual at business lunches, family gatherings, sporting events and romantic trysts. We drink to seal marriages and to celebrate the birth of children; we drink to steady ourselves in the face of death. Even drunkenness is sometimes acceptable—on New Year's Eve or prom night. In this context, the borderline between "social" drinking and alcoholism, indulgence and sickness, blurs. In much the same way, the Casanova blends into a society that is at once highly eroticized and persistently misogynistic, where the double standard is still somewhat shakily enshrined and commitment—to spouse, job or values —is viewed with ambivalence. When, according to a recent survey, 66 percent of the married men in America have had extramarital sex, how do we distinguish the chronic from the sometime adulterer? When teenaged boys are encouraged to rack up sexual conquests, how do we decide whose score is too high? When the heroes of prime-time television are artful womanizers like Sonny Crockett and Arnie Becker, how can we label one man a Casanova and another a wishful imitator?

When a particular form of behavior is congruent with the standards of a larger society, it is called culturally syntonic. I believe that the Casanova complex is a culturally syntonic disorder. It may have its origins in the psychic history of the individual, but it is also mirrored in the attitudes and behavior of millions of "normal" men, and indeed has been subtly promoted—one could even say encouraged—by our ethical, legal and religious institutions, our economic structure and our mass media. The Casanova is in many ways the true heir of a society whose official ethic of monogamy coexists with what the social scientist Robin Fox has called a "polygyny of the powerful," in which men may no longer take several wives but continue to enjoy greater access to sexual opportunities outside marriage, especially if they have the means to do so. Casanova's division of women into Lucretias and Judiths reflects his culture's ancient tendency to assign women the rigid and mutually exclusive roles of virgin and whore, mother and mistress, and to observe a corresponding dichotomy between love and lust, tenderness and desire. His view of sexual commitment as a sterile and humiliating trap is the same message imparted in *The Odyssey* and *The Aeneid*, in the teachings of the early Christian fathers and in popular media from Westerns to *Playboy* magazine. Finally, the Casanova is the perfect embodiment of Christopher Lasch's "culture of narcissism," a state in which the image is omnipresent and of paramount importance, where everything—including feelings and relationships—is a consumer product and the ethic of entrepreneurialism has made all human interactions suspect and transient.

SONS OF THE SHEIK

A 1968 survey of 807 human cultures found that 708 of them—more than 75 percent—were polygynous, with one man enjoying the sexual and childbearing services of several wives or concubines. There are those who argue that polygyny is the "ideal" male evolutionary strategy, for it enables men to mate with as many women as possible in order to produce the maximum number of offspring. In practice, of course, only those who have the means to support several wives and children—and the power to ensure the legitimacy of their offspring—can truly afford polygyny. It remains the option of the wealthy and powerful, of tribal chieftains, Arab sheiks and the Mormon elders of the previous century.

The polygyny of the powerful gave birth to two institutions. The first was the harem, in which a wealthy man kept his wives and concubines, usually under the guard of eunuchs. The object was not only to house the women but to guarantee their fidelity and ensure that his children were indeed his own. But if the harem represented a sexual monopoly of older, more prestigious men, there had to be some outlet for those too young and too poor to support even one wife, let alone many: the alternative was rape and relentless class and age warfare. Thus the harem bred its antithesis, the brothel, where several men could enjoy the sexual services of a single prostitute. As John Money has observed, the division of women into madonnas and whores begins with these twin structures, the one devoted to procreation, the other to what we now call recreational sex.

The polygyny of the powerful is, of course, a part of the Judeo-Christian tradition as well. It was the ethic of Abraham, Isaac and Jacob, of David and Solomon. For all His sternness, the God of the Old Testament tolerated all sorts of sexual misconduct among the forefathers of Israel, as long as that conduct was fruitful. Lot could lie with his own daughters and Jacob could bed Leah and her sister Rachel without provoking divine punishment. The Seventh Commandment, prohibiting adultery, seems to have been intended less as a curb on male sexuality than as a way of ensuring the purity of Israel's bloodlines, which were then still reckoned patrilineally. It certainly didn't keep the kings of Israel from taking new wives when they wanted sexual variety or favorable alliances with other tribes or wished to father more children. In the New Testament, we find both the courtesan Mary Magdalene and a reference to eunuchs (Matthew 19:12), which suggests that the brothel and the harem were fixtures in Hebrew society. For the Jews, polygyny endured into the Middle Ages: it was not outlawed by the rabbinates of the West until A.D. 1000.

Theoretically, monogamy has been the standard—and the only approved—form of marriage in the West since the Christian era. The Christian fathers listed adultery and fornication among the four sins against the body. But in practice Western monogamy has been a kind of sieve, riddled with loopholes that admit men but until recently were sealed to women. The cultural historian André Béjin sums up this double standard as "strict fidelity demanded of the wife, relative fidelity accepted for the husband" and claims that it satisfied the cultural requirements of preindustrial Europe: "it meant that one knew who one's mother was, while one's paternity was a matter of belief." Although the Catholic Church construed fornication and adultery as offenses for which men and women were equally punishable, it seems to have enforced its marital and sexual codes selectively: men, at least, continued to enjoy sex before and outside marriage without much interference.

The harem vanished in the West, but the brothel endured in spite of intermittent crackdowns. In fifteenth-century France, for example, prostitution was not only tolerated, but enshrined as a public institution. Most towns had a municipal brothel or bathhouse. In the larger cities entire districts dedicated to recreational sex were officially protected. The women who worked there enjoyed the status of public servants, and prostitution was considered a respectable occupation for women of the lower and middle classes, even if they were married. While these municipal brothels were theoretically closed to local husbands, there was nothing to prevent a married man from visiting the *prostibula* of a neighboring town. Courtesans were among the chief citizens of sixteenth-century Venice. These erotic technicians not only produced and controlled much of the city's wealth but shaped its mores and etiquette, leading the writer Aretino to observe, "A good pair of buttocks is possessed of greater power than all that has ever proceeded from philosophers, astrologers, alchemists and necromancers."

Even in the most stringently moralistic societies, men largely escaped the penalties attending illicit sexuality. If the noble ladies of the Middle Ages had to endure the chastity belt, their husbands could exercise the *droit du seigneur*, which entitled them to sleep with their vassals' brides on their wedding nights. In his *Memoirs*, Casanova noted that in eighteenth-century Austria the Empress Maria Theresa had unfaithful women imprisoned while turning a blind eye to the philandering of her own husband. In Puritan America prostitution coexisted with the stocks and the scarlet letter. According to Masters and Johnson, a guide to American brothels published on the eve of the Civil War listed 106 such establishments in New York, 57 in Philadelphia and dozens elsewhere. Victorian England, which we so often imagine as a tight little island of sexual repression, had flourishing industries in pornography and prostitution. And more recently a large number of Christian fundamentalists seemed inclined to forgive evangelist Jim Bakker's well-publicized fall from grace. One wonders how his wife, Tammy, would have fared had the sexual transgressions been hers.

Alongside this pattern of chastity for women and permissiveness for men, we note the relative ease with which men, especially rich and powerful men, have been able to escape inconvenient marriages. In the early Middle Ages, for example, the Church was reluctant to condemn divorce and remarriage; it didn't assume its present status as the guardian of marital stability until the twelfth century. Even then, the papal annulment allowed the nobility to continue to put old wives aside and take new ones, as long as they were willing to pay for the privilege. When Henry VIII broke with the Catholic Church, it was less because the pope refused to annul his marriage to Catherine of Aragon than because the English king hankered after monastic lands. After divorce was finally legalized, the laws still perpetuated this masculine bias for some time: in nineteenth-century England, a husband could divorce his wife for adultery; a betrayed wife, however, also had to prove her husband guilty of cruelty, rape or sodomy. Even in the United States today, where divorce codes are relatively gender-blind, men are still more likely than women to seek divorce on grounds of adultery, and more divorced men remarry, within a shorter time, than women. Given the economic consequences of divorce and the enduring disparity between men's and women's earning power, the current system still gives men an advantage that women lack: with enough money, they can divorce and remarry to their hearts' content.

The ethic of polygyny is entrenched not only in our laws, but in our literature and popular myths. In medieval fabliaux the philanderer is a comic but triumphant figure, whose seductions are seen as *exploits*—heroism translated into the sexual realm. He may be an aristocratic rake, but he is just as often a subversive upstart from the lower class, who rebels by seducing the wives and daughters of his social betters. He attains his stature not with a sword, but with his penis, that perpetually erect weapon with which he impales women and flouts the authority of fathers, husbands, laws and church. He is Til Eulenspiegel and the roguish Nicholas of Chaucer's "Miller's Tale" and the hero of a dozen Restoration comedies. In this century he has been reborn as Rudolph Valentino's sheik, Warren Beatty's insatiable hairdresser in *Shampoo*, and a generation of prancing, slithering rock 'n' roll bad boys from Chuck Berry to Mick Jagger and Prince. A rock star's penis is as essential a piece of equipment as his microphone: think of the moment in the movie *Spinal Tap* when an airport metal-detector shows up the foil-wrapped cucumber that a band member has shoved down his pants. Sometimes the Casanova is not just a stud but a swashbuckling satyr like John Barrymore's François Villon or Errol Flynn's Captain Blood, a genuine hero who is equally adept with his sword and his member.

The heroic philanderer rarely falls in love, except in the most breezy and jocular fashion, and never pays for his transgressions: when he vaults from the bedroom window, he lands lightly on his feet. He is a man who toys with women, and he always seems shocked and vaguely disgusted that they take his overtures so seriously. The ease with which he leaves his mistresses is an essential measure of his virility. As the film critic Joan Mellen observes of the characters played by Humphrey Bogart and Clark Gable: "He is always ready to walk out of a relationship or to avoid involvement with a woman. His cynical wariness and inaccessibility are of course assumed to make him more appealing." In *No Man of Her Own*, Gable kisses off a lover with the words, "What gets me is why women can't laugh when it's over."

Coexisting with, and often underlying, our current principles of monogamy and sexual equality, polygyny endures. Until quite recently, boys lost their virginity at an earlier age than girls and were expected to come to their marriages with a résumé of sexual experience that "nice girls" lacked. The double standard informs our reading of "bachelor" (glamorous, eligible) and "spinster" (withered, tragic, embittered), "playboy" and "party girl." It explains why the word "divorcée" has salacious connotations, while its male equivalent is virtually unused. It is why only women are called "sluts." The hidden code of polygyny made it socially acceptable for millionaires like John Paul Getty and Huntington Hartford to take an endless succession of wives and mistresses, while the oft-married Barbara Hutton became a figure of scandal and pity. For many, Hugh Hefner is a modern culture hero, who lives out the fantasies that he purveys to readers of *Playboy*. His closest female counterpart, *Cosmopolitan*'s Helen Gurley Brown, is renowned for her devotion to her husband. In the 1980s the double standard has relaxed long enough for us to see the advent of Madonna and Alexis Carrington, while the specter of AIDS has led to a renaissance of monogamy. It's too early to tell how long this renaissance will last and whether the philandering, polygynous male will finally lose his chic. For most men, the glamour is still there: when I discussed Casanovas with an acquaintance, he exclaimed, "Those lucky devils! Where do I go to take lessons?"

MADONNAS AND WHORES

As we have seen, the division of women into madonnas and whores may have begun with the ancient duality between the harem and the brothel. The women of the seraglio were not only lovers but mothers, the property of one man who guarded their chastity jealously; the courtesans of the brothel were purely sexual creatures, at once no man's property and every man's. Each was a prototype, with a long line of descendants. In the Old Testament the concubines of nomadic herdsmen are reimagined as the matriarchs of Israel. In the New Testament, the prostitute becomes the Scarlet Woman, the Whore of Babylon.

It seems more likely, however, that our culture's ambivalent view of women predates recorded history and has its earliest model in the male infant's relation with his mother. As we have noted, that relation begins as a perfect, symbiotic union and leads to a series of traumatic separations. The child responds to each shock with a fantasy whose aim is to restore the primal union: he dreams at different times of reentering his mother's womb, of devouring her, of possessing her sexually. And, of course, he projects those desires onto his mother and fears being devoured or seduced by her. In place of the real woman who gave him birth and sustenance, the child invents an idealized good mother and a terrifying bad one: the former is at once ethereal and eternally nurturing; the latter is a creature of flesh, but her breast is dry and her womb barren or populated with monsters. The imaginings of the child persist in the unconscious beliefs of the adult and find expression in folklore, the artist's imagination and the institutions of society. The good mother becomes the madonna, universally yearned for and idealized. The bad mother becomes the desirable and dreaded whore.

Whatever its origins, the splitting of women into two mutually exclusive aspects is entrenched in Western culture and mythology, along with a corresponding schism between love and lust. Although motherhood begins with sex, it was symbolically dissociated from the sexual act through the Roman cult of the vestal virgin and the Christian cult of Mary, the virgin mother of Christ. To acknowledge the connection was at once a violation of the taboos against incest and an act of blasphemy: sex was figuratively banished from the wedding altar and the birthing chamber, and Christian wives were encouraged to identify with a line of virginal saints and martyrs, both religious and secular. Although the Church defined sex as a marital obligation, it was considered incidental to the primary purpose of marriage. Better for a wife to be reticent than amorous: in the villages of medieval France a bride who struggled against being carried to her husband's house was viewed approvingly. The marriage manuals of the nineteenth century—largely written by men for women—portrayed sex as something that women might come to tolerate but certainly not enjoy.

The virgin mother was a creature of unearthly radiance. In her shadows, the figure of the whore sprang up like the deadly nightshade of a witch's apothecary. That the Scarlet Woman was an imaginary being may be seen by the way in which real prostitutes were treated during much of the Middle Ages: as we have previously noted, they were often honored municipal employees who as a matter of course might marry and raise children. The whore was incapable of such domesticity; she was as exclusively sexual as the madonna was solely maternal. She was Eve, the despised instrument of man's fall from grace; she was the pagan goddesses Ishtar and Cybele; she was Delilah and Salome, who destroyed the men they seduced. If the madonna was life-giving, the whore was dangerous. The Bacchae tore men apart with their bare hands. Witches were blamed for poisoning cattle and spreading plague. Although the whore was a product of the collective unconscious of the West, the metaphor was all too often projected onto real women: the daughters of Eve suffered for her transgressions as Jews were punished for their ancestors' supposed role in the crucifixion. From the fifteenth through seventeenth centuries—the same period in which the Reformation dethroned the Virgin Mary—witches became the victims of hysterical persecution in continental Europe, England and America. These women, who were usually single or widowed, were thought to do more than cast malign spells: they were the whores of Lucifer, who coupled with him at their sabbats —the madonna's demonic stepsisters.

Men responded to the two archetypes in radically different ways, viewing the madonna with reverence and tenderness, the whore with desire, terror and defensive scorn. The division between the madonna and the whore was mirrored by the split between wife and mistress, mother and lover. "A man who is too passionately in love with his wife is an adulterer," said Saint Jerome. "Nothing is so vile as to love one's wife as if she were a mistress." A strict economy of feeling came to govern all interactions between the sexes, assigning adoration to mothers, affection to wives, and lust to whores and mistresses. The categories were narrow, and severe consequences could befall women of uncertain status: in fifteenth-century France prostitutes, female day laborers, widows and single girls of the working classes were all treated as "fallen women" and could be raped without legal penalties. Two types of literature popular in

nineteenth-century England preserve the distinction between madonna and whore: the marriage manuals of the era portray young
brides as prim and absurdly naive creatures who tremble on their
wedding nights; the pornography of the same period introduces us
to women whose sole role is to satiate and be satiated, who have no
feelings other than the sexual. As Peter Gay observes, "In [the]
pages [of pornography] the separation of lust from love...is
complete....Women in pornography represent, in the most extreme
form, the despised half of the man's split image of the first, and in
some ways always most important, woman in his life—his mother."
Little wonder that the separation of passion from affection became
a crippling disorder for so many Victorians: where these men loved,
they could not desire, and where they desired, they could not love.

As women increasingly speak for themselves, men are coming to
see them more realistically. Still, during my childhood in the
1950s, I grew up with the persistent images of madonna and
whore and the idea that only certain kinds of feeling were appropriate for each. In the movies and TV shows I watched, actresses
were rigidly type-cast in generic roles: Donna Reed, June Lock-
hart and Doris Day were virgins who seemed to pass over into
motherhood without ever encountering a penis; Marilyn Monroe,
Kim Novak and Ava Gardner were the seductive femmes fatales I
craved and feared. Christina Crawford's gaslit account of her
childhood in *Mommie Dearest* only confirmed what I had always
known intuitively: Joan Crawford could never be the kind of
mother who made you chocolate-chip cookies and tucked you into
bed at night. Beginning in the 1950s, the mystique of the mother
was drastically deflated: authors like Philip Wylie and Philip
Roth tore away her otherworldly veil and exposed her as a shrill-
voiced, castrating Medusa. Pornography, though, became more
prevalent than ever before. The whore no longer beckoned from
dim alleys and specialty bookstores; she was an icon on every
newsstand.

We continue to reenact in our culture the schism between love
and lust. Advice columnists still admonish young girls to preserve
their virginity and warn that their reputations will be shattered if
they don't. In slasher movies like *Friday the 13th*, the bad girl is
always the first to die. Women are urged to reclaim their sexuality,
but when they do they discover that old penalties are still on the
books. Until quite recently, an attorney had only to prove that a
female rape victim had been sexually active to win an acquittal for

his accused client. Casanovas in many ways are just the most blatant exponents of a moral code that divides women into camps that
are light-years apart and have no middle ground between them. A
recent popular move called *Fatal Attraction* explicitly reenacts the
split between madonna and whore: when Michael Douglas's perfect
wife (played by Anne Archer) goes away for a weekend, he sleeps
with Alex (Glenn Close), who turns out to be a pathetic yet murder-
ous psychopath, a woman who is all too willing to destroy what she
cannot have. The whore is more arousing than the virgin wife, but
the price of sleeping with her may be terminal.

OF WOE THAT IS IN MARRIAGE

Experience, though no authority
in this world, entitles me
To speak of woe that is in marriage.

> —Geoffrey Chaucer,
> *The Canterbury Tales*

When polygyny is presented as a legitimate option for those with
the means to afford it, and when an invisible barrier separates love
from desire, it follows that men—some men—will view monogamous marriage at best as a necessary compromise and at worst as a
vile imprisonment. By this chain of reasoning, to marry is to forgo
one's natural inclination to sleep with as many women as possible
and to sacrifice passion in favor of affection and companionship.

For our ancestors, this did not seem such a bad trade-off; marriage was seen to confer essential benefits that were not to be found
in any other relation between the sexes. Until two hundred years
ago, marriage was widely viewed as a social, economic and procre-
ative contract in which sexuality had a secondary place, and romantic love none at all. The classical Greek word for woman, *gyne*,
means "bearer of children," and the Greeks saw marriage as nothing more than an instrument for procreation and child-rearing;
passion and sexual excitement were to be found in idealized homosexual relationships. There was, of course, the further incentive of
the dowry, a critical factor in the biblical Middle East, in Europe
until recent times and in most agrarian cultures today: the right
marriage might secure a man anything from cattle to a kingdom.

When Christianity made all sexuality suspect and prescribed a monk's life as the ideal, marriage attained new importance as the sole legitimate channel for the impulses of the flesh. For those uninterested in lives of celibacy, Saint Paul spelled out the alternatives succinctly: it was better to marry than to burn. Even then, sex within marriage had to be of a different order than sex outside it. To love one's wife excessively, as Saint Jerome observed, was to commit adultery. More than eleven hundred years later, Montaigne expounded a similar idea in his *Essais:* "Those shameless endearings, which the first heat suggests unto us in that sportful delight, are not only undecently, but hurtfully employed toward our wives.... Marriage is a religious and devout bond: and that is the reason the pleasure a man hath of it should be moderate, staid and serious pleasure, and mixed with severitie...."

This is not to suggest that marriages of the past were loveless, but rather that love within marriage was not a given. Men rarely admitted to loving their wives, except in wills, and one did not talk about one's feelings for a spouse any more than one discussed one's sex life. Conjugal love was a consequence—not uncommon but hardly guaranteed—of marriage. Husband and wife might come to love each other simply because they had spent so many years together, as one might come to love one's fellow castaway on a desert island, and love often seemed to take them by surprise years after they had taken their vows. Actually, this isn't all that different from what happens to couples today, who often find that their early passion metamorphoses into something quieter and more consistent. We may not realize that our marriages work until that moment, years or decades after the wedding day, when we look at the person next to us in bed and think, Yes, I still love her. I love her more than ever.

As necessary and pleasant as this state might be, the monogamous marriage was a far cry from the sensual fulfillment of polygyny or the joyous irresponsibility of bachelorhood. And from very early on, it was considered a relatively minor condition of a man's life—even a distraction from his true responsibilities. To the Greeks, homosexuality was the noblest arena of the passions—one that combined the physical, the intellectual and the spiritual. Men could love men and still go about the business of making war, ruling the state and seeking the good. In the *Iliad*, Achilles' infatuation with the woman Briseis causes a petty interruption in the siege of Troy. It is his love for his comrade Patroclus that restores him to his heroic destiny. Heterosexual—and especially married—love is portrayed as anticlimactic, a lulling and sometimes dangerous inter-mission in the drama of manhood. Odysseus' sojourns with Calypso and Nausicaä are blank spots in his voyage across the sea, and al-though the goal of that voyage is his wife, Penelope, what transpires after his reunion with her is an afterthought to his adventures.

In Christianity, too, marriage was incidental to man's true call-ing, the worship and service of God. The writings of Saint Paul and Saint Jerome suggest a pragmatic but resigned view of marriage as a compromise for those too fettered by the flesh to follow a life of the spirit. It's no coincidence that the great treatises on sexual mo-rality and sin were written in a monastic setting and dwelt on their significance to men who had taken their vows. The true meaning of desire and the transgressions that resulted from it lay outside the marital union, in the relation between man and God, for one's sins were first and foremost sins against Him. In the Arthurian ro-mances as in the Greek epics, marriage lies outside the arena of heroism and action. A wife is someone a man comes home to when his adventures are done, and everything that happens afterward can be summed up in one sentence: "And they lived happily ever after."

The Middle Ages saw the emergence of a code of romantic love, but such love was by definition adulterous, the exalted but forbid-den union of highborn protagonists like Launcelot and Guinevere and Tristan and Iseult. In opposition to the economic and procre-ative bond of marriage, there arose the idea of passion, which could exist only when the laws of man and God were suspended. But God's laws could not be suspended indefinitely: Chrétien de Troyes and Marie de France saw quite correctly that romantic love is tran-sitory, a truth that generation after generation of lovers keeps for-getting. "Passionate love," Philippe Ariès writes, "was love at first sight: one fell in love. A feverish beginning, a flowering and an end. Cupid's dart was as sudden and unforeseen as death's sting. Pas-sionate love does not last, marriages based on it do not last either."

The epic literature of the Greeks and the courtly aesthetic of the Middle Ages gave rise to a long and durable tradition that pitted heroism against domesticity, romantic love against marital love. The man of action might be married, but his wife was kept dis-creetly offstage. Otherwise, she was bound to get in the way. In *High Noon*, Gary Cooper's Quaker wife wants to turn him into a domesticated store owner; it's only over her objections that he suc-ceeds in doing what a man's got to do. More often, the true hero was a solitary adventurer—a knight-errant, a cavalier, a cowboy or a private eye. He might take a lover or two in the course of his wanderings, but such women were quickly disposable. Humphrey Bogart's Sam Spade loves the treacherous Brigid O'Shaughnessy (Mary Astor), but at the climax of *The Maltese Falcon* he turns her in to the police: "I don't care who loves who," he snaps at her, "I won't play the sap for you." Frequently, he was an unabashed misogynist. In *The Plainsman*, Gary Cooper's Wild Bill Hickock scorns the affections of Jean Arthur's Calamity Jane; when she impulsively kisses him, he wipes his mouth. If a hero married, he did so only at the story's climax, or the marriage had to end tragically, leaving him alone once more: it's hard to imagine Frederic Henry living happily ever after with Catherine in some alternate version of *A Farewell to Arms*, or John Wayne dashing from a shoot-out because his wife needs help with the chores. The heroes of my childhood were not sexless—who can forget James Bond and Napoleon Solo, the tormented eroticism of James Dean or the thuggish gallantry of Jean-Paul Belmondo?—but they were not, and could not be, tied down.

To attain dramatic resonance in literature and film, love had to be illicit, a challenge to earthly, if not heavenly, authority, and it had to have an implied time limit. Usually such love was portrayed from a woman's viewpoint—the story of a Cathy, a Tess of the D'Urbervilles or a Jane Eyre. But there was also a convention of men for whom passion became a species of heroism, doomed perhaps, but admirable precisely because it *was* doomed. If other heroes battled human foes, romantic heroes pitted themselves against the dictates of class, morality and nature itself, wooing women who belonged to the wrong station or the wrong men, or struggling to keep passion alive beyond its allotted span. The lineage of the illicit lover extends from Tristan to Romeo, Don Juan and Jay Gatsby. He is Laurence Olivier's Heathcliff and Leslie Howard in *Of Human Bondage*. In recent decades, he has been reincarnated as Omar Sharif's spaniel-eyed adulterer in *Doctor Zhivago*, as Jean-Paul Belmondo's tragicomic sexual outlaw in *Pierrot-le-Fou* and as Marlon Brando forging, and dying for, a private universe of Eros in *Last Tango in Paris*. Such a man might be a bachelor, a widower or an adulterer: the object of his desire was never his wife. There was nothing noble or exciting about loving the woman one was married to.

What about husbands—faithful husbands? Such figures did appear in literature and film, but rarely in an epic or tragic context.

Conjugal love, with its thankless labors, squabbles and above all its *dailiness*, was the stuff of comedy. Comedy, after all, reaffirms the natural order, and what could be more natural, more orderly, than marriage? From the Middle Ages onward, the husband was largely a comic archetype, a cuckold, a blowhard or a henpecked ninny. At best he might attain some stature as a mentor to his sons, but in such cases he was usually portrayed as old and venerable, not a spouse but a patriarch, whose wisdom in some ways depended on his departure from the sexual arena: to have a clear head one had to have escaped the thralldom of the heart and genitals. That notion was preserved in the ways husbands were characterized in films and on television: they were either patriarchs or buffoons. As patriarchs, we saw Lewis Stone in the Andy Hardy films, Robert Young in "Father Knows Best," Fred MacMurray in "My Three Sons" and Hugh Beaumont in "Leave It to Beaver"; as buffoons we had Blondie's Dagwood, "Bewitched"'s wimpish Darin and "The Honeymooners"' Ralph Kramden, whose physical bulk and constant threats ("One of these days, Alice, you're going straight to the moon!") couldn't disguise his childish dependence on his wife. These portrayals conveyed a subliminal message to generations of male viewers. To be a husband was to leave the traditional male spheres of action and efficacy—to give up one's wits or one's balls.

What is particularly interesting is that such subversive portrayals of husbands proliferated during the 1950s and early 1960s, at a time when marriage had undergone an apotheosis in the popular imagination. The opposing streams of romantic and conjugal love had in theory been reconciled: people now married primarily for love. And far from being a diversion in the career of manhood, marriage had been redefined as an essential responsibility, one of the tasks that a man had to perform if he wanted to escape having his maturity or his heterosexuality questioned. Men were *supposed* to marry, settle down and raise children in the same way that they were supposed to work at respectable, remunerative jobs. To demur was to risk the crushing disapproval of family, employers, clergy and psychiatrists. A 1957 survey revealed that 53 percent of the American public believed that unmarried people were "sick," "neurotic" or "immoral." Only 37 percent viewed them "neutrally."

The problem was that such responsibility came to seem increasingly burdensome, even superfluous. Although marriage was popularly envisioned as a partnership in the corporate mold, that partnership often appeared one-sided to its male members. *They* were the family's sole breadwinners, while the housework their wives performed had been rendered largely meaningless by automation and a growing number of service industries. There was no doubt that women needed husbands, but did men need wives? As the feminist cultural historian Barbara Ehrenreich notes, "A man could live on his own. He might be lonely, unkempt and nostalgic for home-cooked food, but he would, more than likely, get by." It seemed that no sooner had marriage been turned into a cornerstone of American society than it fell under attack. *Playboy* magazine portrayed it as a con game in which hapless, emasculated males toiled to support parasitic shrews; the alternative *Playboy* offered its readers was an eternal bachelorhood, affluent, polygynous and as carefree as childhood. Popular medicine warned that the stresses of breadwinning might send the American husband to an early grave. Psychologists like Abraham Maslow and Fritz Perls and psychological entrepreneurs like Werner Erhard hinted that marriage could be an impediment to "growth" and "self-actualization." The beats and later the hippies rejected it as another rusting artifact of a society that had shackled its citizens with straight jobs, new cars and B-52s. By the end of the 1970s the cornerstone was sadly eroded: the number of men living alone rose from 3.5 million at the beginning of the decade to 6.8 million at its end.

Any man who came of age during the last forty years is bound to have been exposed to critiques—some veiled, some direct—of the marital bond. He defined his virility according to the models of Sean Connery, Marlon Brando or Mick Jagger. He watched the bumbling of television husbands and wondered if he would ever be like them. In all probability he read *Playboy* and *On the Road*. If he didn't actually run away and join a commune, he probably fantasized about doing so. He may have sat in on a nude encounter group at Esalen or a grueling but supposedly liberating est seminar. He may have swapped wives with his next-door neighbor or made a foray to Plato's Retreat in New York City. If he got married, there's a great chance that he got divorced. Of course, marriage is being rehabilitated by a combination of factors ranging from the emergence of the New Right to the red flag of AIDS. Commitment is the buzzword of the 1980s, but one that has a rather plaintive ring to it: it is something more often sought than found, as evidenced by the popularity of books on women who love too much and men who can't love at all. And even the current literature tends to present commitment as an *obligation* to women rather than as an option men might seek for themselves. How can such appeals to duty overcome the promises of adventure and sexual excitement that a man encounters every time he turns on the TV set or passes a newsstand? How likely is any man, Casanova or not, to choose the role of Phil Donahue over that of Arnie Becker? How, in twentieth-century America, can "I should" ever compete with "I want"?

THE CASANOVA IN THE CULTURE OF NARCISSISM

These last questions are especially haunting in a society that offers the immediate gratification of every desire and seems to create new desires as quickly as Detroit assembly lines turn out new Chryslers. Indeed, in the present-day United States the fulfillment of desire has become an obligation, symbolized by the elevation of "Go for it!" to a national slogan. According to Christopher Lasch, the harried pursuit of instant gratification—together with the worship of celebrity, the dread of old age and death and a desperate need for human warmth coupled with an obsessive fear of dependence—are marks of "the culture of narcissism." Narcissism —the underlying character disorder of so many Casanovas—has become the dominant psychic illness of our time, in the same way that hysteria and obsessional neurosis were the prevailing disorders of the nineteenth and early twentieth centuries. If Casanovas are increasingly common, it is because they embody a pathology that has become epidemic in their society.

We have already seen that the Casanova is shaped in part by a family constellation that includes an absent or emotionally distant father and a mother who is at once intrusive yet insensitive to the child's emotional needs. That family constellation is increasingly common in the United States. The father, once the dominant presence in the home, has virtually vanished from it. Beginning in the postwar era, his role as breadwinner—and his society's emphasis on "peak performance"—made him a prisoner of his career, which too often became the major focus of his life. It was taken for granted that he would work nights and weekends, and that the boundary between his work life and private life would erode. Whether he was taking his boss home to dinner or playing golf with a client, his free time was often dedicated to his career, and his interaction with his family was likely to be cursory and distracted: the career man was a clock-watcher at home. And a growing number of fathers were not just distracted but absent. As the divorce rate climbed—and as more and more children were born out of wedlock—there was a stunning increase in single-parent households, in which the parent was likely to be a woman. The effects of this explosion go beyond poverty: more and more children, of all races and classes, have grown up with fathers who were only shadowy presences in their lives. In such an environment, how could any boy acquire a sure sense of what it is to be a man?

The disappearance of the father placed a growing burden on the mother. Even if her family was intact, she often found herself having to fill both maternal and paternal roles. As a burgeoning industry of experts informed her that child care was a learnable skill that could be performed well or badly, she often felt painfully insecure in both roles. Her uncertainty was all the greater if she had a job and suffered the additional strain of being a part-time parent. She could no longer have a baby without reading a dozen books on the subject, and choices that had once been instinctual were now fraught with anxiety: should she go with Lamaze or Leboyer methods? Should she breast-feed the child, and if she did, when should she stop? How could she toilet-train her toddler without making him neurotic? What kind of toys provided the best stimulus? At what age should she teach him to read? If her ancestors had worried about losing children to diphtheria and scarlet fever, the postwar mother was beset with fears that were far more diffuse and that hinged on actions far more delicate than washing and disinfecting. Mothers were simultaneously deprived of real support—for who now had the assistance of her own mother or could afford a nanny?—and besieged by the intrusive and often contradictory advice of experts. The result was an epidemic of mothering-by-the-book, obsessive yet grimly mechanical, solicitous yet emotionally distanced.

In this nervous abdication, parents were by and large *yielding* to the dictates of their culture. When work becomes the new heroism, the principal source of self-definition and validation, a man who fails to devote himself utterly to his career is betraying not only his family but his manhood, as evidenced by the new TV commercials that portray white-collar professionals as cooler, more sophisticated jocks. When mothers are forced to raise their children without real assistance and under the judgmental gaze of school authorities and child psychologists, how can they help doing so in a harried and tentative manner? The society of our great-grandparents, buttressed with obligations and repressions, produced the rigidly constrained individual that the psychoanalyst Heinz Kohut calls "Guilty Man." The society of our parents, affluent, permissive and bureaucratized, produced another kind of personality, "Tragic Man," who suffers from a lack of constraints and whose psyche contains a void that no amount of possessions or stimuli can fill. The Casanova is nothing if not a Tragic Man, a typical member of a society where everything is permissible and nothing important.

THE SEXUAL ENTREPRENEUR

The United States in the late twentieth century has been characterized by three tendencies, each of which has contributed to the making of the Casanova: an obsession with the immediate gratification of desire, the transformation of sex into a consumer product and a mode of performance and an ethic of entrepreneurialism that has made all forms of loyalty suspect and outmoded.

America occupies a special place in the psychology of nations: it was, from its earliest history, the land where one went to improve one's status, to become someone else. The American myth goes something like this: the Puritan colonists came here as religious refugees and were soon the arbiters of a new moral order; the Jews who had been despised outsiders the world over came to America and were assimilated; the Irish, Slavs and Italians who arrived as peasants and manual laborers soon became rich. In the myth of Americanization, the realities of hard work and racial and ethnic prejudice are overshadowed by the fantasy of instant transformation: one need only breathe the American air to become a free man or walk down a city street to pick up a piece of golden pavement. The myth is almost as persuasive to those who were born in this country. The universality of credit makes it possible to buy a car, a house or an education in a matter of days and to forgo paying for it for years. In the popular imagination America is a gigantic changing room in which anyone can trade in his rags for a fine new suit.

The same ethic that urges us to transcend our social or financial status now makes possible other transformations, with as little forethought or effort. We are "born again" with a moment's declaration of faith and a nominal donation to an electronic church. We restore the national morale—battered by defeat in Vietnam and humiliation in Iran—with a comic-opera invasion of a Caribbean island. There are pills that help us lose weight while we sleep, and other drugs that change our mood in the time they take to enter the bloodstream. In the right bar we can find a sexual companion, without months of courtship and for the price of a few drinks, who will disappear conveniently the next morning. We can fly to Reno (we buy the ticket right at the terminal) and divorce a tiresome spouse for no other reason than that we are "incompatible," a nut and a bolt that no longer fit together. Such a society seems tailor-made for the Casanova, that devotee of instant intimacy and hair-trigger passion, who falls in and out of love as easily as one changes channels on a television set.

In a society where everything can be bought, sex becomes just another commodity. This in itself is nothing new: prostitution, after all, is the oldest profession. What is new is that sexuality is now democratic and diffuse. License is no longer the sole prerogative of the rich but an option for anyone who cares to indulge it. The prostitute still flourishes, but she must compete with amateurs of both sexes, as promiscuity becomes more an avocation than a profession, one of the tokens of an adolescence that now extends into middle age. To assist these amateurs there has evolved an entire stratum of businesses dedicated to sexual consumption: sex clubs, singles bars and gay bars, glossier and more sophisticated pornography and sex shops selling everything from whips to vibrators. Far from promoting a more relaxed and playful approach to sex, these businesses have subjected Eros to the laws of mass production, in which quantity, speed and efficiency are of paramount importance. As one observer comments, "Such activities, born of social leveling and reeking of boredom, can be reduced to two paradigms: the crowd's watchword 'move on,' and the queue's 'next please.'" The fear of AIDS may have curbed the promiscuity of the general consumer, but it has also launched an industry of telephone sex that is at once cheaper, safer and less taxing than its predecessor. If the true product of the erotic industry is orgasms, orgasms in maximum quantity and without the frills of seductiveness, commitment or intimacy, the telephone prostitute offers them in their purest form.

But while sex itself has been leeched of its erotic content, other arenas have been eroticized. Sex is now used to sell everything from cars to rock 'n' roll bands, soft drinks and politicians. The promise of sex is sometimes blatant: advertisements make it clear that anyone who drinks the right brandy, wears the right jeans or daubs on the right cologne will be rewarded with a terrific sexual partner.

Part of *Playboy*'s commercial triumph came from the way in which it gave every product advertised in its pages an erotic patina, so that a wristwatch or a piece of stereo equipment became as essential to sexual achievement as a king-sized bed or fur-lined handcuffs. Sometimes sexuality is just a package that is used to make any product more appealing, in the way that a spray of water and glycerine is used to make aging vegetables look fresh: can there be any doubt that the success of Ronald Reagan and Gary Hart depended less on their particular views than on their differing types of sex appeal, or that so many boutiques are designed to look as much as possible like S and M boudoirs? Even as its public morals tend more and more toward repression, an entire nation has taken on a climate of free-floating lubricity, in which even pieces of legislation are said to be sexy.

When sexuality is democratized and diffused, it stops being a private pursuit. Instead, every act of love becomes a crowd event, subject to the same performance ethic that governs other forms of public activity. What was once an exchange between two people acquires dozens of imaginary spectators—our previous partners, our partners' partners and a host of sexual authorities, against whose recommendations we measure our performance. Sex is now as goal-oriented as work, and its goal is the orgasm. We judge our effectiveness as lovers by the number and intensity of orgasms we give our partners. Men, already subject to the work ethic in so many other areas of their lives, are particularly likely to adopt this criterion in their sexual relations and to recast themselves as expert givers of orgasms. To become an expert means reading the right books—*The Joy of Sex, The Sensuous Man, How to Make Love to a Woman*—and perhaps consulting a sex therapist. It may also mean honing one's technique on different partners, so that promiscuity becomes an obligatory rite of passage in one's search for the right mate. Each woman is a stepping-stone to the next. Every encounter is a "learning experience," where what is learned are the erotic skills that will make future encounters more rewarding. The Casanova is the paradigm of a society that has turned sex into a mass commodity and sexuality into a mode of performance. Professionally seductive and obsessively goal-oriented, he is the consummate collector of sexual experience, the man who scores with the most women and gives them the most orgasms. Even his inconstancy is an asset, for it enables him to race to the next partner more quickly.

In this the Casanova does not resemble an assembly-line worker so much as he does one of the ruthless, entrepreneurial titans of contemporary American business—a T. Boone Pickens or an Ivan Boesky. He embodies, not thrift and industry, but acquisitiveness and self-promotion. His rise has less to do with loyalty than opportunism and depends on his ability to make and break alliances at a moment's notice. He is not a member of any organization, but a self-made man in the new American tradition identified by Christopher Lasch: "He practices the classic arts of seduction and with the same indifference to moral niceties, hoping to win your heart while picking your pocket. The happy hooker stands in place of Horatio Alger as the prototype of personal success."

If the Casanova is increasingly prevalent in the 1980s, it's because so many of his values are shared by the arbiters of his society. For all its vaunted conservatism, that society has further eroded the old loyalties and responsibilities it seemed so intent on reinstating. Instead, the new America has seen a triumph of rapacity and moral evasiveness in individuals and institutions alike. In its public policies, the United States has forsworn its obligations to a growing number of its citizens—the poor, the elderly, women, children and minorities. Much of government has been privatized, effectively sold to the highest bidders: our national lands are now administered by oil companies; our defense has been auctioned off to military contractors. Even our foreign policy seems to have been taken out of the hands of the State Department and placed in the care of retired military officers and shadowy businessmen. Laws and regulations are treated as so much red tape, and the maverick who cuts through them is no longer a misfit but a heroic figure like the patriotic gun-and-drug-runner Ollie North.

Bewildered by the monolithic nature of its institutions, the American public has once more deified the individual, and especially the individual who seems to challenge a larger organization. By a peculiar twist of logic, the new paradigm of individualism is not the self-proclaimed outlaw or anarchist but the entrepreneur, who often breaks laws just as flagrantly and is motivated by nothing but his own greed. In the new moral order, the freebooting auto magnate John DeLorean and the corporate raider Ivan Boesky are role models, their breaches of ethics justified by their personal style and overwhelming success. But when loyalties to employees, consumers and stockholders are viewed as outmoded, can other ties remain intact? The same climate that produces corporate raiders can just as easily give birth to traitors like John Walker and his unfortunate son and brother. These men, too, must have chafed under the restrictions of the organizations that employed them, and like other entrepreneurs, they struck out on their own: their only problem was that they sold their secrets to the wrong buyer, and for piddling rewards. In a culture that glorifies expediency and views all obligations as suspect, a vow of marriage is as vulnerable as an oath of office. The Casanova becomes an erotic entrepreneur, who lives by a code of conduct that is wholly private and that changes whenever the situation calls for it.

The heir to a long tradition of polygyny and misogyny, envied and often imitated by other men, the Casanova is nevertheless an anomaly in Western culture. Where most men's sexual experimentation is part of a search for a long-term partner, the Casanova never stops searching. Where most men stray intermittently, the Casanova's infidelities occur so frequently that they can no longer be called straying. What for most men is the stuff of adolescent daydreams becomes for him a way of life, dragging him, despite guilt and loneliness, on a course unchecked by divorce, pregnancy or the threat of disease. Yet the Casanova is common enough to be an archetype. He represents tendencies that have always been present in his culture, and he acts out the fantasies popularized in its myths, literature and electronic media. His pathology is private, with its own private origins, but it is widely mirrored in the world around him. When women are treated as property and sex as a consumer product, the Casanova will appear to be nothing more than a particularly successful consumer. In a society that views marriage as a dreary but obligatory compromise and denigrates all forms of commitment, his flight from love will be seen as a triumphant escape.

PART FOUR

—◆—◆—◆—

Casanova's Women

I grew to love him better than virtue....He broke my heart, and still I love him.

—Lady Caroline Lamb

CHAPTER TWELVE

"He Broke My Heart, and Still I Love Him"

THE EXAMPLE OF LEE HART

With its exposures, humiliating exits, and sudden reentries, the Gary Hart affair came to resemble Restoration comedy translated into the realm of contemporary American politics. But earlier on, and with a little indulgence, we could read it as Shakespearean tragedy. An ambitious man, who seems ideally suited by looks, temperament and charisma to occupy the most important office of his time, is overthrown by a single flaw: his blind and self-destructive pursuit of sexual opportunity. Seen in this light, it doesn't matter whether Hart had the true potential for greatness or whether the Casanova complex is a genuinely tragic affliction. What endures is our ancient fascination with a man's plunge from grace, whether because he has misjudged his footing or because the state of grace is inherently precarious.

Because of Hart's stature—and because in any drama of adultery, the adulterer usually occupies the spotlight—we tend to overlook his wife, Lee. But then, being overlooked is intrinsic to the role of political wife. With very few exceptions, she stands in the background, serving as the implicit reassurance of her husband's sexual preferences, potency and responsibility. The candidate's wife is to the candidate as a frame is to a picture: something that sets it off and holds it in place. Lee Hart seems to have played this role exceptionally well, serving her husband's career while gently effacing herself from public scrutiny. She was stylish and attractive, but not unnervingly so, like Jacqueline Kennedy. Indeed, she allowed her husband's glamour to eclipse her own: like Dorian Gray's portrait, she aged while he stayed youthful. She was devoted enough to return to him after two separations, but her devotion never seemed obtrusive or worshipful, like Nancy Reagan's. As she calmly sloughed off the rumors of Hart's infidelity, she seemed to be made for tolerance and quiet suffering, but she never projected the aggressive stoicism of a Pat Nixon. When queried about her marriage, she always reaffirmed her love for her husband, even though his aides sometimes had to remind him to kiss her during public appearances. Every aspect of her character seemed a complement to his—an afterthought that threw his best qualities into relief while negating the worst ones. To be loyal in the way that Lee Hart was is to be eternally an afterthought.

In the days after Hart's extramarital affairs became public knowledge, Lee's devotion stopped being an afterthought. Instead, it became almost as emblematic as her husband's womanizing. According to published reports, she urged him to stay in the race. Where Hart responded to the press defiantly, she seemed inclined to minimize his actions. When a man continually betrays his wife, the question, "How does she put up with it?" hovers on people's lips. For Lee Hart the answer might have been ambition, a motive that *she herself discounted: "If we were such political animals, why did we separate in the first place?" Her only public response to the question of her husband's infidelity showed a loyalty so extreme that it became a kind of pathology: "If it doesn't bother me, I don't see why it should bother anyone else." Her answer was at once ingenuous—it assumed that the issue was Hart's morals rather than his suicidal lack of judgment—and provocative: it attempted to place her husband's conduct within the private, domestic sphere, implying that its sole significance lay in her response to it. In that moment Lee Hart claimed for herself—perhaps for the first time— an importance equal to her husband's, positing herself as the sole arbiter of his behavior. And she also demonstrated a possessiveness that had previously gone unnoticed: just as she claimed her own significance, she also claimed her husband for herself, defending him against his interrogators as though they were her rivals. She responded to their grilling as if to say: "Gary Hart does not belong to you. He belongs to me. And I will see him as I want to see him, even if that means wiping out the rest of the world."*

There was a time—incredibly, not that long ago—when a woman might go through life without more than a casual encounter with a Casanova. He might be the fellow in promotion who kept asking her out to lunch even though everyone knew he was married, or the neighbor who was notorious for making passes at cocktail parties. The same factors that constrained a woman's life also insulated it: between the security of her childhood home and the security of marriage there was only a short leap. The distance she traveled as a young, single adult was no greater than the distance between two trapezes, and typically there was a strong arm at either end, and a safety net below—the mores that governed sexual conduct. Those customs may have enforced purity—or something approaching it —before marriage and fidelity afterward, but they also reassured a woman that no man of reputable character would try to "take advantage" of her unless he had serious intentions of sharing his future with her. More than that, they gave her reliable standards for judging his character beforehand. A fellow who had kept a string of mistresses or been involved with more than one woman at a time was not a decent man. Until the 1960s, even a divorced man was considered suspect. Such unspoken rules may have been suffocating—and they certainly could not guarantee a man's conduct after marriage—but at least they offered a woman the illusion of safety.

For better or worse, the distance most women must travel in their lives has grown, from a brief leap to a long and often bewildering passage, and the standards that once governed their transactions with men have largely vanished. Women must now map out their own sexual and romantic itineraries, choosing their own destinations and their own landmarks along the way. The longer a woman remains single and the more numerous her romantic involvements, the more likely it is that she will eventually meet up with a Casanova. In an age whose sexual mores are often improvised on the spot, Don Juans are no longer easily identifiable as suspicious or dangerous characters. Indeed, the very notion of the suspicious character seems as antiquated as that of the mustached and brilliantined villain. Until recently we were more likely to be suspicious of a man who seemed too pure than of one with a long and variegated sexual history. Even now that sexuality is once more suspect, Casanovas often appear to be simply enjoying the prerogatives of extended youth—the freedom to have casual sex at first encounter and with no assumptions about a future, the freedom to make erotic variety an end in itself, the freedom to keep relationships open and elastic and to end them at will.

THE LOVER AS DESSERT

Until now we have seen these men at such close range and examined their obsession in such detail that it may come as a shock to remind ourselves how attractive they can be to the opposite sex. We are like spectators at a performance of *Don Giovanni* or *The Rake of Seville* who, having eavesdropped on the hero's leering soliloquies and asides, wonder how any woman can fail to see through him. But the traits that identify Don Juans or Casanovas are often the very ones that make them successful seducers. What woman has not responded—at least once—to the sexual directness of a hitter, the expert manipulations of a juggler or the operatic passion of a romantic? Alcoholics are sometimes defined as people who can find a drink on a Friday night in Teheran. Similarly, Casanovas are men who can find women under any circumstances and charm even the most skeptical among them. These men are addicted to sexual conquest, which holds for them the same ephemeral comfort and reassurance that alcohol supplies for the drunk. Their addiction has given them a powerful affinity for its object, a tolerance for the most arduous discomforts associated with it. A hitter will search for a sexual partner until he finds one or the last bar has closed, and reenact his search the next night in spite of a screaming hangover. The alarms of a tomcat's conscience never seem to check him in his adulterous rounds. For Casanovas seduction is not a diversion but a central preoccupation, one that burns like a sun in a cloudless sky and gives other areas of their lives the sketchy, wavering character of a heat mirage. Their success with women is not contingent on their looks, intelligence or personal prestige: it arises directly from their pathology, which endows them with a romantic urgency and persuasiveness that most other men lack. They are living embodiments of the dictum that those who want something badly enough and are willing to sacrifice enough for it will eventually get it.

My interviews with women suggested that the initial appeal of these men is to some extent universal. Casanovas attract women of every economic stratum and ethnic background, and from every profession. In their approach to courtship, these men embody so many of the popular stereotypes about romantic love that their partners often find them irresistible. Ardent and impetuous, they express their desire quickly, without ambiguity. In their compulsive scramble for sexual and romantic fulfillment, Casanovas sweep women off their feet, evoking images of fantasy lovers from Heathcliff to Marlon Brando. In the early stages of their affairs, they often see their partners as idealized Lucretias and give them an adoration that is easily mistaken for love. At the same time, Casanovas subtly project the self-absorption, the childlike luxuriance in self, that is the mark of all narcissists and which may exercise a regressive allure for even the healthiest women.

Common sense is no defense against these charms. Indeed, many women report having been sexually and emotionally overwhelmed by men they could never bring themselves to trust. As Helen Gurley Brown observed not long ago: "Casanovas are so romantic, running out on the ramp of the airplane to say good-bye. Never mind what their motives are, they're lovely." In such encounters, women seem as capable as men of disengaging their intellects and operating on pure feeling and sensual pleasure, which, after all, constitute the core of the Casanova's appeal. Involvement with these men often means making an implicit choice against true intimacy and commitment in favor of momentary passion. Casanovas owe much of their success nowadays to the fact that many women have come to embrace the basic terms of their argument: that sex is a separate mode of experience, no more crucial or momentous than any other human interaction. When a best-selling book tells women that "men are just dessert," a love affair with a man who leaves or proves unfaithful becomes nothing more than an insubstantial confection, all meringue and spun sugar, dissolving instantly and leaving only the faintest memory of its taste.

LADY-KILLERS' LADIES

This is not to dismiss the genuine pain and disillusionment that many Casanovas cause their lovers, especially those who saw in their tenderness and enthusiasm the possibility of something lasting. Some women seem particularly drawn to Casanovas, for reasons that have as much to do with their own unresolved emotional issues as with the innate seductiveness of their partners. These are the women who keep falling in love with the wrong man, whose romantic biographies are rife with abandonment and betrayal. They are the ones who respond to Casanova as though to some noble cause, worthy of the gravest sacrifices. When they fall in love, it's with an ardor that eclipses the rest of their lives and tolerates no hesitation or second thought. Often, they idealize the Casanova and ignore or rationalize his most disturbing flaws. They treat his deceptiveness, infidelity and unreliability as inconveniences that can be made to disappear with enough time, love and devotion. Indeed, they often blame themselves for his failings. When he is unfaithful, they strive to please him better. When he leaves, they pursue him; when he says he no longer loves them, they love him harder. When he stops calling, they wait by their telephones, prisoners of a hope that is by now indistinguishable from despair. For most women the allure of the Casanova is powerful but short-lived: to speak of lady-killers' ladies, though, is to enter the realm of heartbreak and obsession.

Such women, I believe, are victims of a pathology that is fully as crippling as the Casanova complex. Freud discussed its masculine counterpart in his paper "A Special Type of Object Choice Made by Men" (1910), a study of men who were drawn to what were then known as "fallen" women. Any woman who has a history of involvements with Casanovas—or has had a long and painful relationship with a nester, juggler or tomcat—would do well to read that essay or Robin Norwood's *Women Who Love Too Much*, which examines the causes of a similar, but far more destructive, condition in women, describes the forms it takes and suggests a program of recovery. Lady-killers' ladies have a mirrorlike affinity for Casanovas. Like those men, they come from dysfunctional families, in which they received little nurturance or recognition. Like them, they treat their romantic partners as transitional objects—substitute sources of the comfort they never experienced in childhood and thus never learned to provide for themselves. But where the dynamics of the Casanova complex impel those men to run from object to object, lady-killers' ladies tend to remain fixated on one lover and will go to drastic lengths to keep him in their lives. Among such women, I encountered one who had allowed her live-in boyfriend to take another woman into their bed while she watched television in the next room. Another continued to support her husband after he had gone to live with a new girlfriend. Several women I interviewed remained emotionally in thrall to men who had walked out months before, keeping the belongings they'd left behind in pristine condition and avoiding new involvements in the forlorn hope that their lovers would return to them.

For most women, the appeal of the Casanova diminishes after a few episodes of infidelity and rarely outlives the breakup. One does not mourn long for a man one never trusted. Lady-killers' ladies, however, respond to different traits in this man, and their attraction to him seems to increase in direct proportion to the pain and frustration of the relationship. Much of that attraction seems to spring from the peculiar affinity between their pathologies. In Casanova these women perceive their own desire for instant, effortless intimacy and a fusion so intense and all-encompassing that it resembles adult love less than it does the primal bond between mother and child. Far from being scared off by his checkered sexual history or repelled by his fickleness, lady-killers' ladies are aroused by the challenge of wresting him from the other women in his life and galvanized by the threat of losing him to female rivals. With the insight of fellow sufferers, they see through the Casanova's facade of virile self-sufficiency to the wounded core of his personality and dedicate themselves to nursing it to health. Beneath the capacity of such women for unstinting devotion and self-sacrifice lies a profound discomfort with the quiet of true intimacy, and an unconscious belief that love is to be found only in suffering and struggle —things that Casanova supplies in plenty.

The disorder that afflicts these women is rooted in the circumstances of their childhoods. The families of lady-killers' ladies were often scarred by alcoholism, drug addiction, incest, infidelity or mental illness. One woman I spoke with, for example, was the daughter of an alcoholic father and a mother who determinedly ignored the evidence of his drinking; another had grown up with a mother who was an untreated manic-depressive, who sometimes assaulted her children and at others withdrew into catatonic stupors; still another had been sexually abused by her father. The daughters in such families received little emotional nurturance, or even recognition. Their perceptions were consistently denied: "Daddy isn't drunk," their mothers told them, "he's just resting." They grew up in a climate of continual emergency; their early lives were soap opera. Often, they were thrust prematurely into the responsibilities of adulthood, forced to care for younger siblings or ailing parents, to run households whose adult members had abdicated authority, to maintain polite fictions of normalcy in the face of daily chaos. They had in effect had their childhoods stolen from them, and very early on they learned to act as though they were little grown-ups while concealing the fears and yearnings of the child inside.

As adults, lady-killers' ladies are often gravely responsible, with a gift for managing their own lives and a penchant for helping others. In other ways, they seem peculiarly undeveloped, so that they remind the observer of nothing so much as the courageous, "womanly" orphans of Dickensian novels. Thoroughly mature in their conduct, they remain inwardly haunted by childlike needs for acceptance, nurturance and emotional fusion. That they are repeatedly drawn to men who are incapable of supplying those things seems paradoxical. But they are only recapitulating the experience of childhood, in which they appealed for—but rarely won—the love of abandoning, ineffectual or infantile parents by taking on the parental role. For these women the Casanova's thinly disguised weakness and dependence exert a strong appeal, serving as unconscious reminders of a weak and dependent parent. An affair with such a man provides them with an opportunity to act out behavioral patterns that have the attraction of long familiarity. It allows them to experience the only kind of love they know.

The fact that this love is unrewarding means little. Indeed, lady-killers' ladies respond to romantic disappointment by plodding the familiar paths of caring, helping and rescuing with greater tenacity. As children, most of them were conditioned to take the blame for the failures of their parents. If their fathers ignored them, if their mothers abused them, it could only be because *they* were somehow at fault. However painful that explanation, at least it left them with the hope that they might one day get the love they wanted. As adults, they unconsciously cling to the notion that, with enough effort, the goals of childhood are still attainable. All that remains is to find an appropriate surrogate for the parental taskmaster—a man to strive for, to care for, to love with unceasing, selfless diligence until he eventually loves them back.

The line that separates "normal" women from lady-killers' ladies is often thin, and even the healthiest women at times behave in ways that later seem irrational. Who would not warm to the concentrated heat of a Casanova's desire, or feel flattered to be the momentary center of his universe? And who, for that matter, has not at one time wanted to dissolve in a lover's embrace and put down the burden of separateness, at least for a little while? The following quotes and excerpts from my interviews illustrate how different women respond to Casanovas and suggest both the normal and pathological aspects of these men's appeal.

HOT PURSUIT

Don Juan: If you loved me, you'd ease my soul.
Thisbe: I'm yours.
Don Juan: If you were truly mine, heart-whole,
  How could you kill me thus and make me wait?
Thisbe: It is love's punishment at last I've
  found
  In you, and that's what makes me hesitate.
Don Juan: If my beloved, I live solely in you
  And ever so to serve you will continue
  And give my life for you, why do you tarry?

—Tirso de Molina, *The Rake of Seville*

Joanne, 32: "I met Gary at a rock club in Boston. He asked me to buy him a drink. That was new, at least, so I bought him one. Halfway through it, he told me that he wanted to make love to me. If anybody else had said that, I would have walked away. Instead I said, 'What makes you think I'd go to bed with you?' He said, 'Because I want you, and I'm used to getting what I want.' I found that enormously exciting. He was so arrogant and so direct, as if he was so attracted to me that he didn't care what kind of impression he was making. I ended up going home with him."

———◆·◆———

Linda, 27: "My first date with Brad was okay, nothing really special. But *he* acted as though it was, and that same night, after taking me home, he called and asked me out again. Within a month we were seeing each other two nights a week and spending weekends together. I never had to wait for him to call, not until much later, when he started backing off. But in the beginning he was very enthusiastic. I suppose his excitement carried both of us. One of the things you learn in adolescence is you don't call a man, you don't push him, you don't tell him you're really interested in him, because that'll just scare him off. Well, Brad did all the calling and all the pushing. On our third night together, he told me that he loved me. When I think back to what it was like then, I realize it was the first relationship in which I didn't feel afraid. The fear came later."

———◆·◆———

Lynne, 43: "How could I have guessed that Ray would be the kind of guy who runs? On our second date, he pinned a pearl brooch on me. On our third date, he talked about taking me to meet his mother! He was planning our summers together, what we'd do with our kids. Everything about him said 'I love you and I want to settle down with you.' And then out of the blue he tells me that he can't handle commitment."

———◆·◆———

One of the trademarks of the Casanova is haste, a romantic impetuosity that demands instant fulfillment. Whether his goal is a night of sex or a long relationship, he pursues it urgently, hustling through the stages of courtship or come-on like a real-estate agent rushing a prospective client through the rooms of a crumbling house. Such manic pursuit corresponds to many of our ingrained preconceptions about romance. No one who has grown up in this culture is immune to the idea that true love arrives suddenly, with the sting of Cupid's dart. The whirlwind romance is a fixture in our literature, plays, movies and popular love songs, and any man as impetuous as Brad or Gary or Ray has hundreds of years of tradition on his side—the tradition of Tristan and Romeo, Don Juan and Lord Byron. We see his haste as a mark of authentic passion: we forget that one can as easily blurt out a lie as the truth. For many women, recklessness makes an otherwise ordinary stranger mysteriously attractive, lending him an aura of romantic excitement that they had previously associated only with the great lovers of film and fiction. They fall in love with men who act like lovers.

Much of the excitement women feel at being so eagerly pursued has less to do with falling in love than with being caught in a process over which they seem to have no control, in which there is barely time to think out the next move, let alone assess their feelings. Again, they are responding to a cultural stereotype, the notion of love as surrender. Our culture has for centuries imparted the message that true love is irrational, a short circuit of the will. It informs all the stories in which men and women are brought together by spells or potions; it is the central conceit in songs like "You Made Me Love You" and "That Old Black Magic." To surrender one's will is both threatening and titillating, and for some women the borderline between anxiety and excitement is blurred: all too often, they mistake one feeling for the other. The sensations that many associate with passion—dryness of the mouth, a fluttering of the stomach, the feeling that the heart is rising into the throat—are also the symptoms of panic. To surrender one's will is dangerous, especially when the man one yields to is an unknown quantity. Is this stranger a lover or an assailant? When women succumb to a whirlwind courtship, they are in part falling in love with the danger of their situation, which in so many ways resembles the prelude to a rape. That, too, begins suddenly, with an abrupt and unequivocal demand, and entails a total submission to the other's will.

To surrender to the momentum of another's courtship is also comforting, a way out of the difficult choices that all lovers must ultimately make. Women may have doubts about the men who are so suddenly and overwhelmingly interested in them, but the speed and aggressiveness of courtship makes acting on those doubts unnecessary: they feel they can just go along for the ride.

One of the great risks of loving is facing responsibility for what happens if love goes wrong; yielding to another's passion absolves us of responsibility, allows us to see ourselves as blameless victims of forces beyond our control. Falling in love is infinitely easier than loving. It depends not on choice but on vertigo, which the writer

Milan Kundera has described as "the intoxication of the weak." And it replaces the hard work of choice with the unthinking swiftness of reflex.

If a woman is at all unsure of herself and has had her confidence shaken by the pain of earlier abandonment, there is a further allure to being the object of a whirlwind courtship. One of the reasons that Casanovas hurl themselves into their love affairs is their implicit awareness that their passion cannot last. As children, they probably learned that their mothers' love was unreliable and might be withdrawn at any moment. As adults, they have seen their own feelings wax and wane with wild irregularity. The only way they know to assure themselves of love is to grab hold fast and wring what they can from it before it vanishes. That psychology is hardly unique to men. Any lover fears losing the beloved, and women who were abandoned, neglected or loved inconsistently as children are especially prone to that fear. As adults, they must battle the impulse to dive into relationships before testing their depth. Of course, fighting that impulse is difficult when a Casanova is urging them to surrender, to do what comes naturally. Every hint about the future, every erotic escalation, is at once a promise of further intimacies and a subtle threat of rejection. Two fears come together and interlock, creating a climate of romantic hysteria in which caution is seen as betrayal. Implicit in every whirlwind romance is a deadline —usually imposed by the Casanova—a summons to act quickly or give up the possibility of love. As the rock band X warns: "It's very bad luck to draw the line on the night before the world ends."

The breathless momentum of a Casanova's courtship is a tidal force on which his partners are swept away. It speaks to women's most deeply ingrained preconceptions of romantic love. A whirlwind romance encourages them to take the easy route of falling in love over the arduous path of loving, to surrender instead of choose. And it constitutes a kind of covert blackmail, in which the alternatives are to submit totally to the assault of love or be left behind forever.

ENCHANTED MIRRORS

...The consciousness of success in his determination to please, inspired him with a new delicacy of perception, and made it, subtle as it was, more easy to him. If any one had told me, then, that all this was a brilliant game, played for the excitement of the moment,

*for the employment of high spirits, in the thoughtless love of superi-
ority, in a mere wasteful, careless course of winning what was
worthless to him, and next minute thrown away: I say, if anyone
had told me such a lie that night, I wonder in what manner of receiving it my indignation would have found vent!*

—Charles Dickens, *David Copperfield*

Linda: "In the beginning nothing was too much for Brad. He'd
drive miles out of his way to pick me up from work. If we couldn't
get together that evening, he'd come over and eat lunch with me in
the office. When he was traveling on business, he called me every
night to tell me how much he loved me, because he knew it helped
me sleep better. How was I supposed to know that there was always
another woman with him in his hotel room? To this day I'd like to
know if he was as devoted to the others as he was to me. Cross that
out. I'd rather believe it was just me."

———◆·◆———

Claire, 38: "I still can't believe that Hank didn't love me. I don't
know, maybe our definitions of love were just different. I wouldn't
have fallen for him the way I did if he hadn't seemed so completely
in love with me. He wanted to spend time with me even if I was
working on a free-lance project and was too busy to talk to him. As
long as we were together, I could do no wrong. Here was a man who
thought I was beautiful first thing in the morning! He was very,
very generous: expensive restaurants, the best wines, gifts like the
crêpe de chine blouse he gave me to celebrate our first night of
lovemaking. There were no limits to the time he'd devote to me or
the attention he'd give me. How could all that be a lie?"

———◆·◆———

A truth known to every con man is that human beings want to
believe the best about themselves. If a tarot reader tells us that we
have a passionate heart, hidden talents and deep insights into
human nature, we gasp in recognition and exclaim, "You've described me perfectly!" All too often a Casanova's lover responds to
him because he seems to see the best in her; indeed, he sees her as
the idealized embodiment of all that he feels lacking in himself. His
excitement—the excitement of a man glimpsing his missing other
half—overcomes any diffidence she may feel. He may be physically

unprepossessing, of ordinary intelligence, with all the style of a fire-plug, but those shortcomings are eclipsed by his obvious enthusiasm for her. A woman does not fall in love with such a man so much as she succumbs to his love for her, giving herself over to a climate of adoration as seductive as it is diffuse. The Casanova's endearments, his gifts and his willingness to devote all his time to her convince her that she is important to him. In time, they make him equally important to her.

The idea of being important is especially compelling to those who felt unimportant as children. Every child wants recognition, but all too many children were overshadowed by their siblings or neglected by parents who were too busy, too ill or simply incapable of truly valuing the offspring they had brought into the world. The women who are most vulnerable to Casanovas are very often still searching for the validation they never received as children. Casanovas appear to offer it. Indeed, their extravagant praise and gestures of affection appeal directly to their women's lingering fantasies of being their parents' adored little girls. Here is another instance of the mirrorlike symmetry between Casanovas and the women who love them. Consumed by their own childish longings for attention and recognition, these men intuitively know that the best way to become the center of a woman's life is to make her the center of their own, if only for a little while. The bond between Casanovas and their partners is thus a bond between similarly damaged individuals, who see in each other the potential for healing the lasting wounds of childhood.

Such relationships are inherently narcissistic, and the force of this narcissism is often stronger than that of love. The lovers serve each other as enchanted mirrors, reflecting selves that are eternally young, admirable and alluring. To be desired so intensely, to be the obsessive focus of another's attention, can be a drug in its own right, as so many celebrities have discovered: stars like Judy Garland often seemed to need their fans as much as their fans needed them. Such adoration creates an emotional high that is easily confused with the euphoria of love. It's also terribly easy to confuse this euphoria with the person who evokes it. Casanova makes women feel wonderful; therefore, *he* must be wonderful. Just as he idealizes his partners, so they come to idealize him, overlooking his flaws and seeing him in the cosmetic glow of requited narcissism. Casanova briefly turns his lovers into stars. And those stars, of course, are endlessly grateful for the fan to whom they owe their stardom.

In extreme cases, the idyllic memory of a Casanova's adoration may blind a woman to the evidence that he no longer loves her. As their relationship deteriorates, she may increasingly deny its ambiguous present and cling to her memories of the past. In her nostalgic fantasies, his growing lack of interest is only a momentary aberration. She tries desperately to explain it; she keeps hoping it will go away. The drug of his attention is so potent that it may work on her for months after it has been withdrawn. Her euphoric memory of the affair, her plaintive insistence that he *must* have loved her, is as self-deluding as an addict's memory of his last good high.

At the onset of their love affairs, Casanovas give their partners a precious gift, an attention that briefly elevates its object to the status of a goddess. This kind of attention is seductive and easily mistaken for love. And in the pleasure of being loved, women sometimes ignore their own perceptions of the men who seem to love them. In Robin Norwood's phrase, they end up asking " 'How much does he love (or need) me?' and not 'How much do I care for him?' " Gratitude disguises itself as love and comes to take love's place. In some women, the Casanova's adoration forges an addictive bond that persists even when adoration is withdrawn. In the hope, the need, of regaining it, women may deny that their relationships are now bankrupt and that their partners' attentions are directed elsewhere.

SPECIALISTS IN THE ORGASM

He loves to please women, because by pleasing them he pleases himself....His lovemaking secret is that he practices an Egyptian technique called Imsak. No matter how aroused he becomes, he doesn't allow himself to complete the act. What he enjoys about it is the sense of control he achieves over his own body while exciting the woman beyond control, beyond the threshold. His pleasure derives from totally arousing his partner while he remains aloof, the absolute master of the situation.

—Barbara Hutton, describing her lover and
soon-to-be fifth husband, Porfirio Rubirosa

Joanne: "He was very good in bed. By that I mean that he paid a lot of attention to me, to my body, to what gave me pleasure. With a lot of men, I've felt that I was being used. Gary more or less encouraged me to use him: 'I know what you want; let me give it to you.' "

———◆•◆———

Claire: "How do you know if a man loves you? That's what I keep asking myself, even now. Because Hank made love to me as though he really loved me. He used to tell me that he *reveled* in me. I'd never much liked my body. I thought it was too fat in some places and too skinny in others. I thought my breasts were too small. Hank made me like my body because he did. He loved making love to me. He couldn't get enough of me. It was never, 'Okay, I'm done, time to get some sleep.' Usually, *I* was the one who had to stop. And it was like that until the day we broke up. How could I have known he'd fallen out of love with me? It sure didn't show in bed."

———◆•◆———

Christine, 27: "Toward the end, Stewart would only see me every other week—in between we'd make plans to get together, but he'd always end up breaking them. He'd hardly talk to me, and anything I said he saw as pleading or manipulation. It should have been obvious to me that our relationship wasn't going anywhere. But there was still the sex, and that was good. It was even better than in the beginning. All the differences between us went away in the bedroom—all the suspicion, all the hurt. It was just endless loving. That was all I had left of him. And I hung on to it for dear life."

———◆•◆———

The bedroom is the Casanova's true arena, the place where he feels most powerful and proficient, most securely insulated from his own pain. Not surprisingly, he is often a "good lover," if we reduce a good lover to a successful giver of orgasms, as we so often do. Good sex is, of course, enormously compelling in itself, and especially so in a culture as eroticized as our own. Increasingly, and irrespective of gender, we tend to see sexual satisfaction as our birthright, a given in any relationship between man and woman. From there it's only a short step to viewing sex as the relationship's primary determinant—the thing that makes it "good" or "bad." When Eros goes public, sexual prowess is equated with love-worthiness, and the pleasure a man gives a woman in bed becomes a sign of his love for her. Orgasms come to signify feelings that may or may not actually exist. Casanovas, as we have seen, are quite capable of enjoying sex with partners for whom they feel nothing and often derive the greatest satisfaction from anonymous one-night stands. For them, the equation between sex and love breaks down: a woman who interprets a Casanova's sexual virtuosity as a sign of his love for her might as well pluck petals off a daisy while chanting "He loves me, he loves me not."

Unfortunately, many women also use sex as a way of deciphering or clarifying their own feelings. In the bedroom the ambiguities of interpersonal relations give way to the blunt certainties of the body. How much easier it is to tell if we have had an orgasm than to decide whether we genuinely like someone. Lady-killers' ladies in particular seem detached from their emotions: for them the body is often the only barometer of the heart. As one woman told me, "I knew I loved Al because I never wanted him out of my sight. I never wanted him out of my bed. Sexually, he turned me into a wild woman. As far as I was concerned, that was love." Again, we see a confusion between a physical sensation and an emotional state, a reduction of love to so many erogenous responses. It's not surprising that some women experience great sexual pleasure with Casanovas—these men are, after all, specialists in the orgasm. But women who succumb to them very often fall in love with the *sensations* aroused in them, with the dreamlike raptures of extended lovemaking and multiple orgasms.

This is especially evident as their relationships draw to a close. As communications between Casanovas and their partners break down—as dates are broken and conversations falter and die—sex can acquire increasing significance. It is the only thing that still works. Lady-killers' ladies, especially, are likely to use sex as a solution for the multiplying problems in their relationships. For these women, as for Casanovas themselves, intercourse comes to serve as a substitute for speech, for nonsexual touch, for tenderness and intimacy. Only in bed do they feel safe, for it is only here that their partners seem to want them. Terrified of rejection and sensing that their lovers are drawing away from them, they cling all the more tightly in the sexual embrace. Because it carries a weight of inarticulate messages, the sex between Casanovas and lady-killers' ladies is often very "good" sex indeed. It is a last-ditch holding action, the labor that redeems a ruin.

But sometimes we find that sex, too, diminishes in the closing phase of a Casanova's relationship. As the good mother turns inexorably into a bad one and his feelings of attraction give way to panic and resentment, he begins to experience bouts of impotence or simply avoids his partner; a single incident of impotence may lead him to shun coitus altogether, lest his humiliation be repeated. The Casanova's lover may blame herself for his sexual dysfunction, especially if he accuses her—as he often does—of causing it. She treats her man as a sexual invalid and anxiously takes on the role of erotic nursemaid in a vain effort to heal his wounded penis and restore the ardor that he has so mysteriously lost. She experiments with new positions, exotic costumes, the whole arsenal of Marabel Morgan and Alex Comfort, with the frantic ingenuity of a mother trying to find the one food her child will eat before he starves to death. Even in its absence, sex exercises an obsessive authority. It becomes a missing grail, and the search for it blinds her to the multiplying signs that her man now values her only as a caretaker.

Sex is Casanova's principal way of relating to his lovers. Not surprisingly, therefore, sex becomes his lovers' only way of holding on to him. Eros becomes a substitute language, a vehicle for feelings and desires that neither partner dares express directly. The sex in these relationships thus acquires great power, an urgency that derives from each partner's effort to decode the "utterances" of the other and to read meaning into his or her own sexual responses. Her orgasms tell him that she loves him; his erections tell her that he still wants her. As other lines of communication fail, sex becomes a cry for attention, an appeal for care and the justification for a relationship that might otherwise have ended long before. The sex is all that matters because the sex is all that is left.

THE INTRIGUE OF SELF-LOVE

You can dance. You can make me laugh. You've
  got x-ray eyes.
You know how to sing. You're a diplomat.
Everybody loves you.
You can charm the birds out of the sky.
But I've got one thing: I loved you better.

—Laurie Anderson, "Gravity's Angel"

Claire: "The thing that attracted me to Hank was the same thing, I think, that attracted me to Lewis. They reminded me of the guys in high school who were very good-looking or very athletic, and who *knew* it; they had no use for anybody who wasn't as good-looking or popular as they were. And, of course, that made me want them all the more. So you see, Hank and Lewis were like those guys grown up. Not that they were that handsome or successful, but they had that same self-confidence and self-absorption. And when they paid attention to me, it was as if the captain of my high-school football team had suddenly asked me out."

Christine: "For all that he said he loved me, Stewart's ultimate concern was himself. He was totally wrapped up in himself, how he looked, how he came across to others and, for a while, how he came across to me. When I got angry with him, say when he broke a date or came on to another woman or went days without calling me, well, that was *my* problem: he hardly ever apologized for anything. I had to accept him on his terms or none at all. It would have been infuriating except that he was so charming and passionate. Instead, it was like some peculiar integrity on his part. Whatever else he may have been, he sure wasn't a wimp."

In a society that widely equates psychic health with the apparent absence of conflict, narcissism is easily mistaken for well-being. To the women who become involved with them, Casanovas—those supremely narcissistic men—often seem admirably free of hang-ups: certainly, that is how many Casanovas see themselves. While they feed off the admiration of their partners and are in constant need of external gratification and reassurance, they present the world with a mask of magisterial self-confidence. In this, they are rather like cats, those engaging predators that seem completely independent of those who give them food and shelter and somehow manage to make us feel immensely flattered when they alight, however briefly, in our laps.

It is this apparent self-sufficiency that gives their gallantry an aura of largesse; a Casanova's attentions do not seem motivated by need so much as by a sense of noblesse oblige. Similarly, he displays an aristocratic disdain for his partners' expressions of displeasure. Women who take him to task for infidelity or neglect are likely to hear themselves accused of being possessive and insecure. Often, they end up believing their accuser, who himself seems a stranger to indecision or self-doubt. There is something almost awe-inspiring about such unshakable aplomb. We have only to reread the interview fragments that begin this section to see the grudging admiration that Casanova evokes even in women whom he has bitterly disappointed.

This admiration, I believe, is really a kind of nostalgic envy. In his essay "On Narcissism," Freud notes that "one person's narcissism has a great attraction for those who have renounced their own narcissism and are seeking after object-love; the charm of the child lies to a great extent in his narcissism, his self-sufficiency and inaccessibility." Casanovas, indeed, often seem extraordinarily youthful, like so many Dorian Grays. It's not that they are immune to the aging process: rather, they seem young because they are in some way frozen in the attitudes of childhood. Every Casanova remains at heart his mother's little prince—or, alternatively, her naughty little boy. Their youthfulness endows these men with a typically American sex appeal, the allure of the eternal boy. They hold out to women an invitation to a second childhood, in which pleasure is there for the taking, without consequences or obligations. The invitation is especially attractive to those women who feel most burdened by the responsibilities of adulthood. Certainly, it appeals to lady-killers' ladies, who so often see life in terms of duty and obligation. No one responds to the fantasy of a renewed childhood more eagerly than those who renounced childhood too early.

The Casanova's dependency is hidden by a narcissistic facade of self-sufficiency. He seems to want women without ever really needing them, to love them from an Olympian plane, removed from insecurity, guilt and doubt. To be loved by such a man—with the implication that one has somehow broken through the screen of his self-absorption—can be immensely flattering. It is as though one had been singled out by a god. The Casanova's narcissism also recalls the blissful solipsism of childhood; when he offers women his love, he also offers them a symbolic return to a time when they too were exempt from the burdens of maturity. An affair with a Casanova thus represents a second chance at childhood, and at the narcissistic freedom and irresponsibility that childhood confers.

THE MYTH OF INSTANT INTIMACY

As for this everything I desire, it suffices for its fulfillment...that each of us be without sites; that we be able magically to substitute for each other: that the kingdom of "one for the other" come..., as if we were the vocables of a new, strange language, in which it would be quite licit to use one word for another. This union would be without limits.

—Roland Barthes, *A Lover's Discourse*

Marilyn, 40: "From the moment we started talking, it was as though the rest of the room and everybody in it disappeared. Gregory told me everything about himself, his hopes, his dreams, his deepest fears. How his marriage had broken up, about his gambling problems. He held nothing back from me. So I felt that I could reveal myself to him—right away, too."

———◆◆———

Phyllis, 52: "When I look back at it, I realize how one-sided my relationship with Joe was. It was always *his* goals, *his* priorities, *his* career. When he tried to rebuild his law practice, I put my career on hold and stayed up nights typing his briefs. Here I was a practicing attorney, and I was doubling as his secretary! The irony was that while I was patching up his practice, he was out running around with other women. The bigger irony was that even after I found out, I kept on typing his briefs."

———◆◆———

Janet, 34: "Jim moved in with Marissa, but he was still hitting me for money to pay his bills. And I never turned him down. He'd call me up and he'd be drunk and crying because of something she'd done, and he'd ask to come over. I suppose I always believed that maybe this time he'd come back to stay, but he never did. And even after reality sunk in, it was impossible for me to say no to him. I felt his pain. I knew how humiliated he was to be bouncing from job to job. I could remember what he'd suffered with alcohol. I could even empathize with what he was going through with his girlfriend and relate to him as a fellow sufferer—even though *he'd* hurt *me*. We'd been so close for three and a half years. I couldn't pretend that closeness had never existed. And so I felt everything that happened to him as though it were happening to me."

———◆◆———

Behind the Casanova's cycle of pursuit and abandonment lies an infant's longing for fusion with its mother and an equally great fear of the consequences of such a fusion: to become the other is to lose the self. At the onset of his love affairs, he promises women what he himself needs and fears—a seductive illusion of closeness. So much of his behavior imparts the message, "I want to be close to you." And nowhere is this message more direct than in Casanova's creation of a climate of instant, if spurious, intimacy between his partners and himself. He reveals himself as easily as he loosens his tie and can give a lie the sincerity of a whispered confession. From the moment he meets them, he gives women a sense of complicity —sudden, exclusive and erotically charged—in the mystery of himself.

The appeal of instant intimacy is especially strong in a country whose sprawling distances and code of individualism leave many people feeling lonely. As a people, we long to be close to others with as little effort as possible, a yearning that AT&T's "Reach out and touch someone" commercials attempt to exploit. The desire for instant intimacy underlies our readiness to call strangers by their first names, our fondness for encounter-type therapies and even our national obsession with the private lives of public figures. To read *People* magazine or watch "Lifestyles of the Rich and Famous" is to gain a momentary and one-sided closeness with people we will never meet. When the Casanova opens himself to a new woman, her response is often a galvanic mixture of curiosity and gratitude. Because he has *chosen* her to be his audience, she feels not like a voyeur but like a coconspirator. She believes that, through some unknown process, he has judged her and found her worthy to share in his secrets.

Lady-killers' ladies are especially vulnerable to this kind of praise, for theirs is the loneliness of those who have never enjoyed true human closeness. Their desire for intimacy is as compelling as any Casanova's and, like his, it stems from spending a lifetime behind a mask. Yet because of the different circumstances of their childhoods and the different imperatives that this culture hands men and women, they lack his capacity for easy revelation: as a child, Casanova learned to *perform* for his parents; lady-killers' ladies generally had to *serve* them. Yearning for recognition yet terrified of rejection, these women find it difficult to open up and do so only with those they trust. Casanova at first does everything he can to make them trust him.

Spurred on by erotic excitement and the comforting illusion of trust, the relationships soon escalate into emotional fusion. The Casanova quickly becomes dependent on his lover for nurture and support. Just as quickly, she comes to identify with him, to share his pain and his hopes, his anxieties and goals. Her moods shift with his. She wants what he wants and will gladly sacrifice her emotional and professional needs to serve his. Like Phyllis, she may end up neglecting her own career to type legal briefs for a man who cheats on her incessantly. The swiftness with which such fusion occurs is matched only by its persistence on her side. A Casanova disengages from his partners quickly and almost effortlessly: a lady-killer's lady may continue to sacrifice her needs and well-being for months after their relationship has effectively ended. Janet's symbiosis with Jim was so enveloping that even after their separation she kept on ministering to his pain as though it were her own, responding to every crisis with more money and an empathetic twinge of anguish.

The powerful attraction of fusion is in part a vestige of our culture's old definitions of romantic love. For a woman to love a man was to become one with him, to subordinate her life to his. Her life, her desires, had never counted for much to begin with, and the assumption was that his life would be big enough for both of them. A common joke among married men in Victorian England was: "My wife and I are one, and I am he." Love was equated with compassion in its literal sense of "feeling with" the other. The growing awareness that romantic fusion was usually one-sided (how many men identified so thoroughly with their women?) led to its obsolescence, and seen from a contemporary vantage point, that kind of self-abnegating love seems both dated and a little sinister, an emotional suicide. We cannot love another person unless we preserve our own identities and remain faithful to them. If we define love as a relationship in which two separate beings briefly transcend their separateness, the *denial* of separateness amounts to nothing less than a betrayal of love.

For a lady-killer's lady, the Casanova's invitation to symbiosis evokes a response whose origins lie in an earlier history of self-abnegation. When a child is forced to act like an adult—to become her mother's mother or her father's lover—she gives up her own needs in favor of the parent's. Even a less dramatic demand—a mother's overly rigid insistence that her daughter conform to her values—may require the same sacrifice. The child's identity is still forming; she cannot understand what she is giving up. All she knows is that by becoming what her parents want her to be she occasionally receives something like love. Years later, when a Casanova holds out the promise of romantic fusion, she responds as she did then: nothing is easier and more exciting than to give up the uncertainty of her own desires for the vicarious gratification of ful-filling another's.

As ill-equipped as they are for genuine intimacy, Casanovas are adept at simulating it. They seem to open up quickly, with a studied artlessness that many women find convincing and that appeals to their fantasies of immediate, effortless closeness. What they offer, though, is not love but a brief interval of symbiotic oneness, in which their desires, their feelings and goals, are the only ones that matter. For lady-killers' ladies, that one-sided promise has a power-ful regressive appeal. Raised in families where their own needs were consistently denied, they unconsciously equate love with self-abnegation and seek nothing so much as to reenact the familiar childhood scenario. Underlying every relationship between a Ca-sanova and his lady is an unstated bargain: if she gives up her au-tonomy, he may give her his love.

THE SPECTER OF THE OTHER WOMAN

Then it occurred to her that there might be a way to avoid the condemnation she saw in Tomas's infidelities: all he had to do was take her along, take her with him when he went to see his mistresses! Maybe then her body would become the first and only among all others. Her body would become his second, his assistant, his alter ego.

—Milan Kundera, *The Unbearable Lightness of Being*

Marilyn: "The first thing we talked about when we met was an-other woman, his ex-wife. For two hours Gregory told me how she'd stomped on his heartstrings and then walked out on him. And of course I thought, That awful bitch! and, You poor, poor thing! Let Marilyn make you all better. It was a challenge for me to restore his confidence after what she'd done to him. I was going to succeed where she'd failed."

———◆·◆———

Janet: "A couple of months after we moved in together, Jim de-cided he wanted to try getting back together with Trudy, his ex-wife. Actually, they were still only separated then, but it was a total shock to me. All I'd known before was that she'd been this castrating (Jim's word) monster whom he never wanted to see again. Then all of a sudden he was telling me that Trudy wanted a trial reconciliation. He said that, as a Catholic, he couldn't just blithely divorce her, and that even though he loved me he felt it was his responsibility to give his marriage another shot. All he had to do was say it was his responsibility and I couldn't be angry at him. I mean, I'm Catholic and I know what a sacrament means. I was angry at *her*, all right, and heartbroken. But I told him, 'Go ahead and do what you have to do.' How could I blame him? And when he came back three months later, the only thing I felt was relief."

———◆•◆———

Carol, 33: "There were a lot of signs that Paul was having affairs, or at least sleeping around. He was always surrounded by women. He'd get calls from them at all hours of the night. We couldn't go out without him running into a woman he knew. Every time I walked into a room with him, I'd be sizing up the threat and thinking, Did he do it with her? Or her? What does *that* one have on her mind? I'd be so keyed up with anxiety that I couldn't enjoy myself anywhere. And the incredible thing was, it never occurred to me that he was cheating. The way I saw it was he *had* slept with so-and-so or he *might* sleep with this one. The women were all in his past or in his future. I never held him responsible. It was always the women's fault. I saw Paul as this fabulous prize that everyone else was trying to snatch away from me, and I never credited him with the power to decide whether he was or wasn't going to be faithful. I guarded him the way a dog guards a bone. And I didn't dare get angry at him, because then he'd surely leave me."

———◆•◆———

The growing fear of AIDS among heterosexuals may be making an eventful erotic history a liability; nevertheless, most women still assume that a man should have a foundation of romantic experience and a lively, active enthusiasm for the opposite sex. Among lady-killers' ladies we often encounter this attitude in an exaggerated form. They seem particularly drawn to men who have recently been involved with other women. The men may be newly divorced or separated from girlfriends with whom they had lived for some time. They may be "half-involved," thrashing in the coils of impossible relationships and desperately seeking a way out. Some lady-killers' ladies start out as third parties in romantic triangles and end up being "promoted" by grateful Casanovas. Others rush in to fill the empty space in these men's beds.

It is easy to feel sorry for a trapped or bereaved man. Lady-killers' ladies often respond to the Casanova's complaints of conjugal misunderstanding, hostility and neglect with an outpouring of credulous sympathy. Many of the women I spoke with claimed that their own histories of abandonment and abuse made them identify with men who had been treated similarly. Yet this sympathy seems to arise from a deeper emotion, a veiled yet fiercely competitive antagonism toward other women. When they describe their predecessors, it's often in language as misogynistic as the most virulent Casanova's—as "bitchy," "coldhearted" and "castrating." Other women are always to blame for his breakups. They see their own role as one not merely of compassionate solace but of vengeance. By loving Casanovas, they will win what no other woman could hold on to. For lady-killers' ladies, Casanovas are prizes in a struggle all the more fierce because it is waged against invisible rivals.

Whenever we encounter someone with a propensity for such symbolic sexual struggles with other women, we are usually seeing the ripples of conflicts that date from childhood. These conflicts are generally of two kinds. The hostility may be the remnant of anger at an abusive or indifferent mother, or it may derive directly from unresolved sexual feelings toward the father. Most girls at some point enter into a rivalry with their mothers for the love of their fathers. The struggle is usually resolved in the same way that it is among boys, through an identification with the same-sex parent. But sometimes that identification never takes place: the mother may have been too cruel or threatening, or the father may have encouraged his daughter's fantasies or, worse, subjected her to his own incestuous advances. On some level, then, the child continues to compete with her mother for the father's attention. Any woman whose Oedipal scenario remains unresolved is likely to be drawn into struggles with other women, to gravitate toward men whom she perceives as other women's "property." By winning them from their wives or girlfriends, she can reenact the old familial battle in a safer arena, one in which the taboos against incest no longer operate.

The problem is that the Casanova, like some eternally disputed no-man's-land, can never be won. No woman, no matter how loving, generous or understanding, can satisfy his addictive needs or keep him from seeking other partners. As soon as she defeats one rival, others rise in her place. The realization that her man is chronically and constitutionally unfaithful is often too painful to bear: instead, she absolves him of any responsibility for his affairs and sees his other women as ruthless predators. The constant threat posed by other women gives her relationship a piquancy and drama that compensate for her lover's shortcomings. In Carol's words, he becomes a "fabulous prize," all the more desirable because other women want him.

In order to cope with her partner's infidelities, a lady-killer's lady generally resorts to the same three alternative modes of collusion discussed earlier in the chapter on tomcats and their spouses. Her *denial* of his role in these incidents sometimes leads her to blind herself entirely to the evidence of his betrayals. She eagerly subscribes to his excuses of working late, of needing time with his friends; she pretends that his relations with his many female "friends" really are innocuous or, alternatively, sees him as a passive victim: those bitches just can't keep their hands off him. I spoke with one woman whose denial was so extreme that she blacked out on finding another woman's clothing in her boyfriend's apartment. In *policing*, a Casanova's partner wastes a great deal of energy keeping track of his movements, monitoring his phone calls and checking his alibis. When she finds the proof she both wants and dreads, she explodes angrily but rarely ends the relationship: he goes on cheating; she goes on warning, investigating and scolding. Finally, she may engage in the empty and degrading rituals of *appeasement*. Seeing the Casanova's affairs as responses to her own inadequacy, she strives to fill the roles of mistress, housekeeper and therapist—whatever she feels her man may be seeking elsewhere. With each disappointment she redoubles her efforts: if only she can become the woman her man really desires, he will at last magically become the lover she wants him to be.

But none of these responses can change a Casanova, nor do they make living with his infidelity less painful. One adult simply cannot change another's behavior. As long as she attempts to do so, the Casanova's lover substitutes the fantasy of controlling her errant partner for the real possibility of caring for herself—caring enough, perhaps, to leave him.

But for these women collusion is so familiar a response to pain that its appeal is irresistible. Very often they behave in their relationships with Casanovas in the same ways they did as children in dysfunctional homes. Back then, collusion was quite necessary, for they were powerless to leave the people who exercised such destructive control over their lives. These children were often compelled to deny their parents' alcoholism or mental illness. We hear of some whose family chore was to hide a mother's whiskey bottles or keep a violent father from beating the other children too badly. And we see those same children striving to compensate for the inadequacies of their parents, caring for those who should have cared for them, requiting abuse with obedience, inconstancy with responsibility, neglect with devotion. For all their outward maturity, lady-killers' ladies are very often trapped in the coping behavior they learned in childhood, and they gravitate toward men who give them the chance to practice that behavior anew. The denial, policing and appeasement that were once so necessary to them are now habits, at once painful and oddly soothing.

To become involved with a Casanova is to become one of a series of women in his life. To be one of a series is rather demeaning—unless, of course, one aspires to be the last, the one who triumphs where so many other women have failed. To become involved with a man who is habitually unfaithful is to be vicariously involved with his other women, to compete with dozens of past and present rivals. For some women such a struggle is familiar and exciting. Here is the chance to wage the Oedipal warfare of childhood on new terrain, against mothers to whom they owe no loyalty, for fathers who are not forbidden prizes. The Casanova's other lovers enhance his allure and lend to an affair with him the suspense of an endless battle. They serve as convenient objects of the anger and disappointment that might otherwise—and more realistically—be directed at the womanizer himself. The Casanova's involvements with other women thus often make him perversely attractive to his primary partner, who might well ask herself: "Would I want him so much if other women didn't?"

THE APPEAL OF THE WOUNDED MAN

The big man was a bundle of needs; he was a chasm that sucked her heart out of her chest.

—John Updike, *The Witches of Eastwick*

Phyllis: "Joe was a weak man. Truly weak. But I guess that was what I wanted. When I met him, he'd flunked the bar and was living off his parents. That didn't put me off. In the course of our marriage, he screwed up two law practices, one business and I don't know how many girlfriends. I was always the one who put his life back together. I helped him out at work; I settled his debts. Whenever there was an emergency I was the one who was there for him. And you have to understand, I *loved* it. It made me feel so necessary!"

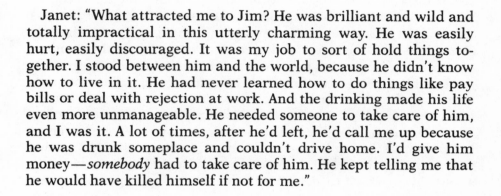

Janet: "What attracted me to Jim? He was brilliant and wild and totally impractical in this utterly charming way. He was easily hurt, easily discouraged. It was my job to sort of hold things together. I stood between him and the world, because he didn't know how to live in it. He had never learned how to do things like pay bills or deal with rejection at work. And the drinking made his life even more unmanageable. He needed someone to take care of him, and I was it. A lot of times, after he'd left, he'd call me up because he was drunk someplace and couldn't drive home. I'd give him money—*somebody* had to take care of him. He kept telling me that he would have killed himself if not for me."

Diana, 43: "Our relationship was based on this unspoken bargain —actually a few bargains: Bret would put romance into my life and I'd put stability in his. Because he was so open about telling me his troubles, I felt that here was someone who would finally listen to mine—the legendary 'Sensitive Man.' It was important for me to feel needed, to do his laundry and cook his meals and help him in his career. I assumed that when I needed something I'd get it in return. But the minute *I* needed anything, he was gone. He once told me, 'You handle your own shit.' But I had to handle his shit, too."

Outwardly, the Casanova often seems dynamic and self-assured, secure in his good looks, professional competence and sexual expertise. But these things cannot compensate for deficiencies that are experienced at the very center of the self. Sooner or later even the most successful Casanova reveals his sense of emptiness and loss, usually in a veiled appeal for rescue from an appropriate woman. A prosperous executive tells his secretary that he is unhappily married. Lord Byron sighs, "I have not a friend in the world!" within earshot of an impressionable young girl. The Casanova's intimacies contain a seductive cry for help, pitched at a frequency that only the right woman can hear.

The right woman is the lady-killer's lady, who suffers from psychic wounds of her own. She is acutely sensitive to his frailty and responds to it galvanically where another woman would flee. For the lady-killer's lady, a man's alcoholism, drug addiction and emotional instability are not liabilities, but signs that he has been victimized by heartless women or an unfeeling world. They bespeak vulnerability, sensitivity, a potential that can be realized if she dedicates herself to loving this injured man back to health. Doing so means being more than a mistress: it means taking on the roles of mother, nursemaid, secretary and confessor. As the relationship deteriorates (for sooner or later he will withdraw from her and turn to other women), those roles become more important. His need for her blinds her to the likelihood that he does not love her; often it keeps her from questioning her love for him, which increasingly is giving way to panic, anger and disappointment. The Casanova's weakness allows his partner to deny her own paralyzing dependency and compensates for her own powerlessness. As Janet recalled: "A couple of times I threatened to leave Jim, and he'd cry and beg me to stay. When he left me, I figured he'd eventually come back because, after all, who would take care of him the way I did?"

As Robin Norwood observes, the appeal of the damaged man suggests "a sexually role-reversed version of the tale of Snow White, who slept under a spell, waiting for the liberation that comes with her true love's first kiss." This fantasy is not one-sided: Casanovas often see themselves as wounded and look to their sexual partners to make them whole; lady-killers' ladies respond to this summons and eagerly jump into the role of prince. The enduring power of myths and fairy tales lies in their expression of collective needs, fears and truths, their coded communiqués. What messages are encoded in the myth of Snow White? The first and most obvious is that a love that is selfless and persevering can overcome any obstacle, undo the most obdurate spell. In the logic of fairy tales such love is always rewarded: when Snow White awakens, she falls in love with her savior. The damaged man exercises an even deeper and more poignant hold on the imaginations of his partners: he offers them the assurance of being needed, he appeals to their desire to control their relationships and he serves as a symbolic surrogate for their absent parents and their damaged selves.

To fall in love is often to come to the unhappy realization that love is as unfair as life. In the world outside fairy tales, kindness, patience and beauty of soul are not necessarily rewarded. How comforting then is the economy of Snow White, in which love is repaid in exact kind. No one longs for justice more keenly than those who were consistently denied it, and when we look at the childhoods of lady-killers' ladies what strikes us is how grossly unfair they often were. As children, they often had to do without the unequivocal parental affection and acceptance that most people take for granted. What love they received was given only conditionally, and the conditions often changed unpredictably. One result of such an upbringing is a lasting desire for fairness. Unable to find it in childhood, lady-killers' ladies tend to make reciprocity a conscious goal of their adult relationships, approaching every affair as a labor of love for which they hope to be repaid. Their unhappiness lies in the irony that they are so often drawn to men who are incapable of giving back.

The very nature of the search makes this misfortune inevitable. It is not just that the lady-killers' lady seeks out the wrong men; she searches for the wrong thing. If we look back to the fairy tale, we see that Snow White loves her prince for a reason: his kiss has restored her to life. The wounded heart responds to the one who heals it. This logic underlies much of the fatal appeal that Casanova has for this woman. Very often she is drawn to him precisely because he *is* damaged and because she has made an unconscious—and mistaken—equation between need and love. Every time her lover calls to her, every time he asks her to salvage the wreckage of his life, his love is reaffirmed. The Casanova's admission of need means more to her than any other man's desire. No caress moves her so much as a cry for help.

Lady-killers' ladies come to confuse dependence with desire for much the same reasons that Casanovas do. The message they received in childhood was not that their parents loved them, but that they needed them. Whereas Casanovas were usually required to repair their mothers' narcissistic wounds, these women had to fill more elemental roles. Very often, it was they who held their families together. When they failed to do so, they might be punished with physical or psychological violence. One woman recalled that the one time she balked at taking care of her bedridden mother, both parents refused to speak to her for weeks. Such messages are bound to damage any child's self-esteem. The unconscious certainty that she is unworthy of love, that the most she can expect in life is the dependence and occasional gratitude of personalities as crippled as those who reared her, persists into adulthood. On some level, such women feel that their usefulness is all that lies between them and abandonment. Although their efforts on their partners' behalf usually go unthanked and place heavy burdens on their own lives, they cannot conceive of love in any other terms. Even if they could, the uncertainties of real love, which comes with no guarantees, would probably strike them as intolerable: if a man doesn't need you, how do you know he won't leave you?

This bargain—like so many other transactions between Casanovas and their lovers—is inherently one-sided and doomed to failure. In the world outside fairy tales, pathological need rarely blossoms into love and the neediest individuals are usually the ones least capable of loving. When asked to give of themselves in return, they are most likely to respond as Bret did: "You handle your own shit." Nor is need any insurance against abandonment: it is easy for Casanovas to find other women to lean on. If wounded men can never reciprocate their lovers' attention, then such relationships must offer other kinds of satisfaction. A great deal of that satisfaction lies in the act of love itself. To love a wounded man is to reassure him, to wait for him, to nurse him; above all, it is to help him. But help is often a disguise for control. Every time a woman rushes to a Casanova's rescue, she is in some way attempting to control her situation. On one level any control she gains is illusory, for all her efforts to manage his life cannot hold it together or keep him faithful to her. But in ceaselessly acting on her lover, she can at least deny the reality of her powerlessness. Her salvage attempts become the meaningless but comforting busywork of a sailor swabbing the deck of a sinking ship.

The psychic origins of the need for control are much the same as the origins of magic and religion. All three stem from a sense of uncomprehending helplessness. Any child who grows up in a chaotic environment is likely to try to control it. It doesn't matter whether her efforts are successful: children think magically, and they make the same connections between their own actions and their parents' behavior that preliterate tribesmen draw between their rituals and the next day's weather. In all probability, the lady-killer's lady spent her childhood in a vain yet ceaseless attempt to impose order on the family maelstrom. Regardless of its outcome, her activity gave her a buffer against feelings of panic, rage and helplessness that might otherwise have overwhelmed her. As long as she kept nursing the sick, placating the angry and intervening in her parents' quarrels, she was not the victim of this domestic melodrama, but its heroine, the good little girl whose precocious industry and courage kept the family together.

The true purpose of controlling behavior is never to repair the other: the child is as incapable of fixing her mother as the grown woman is of loving a Casanova back to health. The only purpose such behavior serves is to ward off feeling. Any behavior that is used to anesthetize pain is likely to become addictive, as drinking is to the alcoholic and womanizing to the womanizer. The relation between Casanovas and their women is thus an alliance between fellow addicts, each of whom uses the other as a transitional object. He needs women to give him a momentary sensation of being nurtured and complete. She needs men whom she can heal, successors to the parents she nursed in her childhood. In healing Casanova, she unconsciously hopes to heal herself, for what is the transitional object if not a stand-in for some missing aspect of the self? The fact that healing never occurs—that these men go on leaving and betraying no matter what their partners do for them—allows the rite to be repeated indefinitely. We can see this addictive play operating in most long-term relationships between Casanovas and their women.

The coping strategies we learn in childhood are the ones we are most likely to practice as adults. This is especially true for those who remain emotionally trapped in childhood. Lady-killers' ladies, who were compelled to assume adult responsibilities before they were truly equipped to do so, have bypassed the processes essential to genuine growth. They have never escaped the emotional turmoil of their early years; they have only learned to narcotize themselves against it, to act as if they were in control of the chaos around them. The wounded man, spreading chaos in his wake, beckons to these women like a familiar figure from the past and offers them a chance to reenact scenarios that are by now as comforting as they were once terrifying. He represents both the fantasy of righting old injustices and the certainty of experiencing them anew; he offers his lovers the surety of his need for them and a chance to exercise a charade of control. He brings with him an entire repertory of ghosts: abandoning fathers, unpredictable mothers and, most of all, the ghosts of thwarted and neglected childhood selves who can perhaps finally be made whole. When we ask why these women put up with Casanovas, why they are willing to spend years patching the holes such men make in their lives and in the lives of those around them, we arrive at a simple answer: this is what they know best.

The Casanova's appeal is not, however, solely pathological. Ironically, this damaged man is in many ways the perfect embodiment of our culture's popular notions of romance: danger and surrender, ecstasy and fusion, exaltation of the other and denial of the self. His idiosyncratic style of courtship encompasses these themes as neatly as if it had been informed by years of market research. He is, above all, a man with innate insight into women's fantasies and desires, an insight no less keen for its lack of empathy and compassion. Such insight may spring from his primary identification with his mother or from the sheer intensity of his need for feminine admiration and validation. Whatever its origins, it makes him a natural seducer—a formidable predator of the heart.

He is most seductive—and therefore most dangerous—to those women who are driven by their own lingering needs for reassurance and validation. Between Casanovas and the women who are drawn to them there is a psychic "fit" that suggests a parody of Plato's notion of the love between the sundered halves of some primal hermaphroditic self. Raised in similarly dysfunctional families, afflicted with a similar split between false and true selves, starving for recognition and nurturance yet uncomfortable with the demands of genuine intimacy, these men and women suffer from complementary pathologies. Each sees in the other a chance to heal old wounds and redress old wrongs; each ends up turning the other into an actor in a drama whose script has already been written and which neither seems able to change. Each suffers from a disorder that is best addressed by outside help.

PART FIVE

Casanova Unbound

CHAPTER THIRTEEN

———◆◆◆———

The View from the Bottom

There was a point in my active sexual addiction—after several years of psychotherapy whose chief issue, interminably debated and elaborated, was my inability to sustain relationships—when I thought myself well enough to get married. I now understood the convoluted roots of my distrust of women, my neurotic need for constant stimulation, my fear of committing myself to someone who might end up leaving me. At least I thought I did. I had mastered the relational skills that my therapist had prescribed, the same ones that so many other professionals were recommending to

a generation of prisoners of sex. I knew how to talk about my feelings before acting on them. I knew that good sex was not just a
matter of performance and that it had little to do with how many
orgasms I gave my partner. I knew that I could be close to a woman
without making love with her, and that her refusal to make love
with me was not necessarily a rejection. I knew that my manhood
had nothing to do with how many lovers I took. I had learned all
this as a Christian convert memorizes the Bible and now considered
myself saved because I knew my texts by heart.

Yet within weeks of marrying, I realized that my knowledge was
incomplete. Either that, or there was some lack of connection between my brain and heart. Once more I was intolerably drawn to
other women—some I knew and some I just glimpsed across a sub-
way platform on my way to work. I say "intolerably" because what
overcame me in their presence left me trembling and laboring for
breath and sometimes brought tears to my eyes. God knows what
those women thought when they saw a strange man gazing at them
with such waif-like yearning. I had similar compulsions to leave the
woman whom I still loved but now suddenly saw, not as my
partner, but as my burden and my jailer. Every time I did something she asked of me—it might have been only to bring her a glass
of water—I felt as though I were giving up a chunk of flesh, a
bloody cube situated, depending on my mood, in the region of my
heart or my balls. When we went to parties, we no sooner entered
the room than I squirmed away from her and fought my way to
neutral ground, dreading the idea that someone, anyone, would see
me as part of a couple. I knew that this hurt her, so I would periodically slink back to her side and give her a few moments of my time.
I wasn't ashamed of my wife—when I could get away from her, I
saw her as other men must have, as brilliant, spirited and desirable.
I was ashamed of being her husband. Anyone's husband.

I couldn't tell my wife about these feelings. I couldn't discuss
them with my therapist; shortly after my wedding I had pro-
nounced myself cured and triumphantly left her office. I couldn't
talk about them with my friends, for I imagined that they would
either be appalled or amused by the fact that I was appalled. I tried
to medicate my impulses with drugs and alcohol and soon got into
the habit of downing a shot or snorting a line whenever I felt
smothered by my wife or drawn too fiercely to another woman. And
I tried to bargain with these impulses, to set the margins within
which I could give them reign. My wedding band acquired the same

significance as the little red hands Italian peasants used to wear to ward off the evil eye. I would be at the health club working out across from a stranger whose thighs, wedged into a Nautilus machine, kept opening and closing in a hypnotically repeated invitation. I would allow myself to glance at her, smile and, if she smiled back, talk to her. But then I would flash my wedding band at her. Maybe I thought that the sight of the gold ribbon glinting on the fourth finger of my left hand would arouse her conscience. Maybe I thought it would make her vanish in a puff of smoke. The ritual soon became a full-blown tic, a sort of moral Tourettism, so that even as I smiled and flirted with a new woman my left hand was frantically shooing her away.

Later I permitted myself to take women out for drinks on the condition that I told them I was married before things got out of hand. Again, I was counting on the notion that women, being somehow finer in spirit or more morally grounded, would draw a line where I couldn't even pick up a pencil. The dates began innocently enough; then I would start getting drunk and make urgent declarations of misery and longing. Sometimes my companion and I ended up necking in front of a bar or in a lurching taxicab. But having drifted that far, I would then hit a cold pocket of sobriety and declare that regardless of my feelings—which by this time always felt a lot like love—we would have to stay on the safe side of friendship and never meet this way again. I became as good at these renunciations as Leslie Howard, who, in spite of the fact that I had only seen his movies on late-night television, became a model of mine during those months, a prototype of the good man who almost goes too far.

Inevitably, my bargaining position weakened. My disease was far better at making deals than I was. When I yielded a little further and began sleeping with other women, it was at first within a grid of taboos almost as elaborate as the ones that used to govern marriages in the Trobriand Islands: no friends of my wife; no neighbors or coworkers; married, preferably, or involved with other men—I didn't want my lovers asking for more time than I was willing to give them or developing an attachment to me that was anything more than casually erotic. We could only see each other infrequently and in total secrecy. And our affairs were based on the explicit recognition that they would neither last too long nor jeopardize our other relationships. These taboos didn't lessen my guilt: I had been feeling guilty from the moment I first thought of leaving my wife or sleeping with another woman. But they gave me something to appeal to when guilt threatened to overwhelm me. On those nights when I lay sleepless beside my wife and my conscience —which I pictured as an overaged motorcycle cop, slow-moving but implacable—began muttering its toothless reproaches, I could plead, "Look, I hardly know the girl. Besides, she's got a boyfriend whom she's got no intention of leaving, certainly not on the basis of a one-night stand, which is all this was. And not a very satisfying one at that. It's not going to go any further. I promise!"

This phase of bargaining, rule making and arguing lasted for about a year. The moral ground beneath me crumbled. My code of infidelity took on endless loopholes and exclusionary clauses. My arguments with my conscience grew increasingly feeble and monotonous, as though I was getting as decrepit as my motorcycle cop, and they finally ceased when I had nothing more to tell it than "Shut up, shut up, shut up!" Early in 1984, a year and a half after we had married, I left my wife. The ostensible reason for our breakup was my involvement with a woman who lived across the street from us. I had been seeing her twice a week for three months and had gone from forbidding her to call me to telling her that I loved her. At the time I was as sure that I loved this woman as I had once been sure that I loved my wife. I wanted nothing so much as to spend an entire night in her bed and wake up gazing at her face. I used to tell her that: "All I want is to watch you while you sleep." But as soon as I was free, I stopped seeing her, arguing that I needed some time alone to sort my feelings out. By the time they were sorted, I was passionately involved with someone else.

The Casanova complex cannot be cured through prayer or through the measures by which one cuts back on sugar or stops biting one's nails. It is not a simple moral failure or a bad habit. Like other compulsive disorders, sexual addiction overrides the moral restraints of the superego ("I shouldn't") and the pragmatism of the ego ("I can't"). In their pursuit of sexual opportunity, Casanovas violate their own ethical standards—their loyalty to wives or girlfriends, their concern for their reputations and their scruples against promiscuity and deceit. One of the men I interviewed is a devout Jehovah's Witness who commits his infidelities in the continual fear of divine punishment. Guilt is one of this condition's emotional side effects. Those Casanovas who seem untroubled by their consciences often display the symptoms of more profound disorders, which are accompanied by their own corrosive fears. Casanovas suffering from borderline personality, for example, are obsessed by fears of discovery and disgrace, the dread of impotence and, above all, the thinly veiled fear that their lovers will either punish them or devour them.

Often intelligent and successful, Casanovas consistently endanger what they know to be their own best interests. All of them have sacrificed at least one marriage or relationship to their illness. Many have compromised careers by pursuing the wrong woman at the wrong time or by devoting more effort to romantic intrigue than they did to work. Some have organized their lives around their compulsion, like Anthony, who, at twenty-six, continues to live with his parents so that he can spend his money on extravagant evenings with his girlfriends. In their insistence on treating sex as a casual and innocuous activity, all of these men seem to be flirting with AIDS. Few of them admit to using condoms. Instead, they reassure themselves with fantasies of immunity and with the notion that their partners are too "nice" to be anything but safe.

One can argue that most sick people want to be cured of their afflictions, while most Casanovas do not. About half of the men I spoke with claim that their womanizing is not a problem. (One man told me that *"Finding* women is, but womanizing, no.") It is hard to take such claims at face value. Even the happiest of my subjects admitted that they were often lonely, anxious and depressed. In light of such admissions, the equanimity with which Casanovas sometimes view their sexual exploits seems like another variant of the denial that characterizes all forms of addiction. Indeed, their arguments often sound remarkably like the ones alcoholics use to justify their drinking: "I can handle her"; "It's just this once"; "It doesn't hurt anybody"; "My wife will never find out."

Many Casanovas *do* seek to treat their compulsive sexuality, or at least place reasonable limits on it. Some have entered psychoanalysis or other kinds of therapy. A few have consulted with ministers, priests or rabbis. A great many "rotate" addictions, turning from women to alcohol, drugs, gambling or compulsive work whenever the consequences of their behavior become too great. They often go to ingenious and bizarre lengths to curb their womanizing. Alan, for example, has given up one-night stands and stopped sleeping with partners whom he finds "unviable." Casanovas frequently try to limit the duration of their affairs and restrict the number of sexual partners they have at any one time. I spoke with several married men who cheated only when they were away from home. Even Eric, that paradigm of liberated Eros, takes his lovers only from the narrow circles of science-fiction fandom and New Age spiritualism. I sometimes had an impression of a legion of Casanovas, each anxiously tending the machinery of his sexuality, turning a valve here, flipping a switch there, in the hope that he could finally make it stop smoking and shuddering.

The most common fallacy among Casanovas—and among their partners—is that the affliction can be cured by the "right" woman or the "right" relationship. We have already discussed the mythical quality of this belief in the redemptive power of love and its psychic origins in the childhoods of Casanovas and the women who love them. We need only add that in their quest for relief, most Casanovas end up aggravating their condition, leaving woman after woman for the specter of yet another who seems more loving, generous or tolerant and turning indignantly away when she, too, proves unable to fill the vacuum of self. In instances of extreme denial, we see men blaming their lovers for "making" them unfaithful or "forcing" them to leave, while those women assume full responsibility for their transgressions. Love is not a cure for their disorder, only its first casualty. No human being can cure another of the pain of being alive.

My own experience is that none of these self-administered plans of treatment is a solution to the Casanova complex. At best, they give these men an illusory and momentary self-satisfaction—the excuse that they have tried to change and that whatever unhappiness they now cause is someone else's—anyone else's—problem. At worst, Casanovas' attempts to modify their behavior intensify their guilt and aggravate secondary addictions: I stepped up my usage of drugs and alcohol to keep myself from cheating on my wife and found instead that I could cheat when I was too high to speak coherently. Most such attempts end in failure, and even when the compulsion is rerouted it remains as consuming and destructive as ever. I spoke with many men who had shifted their pattern from one-night stands to longer involvements that were superficially more stable; most of them seemed plagued by the same urgency, guilt and sexual dread that had afflicted them from the first. The fact that they were now leaving women they cared for often made those feelings keener and more debilitating.

In the Introduction to this book, I suggested that it was not a self-help manual in the traditional sense. It sets forth no surefire exercises or conversational gambits, no tidy ways of smothering the flames of sexual compulsion. Everything I have learned about this condition—and everything I lived through in my own active addiction—suggests that it will not yield to the struggles of those who are still trapped inside it. The only recourse for the Casanova who wishes to change is to seek outside help. The first and most obvious source of help is psychotherapy, particularly those types that specialize in the treatment of narcissism and compulsive disorders. I would also direct sufferers to clinical programs in human sexuality, like those at the medical school of the University of Minnesota at Minneapolis. A growing body of practitioners views compulsive sexuality as a behavioral problem that can be treated through such techniques as desensitization and flooding. Such therapies attempt to relieve the patient of his symptoms by exposing him—gradually or abruptly—to the sources of his discomfort and teaching him to modify his responses to them. They may sometimes include courses in meditation and relaxation response or anxiety-reducing drugs. The emphasis throughout is on changing the patient's behavior in response to old stimuli.

My own belief is that, while it is essential for the Casanova to change his behavior, he must also change the distorted thinking and feeling that both cause and accompany it. A symptom suppressed has a way of metamorphosing into other symptoms. A Casanova may change from a hitter into a romantic, nester or tomcat. He may "manage" his behavior for months at a time only to have it resurface with all its old virulence. The persistence of symptoms is also evidenced by the number of Casanovas who are multiply addicted, who not only womanize but gamble, drink or take drugs and who sometimes attain momentary relief from one disorder only to plunge headlong into another. A strictly behavioral therapy is unlikely to rid the Casanova of the feelings of emptiness and unreality that underlie his womanizing. A true change of life must be accompanied by a change of heart.

While traditional psychotherapy does address the narcissism from which the Casanova complex stems, it too is subject to limitations. My own course of therapy taught me a great deal about my illness without releasing me from it. How could it, when I was unwilling to take enough responsibility for my behavior to change it, and no amount of treatment could give me the will to do so? The talking cure encounters a peculiar obstacle in the addictive or compulsive patient, who so often wants to have his pain relieved without giving up his drug or fetish. The comfort supplied by a new mistress, a day at the track or a snort of cocaine may be brief and fatally flawed, but it is often the only comfort he knows. To give it up, even for a few days, summons up the dread of the overwhelming anguish that he hoped to alleviate in the first place. What he feels now may be terrible; what will happen when he gives up his shield against the heartlessness of the world and the emptiness of the self? Thus, he is most likely to continue his old behavior while ceaselessly talking about it with a sympathetic professional. He goes on talking, the therapist goes on listening, each hoping that the sheer accumulation of material will provide a key that unlocks the heart and rids the patient of his addiction. The problem is that as long as he continues to act on his compulsions, he is unlikely to experience the need to stop on the visceral level that makes it possible. His heart remains sealed and no external key can unlock it.

The Casanova cannot recover from his condition until he stops using women as drugs. He will not be able to stop for long unless he begins to recover—that is, to revise his skewed vision of the world and establish a benign and durable sense of self that is not dependent on constant sexual reinforcement. To accomplish this he may seek a therapy that combines behavioral and analytic approaches. He should also make use of a combination of psychotherapy and a Twelve-Step program of recovery, such as Sexaholics Anonymous, Alcoholics Anonymous, Narcotics Anonymous or Gamblers Anonymous. There are numerous variants of these fellowships, like Chemical Dependents Anonymous and Sex and Love Addicts Anonymous, some of which are listed in the Appendix. Most of them have meetings throughout this country and around the world. The program most obviously suited for the Casanova is Sexaholics Anonymous, which specifically addresses the problem of compulsive sexuality. But this fellowship is relatively young, and its meetings are still scattered. As a great many Casanovas are also alcoholics, drug addicts or compulsive gamblers, I would encourage them to find help in any Twelve-Step fellowship in which they feel sufficiently comfortable.

The Twelve-Step programs have no initiation fees or membership dues and are based on the principle of total anonymity. They are aligned with no medical center, government agency or religious denomination. They ask nothing more of those who come than the willingness to give up the behavior that brought them there. In return, they offer nothing less than a new life. It is difficult to describe what goes on in a program like SA or AA—so much of the process of recovery is as much a mystery as the process of spiritual conversion—but these fellowships provide the Casanova with a safe place in which he can discuss his problem freely, without being judged and with the encouragement he needs to stop using sex as a drug. The process is not easy—the Casanova, like any other addict, is likely to be plagued by all the emotional symptoms of withdrawal in the first weeks of his recovery and may periodically relapse—but it can be effective if one submits to it fully and lives its principles to the best of one's ability, for the rest of one's life.

The willingness to change—however one chooses to undertake it—is, of course, essential to recovery from the Casanova complex. It is the one thing that cannot be supplied from without. No Casanova will give up womanizing until he has reached a necessary bottom—the crisis that finally cracks his denial mechanism. What does it take to make a Casanova willing to give up a sexual pattern that has become the hub of his life? He is unlikely to be swayed by guilt, or by the pleas and threats of his partners. The pleas may move him and the threats frighten him, but the ramparts of his compulsion are so high that he will in all likelihood remain obdurate. When his lover begs him to stay, he dismisses her as clinging and possessive; when his wife warns him that she will leave if he doesn't stop cheating, he tells himself that she is trying to bully him and feels honor bound to assert his manhood in the only way he knows. And even if he does allow himself to experience shame or fear, he is likely to respond to those feelings with a renewed frenzy of his familiar behavior—to mask his guilt beneath the excitement of a new conquest, to protect himself from being left by being the first to leave. Guilt is an appeal to the sense of what should be; fear is an apprehension of what might be: my own experience is that the Casanova is changed only by his recognition of what *is*.

For many of us in recovery, the willingness to change is at first feeble and conditional: we do not want to give up the drug of seduction and flight so much as we want relief from its accompanying pain. Pain is the great motivator for change, and it may be the only thing that can overcome the layered defenses and rationalizations of the Casanova. Such pain may result from the final dissolution of a relationship he had always taken for granted; it may come when the woman who stood by him through repeated betrayals refuses to stay for more. He may, in the course of his addiction, lose one job too many or estrange the last and most steadfast of his old friends. For all too many of these men, the pain reaches sufficient levels only when they are too old to attract new partners and find themselves alone, without the comforting supports of age, and afflicted with desires that they no longer have the means or health to satisfy. Even this pain may not be enough: at sixty-three, Fred is still desperately seeking new sexual opportunities, though his heart condition makes them potentially fatal.

In recent years the compulsive womanizing of the Casanova has taken on new consequences. In the moral climate of the 1980s adultery is once more a liability: Gary Hart could not conceal his sexual indiscretions as easily as John Kennedy had (perhaps because, unlike JFK, he did not have the press on his side), nor were they condoned as they were in Grover Cleveland's time. More serious, AIDS has spread from homosexuals and intravenous drug users into the heterosexual population and has become a risk attached to any sexual transaction between strangers. We may, like the Elizabethans, once more draw an equation between sex and death: only this time, the death is no longer little.

I can't say what kind of pain or fear will move other men to seek help. I can only describe the terrain I found when I hit bottom. By 1985 I realized that the measures I had always taken to ward off pain had become themselves immeasurably painful: womanizing no longer "worked" for me. I had lost a great deal in the pursuit of my addiction, and my sense of personal emptiness now overtook me within minutes of my last conquest. Sex no longer gave me anything more than the physical release of ejaculation; often enough, I simply couldn't reach orgasm. Women were no longer objects of love, or even of desire. I had reached the point where I loathed my partners even as I entered them, and my loathing was all the worse because I knew how badly I needed them. I had tried to control my compulsion; I had tried to channel it. I had tried to think of it as a bad habit that I could break at any time. When I exhausted all my familiar defenses, I reached a point of readiness that was mine alone and sought help from a therapist and a support group. What was enough for me may not be enough for other men. The moment in which I sought help was the moment in which I truly acknowledged the vacuum inside me and knew beyond doubt that no effort of my own could fill it. I could no longer *take* what I needed from the women in my life: I had to ask for it, not from women but from my fellow sufferers.

The fact that the Casanova's process of decline and renewal is essentially a solitary one means that no woman can make him change. No matter how durable or intense the bond between them, she is powerless over his addiction. Any woman who is presently involved with a Casanova, any woman who contemplates a relationship with such a man, should realize this from the first. If there is a long string of women in his past, chances are there will be more in his future. If he insists on sleeping with other women, it is unlikely that he can be persuaded to be monogamous. If he has left once and then begged his partner to take him back, there is a strong probability that he will leave again. Regardless of whether a woman finds such behavior sinful, unbearable or merely irritating, she should realize that it cannot be altered by such techniques as denial, policing or appeasement. The Casanova will continue womanizing until he reaches his bottom, and nothing a wife or lover does can do much more than slow his fall.

What options, then, are available to women involved with Casanovas? The most obvious is to avoid such involvements in the first place. To do so is less a matter of specific techniques than of observation and common sense. On meeting a man, a woman should find out as much as possible about his sexual history: how many partners he has had before, how long his previous relationships lasted and how they ended. She should be skeptical of any man who portrays himself as a victim of so many heartless shrews. If he expresses an immediate and overwhelming attraction to her, she should wait to see whether it lasts through repeated encounters. If he is flattering, she should see whether his flattery corresponds to her own self-image or, rather, to *his* idealized archetype of a good mother; it would be well to be a litle leery of a man who waxes poetic about qualities she doesn't recognize in herself. If he goes to extraordinary lengths to please her, she should try to find out if he does the same for his family and friends. The point is to pay attention to who he is rather than to the image he presents and to examine his conduct as objectively as possible.

The Casanova typically rushes into relationships. His partner would do well to establish her own pace for intimacy and stick to it. She should reveal herself only when she feels like doing so and postpone sexual relations until she feels comfortable having them. (It goes without saying that she should require him to use condoms.) Establishing a personal pace for intimacy means being in tune with her own feelings and desires. It means knowing whether she genuinely cares for a man or simply enjoys being the object of his obsessive attention and pursuit. It means knowing how much trust and familiarity she needs to be comfortable in bed with a new partner. Above all, it means being firm about her priorities in life and not sacrificing them to please a lover who may want all of her time one week only to disappear the next. I am not advocating a pose of coyness or a strategy that treats men as adversaries. I suggest only that women keep their eyes open, while remaining at least as attentive to their own needs and desires as they are to their partners'.

Such advice comes too late for any woman who is married to a Casanova or lives with one. His behavior is already apparent and has probably gone on unchanged for some time. All that remains is for her to acknowledge that it is unchangeable—at least by her. The alternatives for a Casanova's spouse or lover are to leave or to stay, knowing that her partner will probably continue to act out sexually until he reaches a level of pain that is intolerable to him. Leaving a Casanova may actually benefit him, to the extent that it deprives him of one of his primary sources of denial and leaves him alone with the consequences of his compulsion. Certainly, it provides his spouse with relief from the daily evidence of his disorder and with an opportunity to build a healthier relationship with another man. But leaving may be too painful for some women and too difficult for those who are financially dependent on the Casanova. The woman who chooses to stay with him must find a way to go on living with chronic infidelity and periodic desertions. She must detach herself from his behavior, realizing that it does not stem from any inadequacy of hers and that it will not yield to her most heroic efforts to become a better wife or lover. Above all, she must develop her self-esteem to the point where it is not affected by her partner's transgressions, a superhuman task for any woman who has grown up with the traditional idea of love as "forsaking all others." For most women, this labor is too great to undertake alone. Fortunately, women who love Casanovas can get ample help from qualified therapists or from such self-help fellowships as Al-Anon, Nar-Anon, or the "Women Who Love Too Much" groups that have formed in response to Robin Norwood's book.

Whether she chooses to stay or leave, a Casanova's partner should consider the recent option of a therapeutic intervention, whose purpose is to get the womanizer into treatment. She should not attempt this alone, but rather seek the assistance of others who know him well enough to recognize his problem—family members, friends or coworkers. A qualified professional—a therapist or certified addictions counselor—is essential. The participants in an intervention should compile evidence of the Casanova's disorder and of its effects on the people who love him. They should rehearse the confrontation beforehand and have an immediate course of treatment lined up. To my knowledge, this option has previously only been used with alcoholics and drug addicts, but it has had a high degree of success. Anyone interested in learning more about it would do well to read Vernon E. Johnson's *Intervention: How to Help Someone Who Doesn't Want Help* (Minneapolis: Johnson Institute Books, 1986).

All this paints a rather forbidding picture of the prospects of recovery from the Casanova complex. I can only reiterate that recovery *is* possible—I and hundreds of men like me are now leading sexually sober lives. Recovery offers rewards far beyond the cessation of sexual compulsions. In addiction, the Casanova lives in a dream world in which women are interchangeable objects: in that dream, all women are good mothers or bad mothers, Lucretias or Judiths, who exist solely to be yearned for and seduced, conquered and abandoned, worshiped and then despised. In recovery one is delivered into a world where women are individual presences, many of whom are still desirable but desirable because of who they are rather than what they represent. It is hard to convey the wonder of such a discovery, as though after spending years in a dark warehouse filled with mannequins one were finally to walk onto a sunlit street populated with real human beings. The greatest joy is that one no longer feels so empty of heart and spirit. Once the Casanova stops frantically trying to fill his psychic vacuum, once he enters a program of recovery, the vacuum begins to fill of its own, giving way to a sense of self that needs no conquest to verify its existence. Finding that self and nourishing it may be a lifelong work, requiring much discipline and self-denial. The Casanova usually finds out that he is different both from what he thought he was and what he wanted to be. He is no longer a heartless fucking machine or God's gift to women. He is no longer an anxious child searching for a mother's nurturance and recognition while masquerading as a grown-up. He is a man healing from a grave sickness and perhaps just discovering a capacity for love he never knew existed.

At this writing I live alone, having separated two months ago from a woman I loved for a year and a half. We knew each other awhile before we became lovers; in retrospect, I would have waited longer, but I was fairly sure of my feelings for her by the time we shared a bed. When we separated, it was not because I had lost desire for her or fallen in love with someone else. Throughout our time together, I was faithful to her: it was the longest period of fidelity I have ever known. Knowing about my past, she understandably worried that I would be unfaithful. She seemed to derive little comfort when I told her that to cheat on her would be to deprive myself of peace of mind. How could I throw away what I had longed for all my adult life and finally found at the age of thirty-three? Fidelity was, and is, a large part of my personal solution to my own Casanova complex. I choose it not because it is right, but because it is *comfortable*.

Although I see the Casanova complex as a condition with a strong moral dimension, I am reluctant—really, unable—to say what kind of sexual behavior *is* morally appropriate. Not to exploit or deceive or betray, these all seem obvious. But I don't doubt that some men and women legitimately prefer to lead active sex lives with many different partners, or that some sexually open relationships are genuinely fair and loving. I wouldn't like to see this book used as an argument for enforced chastity or monogamy or as a nostalgic manifesto for the sexual mores of the 1950s—or, for that matter, for those of Puritan New England. If I have learned anything from writing this book and from living the life that led up to it, it is that there is no such thing as a single code of righteous conduct in matters of the heart. A sexual ethic is something that each of us must choose for himself or herself, forging it through repeated trial and error, pleasure and heartache. The tragedy of Casanova is that he never really chose his sexual patterns, but rather had them thrust on him by the exigencies of addictive need. To need something so fiercely and hopelessly is not to choose it. If this book is an argument for anything, it is an argument for choice.

Appendix

A list of self-help fellowships and treatment facilities for Casanovas and the women who love them. Write for information on meetings and services in your area:

Sexaholics Anonymous (SA)
P.O. Box 300
Simi Valley, California 93062

Sex and Love Addicts Anonymous
P.O. Box 1964
Boston, Massachusetts 02105
(East Coast)
or
P.O. Box 99429
San Francisco, California 94109
(West Coast)

Sex Addicts Anonymous (SAA)
Twin Cities SAA Intergroup
P.O. Box 30308
Minneapolis, Minnesota 55403

(612) 339-0217

Since so many Casanovas also suffer from alcoholism, drug addiction and other compulsive disorders, they may seek help from such Twelve-Step fellowships as:

Alcoholics Anonymous (AA)
Alcoholics Anonymous World
   Services, Inc.
Box 459
Grand Central Station
New York, New York 10163

(212) 686-1100

Narcotics Anonymous (NA)
Narcotics Anonymous World Service
Office
P.O. Box 9999
Van Nuys, California 91409

Gamblers Anonymous (GA)
1543 West Olympic Boulevard,
Suite 533
Los Angeles, California 90015

Debtors Anonymous (DA)
314 West Fifty-third Street
New York, New York 10019
and
250 West Fifty-seventh Street
New York, New York 10019

The following centers provide inpatient or outpatient treatment for men and women suffering from compulsive sexual disorders:

Golden Valley Health Center
4101 Golden Valley Road
Golden, Minnesota 55422

(612) 588-2771

Joellen Smith Psychiatric Hospital
4601 Patterson Road
New Orleans, Louisiana 70114

(504) 364-3000

West Bank Center for Psychotherapy
4460 General Meyer Avenue
New Orleans, Louisiana 70131

(504) 367-0707

These organizations help the families and friends of sexual compulsives, alcoholics and drug addicts, utilizing the same Twelve Steps that have proved so helpful to members of AA and NA:

Codependents of Sex Addicts
(COSA)
Twin Cities COSA
P.O. Box 1457
Minneapolis, Minnesota 55414

Al-Anon Family Group Headquarters
World Service Office
P.O. Box 182
Madison Square Station
New York, New York 10159-0182

Nar-Anon Family Groups
P.O. Box 2562
Palos Verdes Peninsula, California
90274

Families Anonymous
P.O. Box 528
Van Nuys, California 91408

(818) 989-7841

Notes

INTRODUCTION

18: Was that pattern: Donald Symons, quoted by M. Daly and M. Wilson, "Male and Female," *The Sciences* 22–24 (March 1980): 24; cited by Jeremy Cherfas and John Gribbin, *The Redundant Male: Is Sex Irrelevant in the Modern World?* (New York: Pantheon, 1985), 133.

CHAPTER ONE: SEXUAL ADDICTION

26: portraying himself: Gail Sheehy, "The Road to Bimini," *Vanity Fair*, September 1987, 135.

26: "He had a real Don Juan complex": Ibid., 189.

27: "I'm not [president]": Tom Morgenthau, Margaret Garrard Warner, Howard Fineman and Erik Calonius, "The Sudden Fall of Gary Hart," *Newsweek*, May 18, 1987, 25.

28: "Gary Hart has been writing": Sheehy, "Bimini," 133.

28: "Addiction is not a chemical reaction": Stanton Peele with Archie Brodsky, *Love and Addiction* (New York: Taplinger Books, 1975), 7; reprinted in Howard Shaffer and Milton Earl Burglass, eds., *Classic Contributions in the Addictions* (New York: Brunner, Mazel, 1981), 335.

CHAPTER TWO: THE BIRTH OF THE SCOUNDREL

31: "a bachelor": Jacques Casanova de Seingalt, *The Memoirs of Jacques Casanova*, ed. Madeleine Boyd (New York: Modern Library, 1929, 1957), *xi.*

32: "If she tries to play": Ibid., 91.

32: "I am neither tender": Ibid., 91.

32-33: "I had intended to marry": Ibid., 77–78.

33: "Casanova loved many women": Ibid., *ix.*

33: "I could still love": Ibid., 188.

34: "the instability": Ibid., *ix.*

34-35: "Casanova's name": Chantal Thomas, *Casanova: Un Voyage Libertin* (Paris: Editions Denoel, 1985), 59. Author's translation.

35: "pleasure becomes": Christopher Lasch, *The Culture of Narcissism* (New York: W.W. Norton, 1979).

37: "A man who abstains": Sigmund Freud, "'Civilized' Sexual Morality and Modern Nervousness," in his *Sexuality and the Psychology of Love* (New York: Macmillan, 1963), 35.

38: "Where such men love": Sigmund Freud, "The Most Prevalent Form of Degradation in Erotic Life," in ibid., 62.

CHAPTER THREE: PATTERNS OF DESIRE

56: one psychologist calls: Cited by William H. Masters, Virginia E. Johnson and Robert C. Kolodny, *Masters and Johnson on Sex, Love and Intimacy* (Boston: Little, Brown, 1986), 217.

56-57: In test subjects: Michael Leibowitz, *The Chemistry of Love* (Boston: Little, Brown, 1983); cited in ibid., 226.

57: "a colorless object": Roland Barthes, *A Lover's Discourse*, trans. Richard Howard (New York: Farrar, Straus, 1978), 31.

60: "the narcissistic person": Otto F. Kernberg, *Internal World and External Reality: Object Relations Theory Applied* (New York: Jason Aronson, 1985), 137.

60: "Within a year": Philip Roth, *The Professor of Desire* (New York: Farrar, Straus, 1977), 261.

70: "Tomas desired": Milan Kundera, *The Unbearable Lightness of Being*, trans. Michael Henry Heim (New York: Harper & Row, 1984), 12.

71: "When the prick": Philip Roth, *Portnoy's Complaint* (New York: Random House, 1969), 128.

72: no correlation: John Money, *Love and Love Sickness: The Science of Sex, Gender Difference and Pair-Bonding* (Baltimore: Johns Hopkins University Press, paperback ed., 1981), 93–95.

78: I stayed home: Charles Bukowski, "Six Inches," in *The Most Beautiful Woman in Town* (San Francisco: City Lights Books, 1967), 24.

82: "any woman": David Herbert Donald, *Look Homeward: A Life of Thomas Wolfe* (Boston: Little, Brown, 1987); quoted in Monroe K. Spears, "Big Bad Wolfe?" *The New York Review of Books*, September 24, 1987.

88: "I believe right now": Suzanne Vega, "Undertow" (New York: AGF Music Ltd./Waifersongs Ltd.)

CHAPTER FOUR: HITTERS

100: "The best": Tirso de Molina, *The Rake of Seville*, trans. Roy Campbell; published in Eric Bentley, ed., *Life is a Dream and Other Spanish Classics* (New York: Applause Theatre Book Publishers, 1986). All subsequent Don Juan quotes from the same text.

CHAPTER FIVE: DRIFTERS

112: A recent fan book: Sally Hibbin, *The Official James Bond Movie Book* (New York: Crown, 1987), 32 passim.

CHAPTER SIX: ROMANTICS

121: A recent article: Bruce Buschel, "Romeo Rising." *GQ*, August 1987, 206–8.
125: "...tender as a mistress": Michel Leiris, *Manhood: A Journey from Childhood into the Fierce Order of Virility*, trans. Richard Howard (San Francisco: North Point Press, paperback ed., 1984), 100–101.
126: "Judith, placid": Ibid., 94–95.
127: "the union": Jacques Casanova de Seingalt, *The Memoirs of Jacques Casanova*, ed. Madeleine Boyd (New York: Modern Library, 1929), 128.
128: "I never could love": Quoted by Leslie Marchand, *Byron: A Portrait* (Chicago: University of Chicago Press, paperback ed., 1970), 183.
129: "a true voluptuary": Ibid., 157–58.
129: "The image of Lucrèce": Leiris, *Manhood*, 42.

CHAPTER SEVEN: NESTERS

135-36: "Love curdles": Quoted by Kenneth S. Lynn, *Hemingway* (New York: Simon and Schuster, 1987), 135–36.
136: "The world's a jail": Ibid., 130.
137: "You really can": Ernest Hemingway, "The Strange Country," in *The Complete Stories of Ernest Hemingway: The Finca Vigia Edition* (New York: Scribner's, 1987), 635.

CHAPTER EIGHT: JUGGLERS

149: "It was better": Quoted by Diana Trilling, *Mrs. Harris: The Death of the Scarsdale Diet Doctor* (Orlando: Harcourt Brace Jovanovich, 1981), 261.
149: "He did all": Ibid, 210.
150: "Get out": Ibid, 279.
160: "The crisis": Roland Barthes, *A Lover's Discourse*, trans. Richard Howard (New York: Farrar, Straus, 1978), 10–11.
161: on men who avoid commitment: Steven Carter and Julia Sokol, *Men Who Can't Love: When a Man's Fear Makes Him Run from Commitment (And What a Smart Woman Can Do About It)* (New York: M. Evans, 1987).

CHAPTER NINE: TOMCATS

169: "The whorehouse": John Money, *Love and Love Sickness: The Science of Sex, Gender Difference and Pair Bonding* (Baltimore: Johns Hopkins University Press, paperback ed., 1981), 57.
169: The psychoanalyst Melanie Klein: Hanna Segal, *Introduction to the Work of Melanie Klein*

(London: Hogarth Press and Institute for Psycho-Analysis, 1973), 3–5; 27–30; 103–16.

CHAPTER TEN: "TRYING TO MAKE SOMEONE LOVE ME": THE FAMILY OF THE WOMANIZER

180: "...[Mrs. Byron] is very amiable": Quoted by Leslie Marchand, *Byron: A Portrait* (Chicago: University of Chicago Press, paperback ed., 1970), 11–12.

180: "My mother": Ibid., 11.

191: "meet[ing] the omnipotence": D. W. Winnicott, *The Maturational Processes and the Facilitating Environment: Studies in the Theory of Emotional Development* (New York: International Universities Press, 1965), 145.

191: "One sometimes": Joyce McDougall, *Theaters of the Mind: Illusion and Truth on the Psychoanalytic Stage* (New York: Basic Books, 1985), 118.

193: transitional object: For a more complete discussion of transitional objects and their addictive qualities, see McDougall, *Theaters of the Mind*, 66–80.

198: The Lover as Fetish: For a more complete discussion of fetishism see McDougall, ibid., 221 passim; Janine Chasseguet-Smirgel, *Sexuality and Mind: The Role of the Father and the Mother in the Psyche* (New York: New York University Press, 1986), 17, 24, 65–79, and *Creativity and Perversion* (New York: Norton, 1984), 26, 43, 80–88; Sigmund Freud, *Three Essays on the Theory of Sexuality* (New York: Basic

Books, 1962), 19–21, 28, 33; Phyllis Greenacre, *Emotional Growth: Psychological Studies of the Gifted and a Great Variety of Other Individuals*, vol. 7 (Madison, Conn.: International Universities Press, 1971), 9–30, 58–66, 162–81, 300–52.

CHAPTER ELEVEN: THE CULTURE OF THE LIBERTINE

201: 66 percent: Shere Hite, *The Hite Report on Male Sexuality* (New York: Knopf, 1981), 1096.

202: "polygyny of the powerful": Robin Fox, "The Conditions of Sexual Evolution," in *Western Sexuality: Practice and Precept in Past and Present Times*, Philippe Ariès and André Béjin, eds. (Oxford: Basil Blackwell, paperback ed., 1986), 11.

202: A 1968 survey: Cited by Jeremy Cherfas and John Gribbin, *The Redundant Male: Is Sex Irrelevant in the Modern World?* (New York: Pantheon, 1985), 114.

203: For the Jews: Lis Harris, "Lubavitcher Hasidim," part 2, *The New Yorker*, September 23, 1985, 84.

203: The Christian fathers listed: Michel Foucault, "The Battle for Chastity," in Ariès and Béjin, *Western Sexuality*, 17–18.

203: "strict fidelity demanded": André Béjin, "The Extra-Marital Union Today," in ibid., 161.

204: "A good pair of buttocks": Quoted by Achillo Olivieri, "Eroticism and Social Groups in Sixteenth-Century Venice: The Courtesan," in ibid., 96.

204: a guide to American brothels: William H. Masters, Virginia E.

Johnson and Robert C. Kolodny, *Masters and Johnson on Sex, Love and Intimacy* (Boston: Little, Brown, 1986), 15.

204: In the early Middle Ages: Philippe Ariès, "The Indissoluble Marriage," in Ariès and Béjin, *Western Sexuality*, 146–47.

205: in nineteenth-century England: Peter Gay, *Education of the Senses: The Bourgeois Experience, Victoria to Freud* (New York: Oxford University Press, paperback ed., 1984), 174.

206: "He is always ready": Joan Mellen, *Big Bad Wolves: Masculinity in the American Film* (New York: Pantheon, 1977), 156.

207: Although motherhood: For an excellent discussion of the Marian myth and the institutions that evolved from it, see Marina Warner, *Alone of All Her Sex: The Myth and the Cult of the Virgin Mary* (New York: Vintage Books, 1983).

208: in fifteenth-century France: Jacques Rossiaud, "Prostitution, Sex and Society in French Towns in the Fifteenth Century," in Ariès and Béjin, *Western Sexuality*, 84–85.

209: "In [the] pages [of pornography]": Gay, *Education*, 369, 376.

211: "Those shameless endearings": Quoted in Jean-Louis Flandrin, "Sex in Married Life in the Early Middle Ages: The Church's Teaching and Behavioural Reality," in Ariès and Béjin, *Western Sexuality*, 127.

211: Men rarely admitted: Philippe Ariès, "Love in Married Life," in ibid., 136.

212: It's no coincidence: Foucault, "Battle for Chastity," in ibid., 14–25; see also Michel Foucault, *Histoire de la Sexualité: La Volonté de Savoir* (Paris: Gallimard, 1976).

212: "Passionate love": Ariès, "Love in Married Life," in Ariès and Béjin, *Western Sexuality*, 138.

213: "I don't care": Quoted in Mellen, *Big Bad Wolves*, 155.

214: A 1957 survey: Cited by Barbara Ehrenreich, *The Hearts of Men: American Dreams and the Flight from Commitment* (Garden City, N.Y.: Doubleday, Anchor Press, 1983), 120.

215: "A man could live": Ibid., 2.

215: the number of men: Ibid., 121.

218: "Guilty Man...Tragic Man": Heinz Kohut, *The Analysis of the Self: A Systematic Approach to the Psychoanalytic Treatment of Narcissistic Personality Disorders* (New York: International Universities Press, 1971). For the notion of a narcissistic culture, I am greatly indebted to Christopher Lasch, *The Culture of Narcissism* (New York: W. W. Norton, 1979).

219: "Such activities": André Béjin, "The Extra-Marital Union Today," in Ariès and Béjin, *Western Sexuality*, 166.

221: "He practices": Lasch, *Culture of Narcissism*, 53.

CHAPTER TWELVE:
CASANOVA'S WOMEN: "HE BROKE MY HEART, AND STILL I LOVE HIM"

227: "If we were": Quoted by Michelle Green, "After Sticking with a Troubled Marriage, Lee Hart Watches a Dream Die," *People*, May 25, 1987, 40.

227: "If it doesn't bother": Quoted by Colleen O'Connor and Margaret Garrard Warner, "Lee Hart's Ordeal," *Newsweek*, May 18, 1987, 31.

229: "Casanovas are so romantic": Quoted by Michael Musto, "Out to Lunch with Helen Gurley Brown and Erica Jong," *Vanity Fair*, July 1987, 132.

236: "the intoxication": Milan Kundera, *The Unbearable Lightness of Being*, trans. Michael Henry Heim (New York: Harper & Row, 1984), 76.

239: "How much": Robin Norwood, *Women Who Love Too Much: When You Keep Wishing and Hoping He'll Change* (New York: Pocket Books, 1985), 39.

244: "one person's narcissism": Sigmund Freud, "On Narcissism," in *A General Selection from the Works of Sigmund Freud*, ed. John Rickman (Garden City, N.Y.: Doubleday, 1957), 113.

247: "My wife and I": Peter Gay, *Education of the Senses: The Bourgeois Experience, Victoria to Freud* (New York: Oxford University Press, 1984), 174.

254: "a sexually role-reversed version": Norwood, *Women Who Love*, 41.

About the Author

Born in 1953 in New York City, Peter Trachtenberg is a graduate of Sarah Lawrence College and holds a master's degree in creative writing from City University.

He was awarded a 1985 Artist's Fellowship from the New York Foundation for the Arts. He is also the winner of the 1984 Nelson Algren Award for Short Fiction. His work has appeared in *Glamour*, *Chicago*, *New Observations* and other periodicals. He lives in Baltimore, Maryland, and is at work on a novel.